APPROVED

This book has been approved by the Department of Homeland Security. It contains no seditious acts or acts of treason. Each word has been examined and analyzed by a team of terrorism experts to insure that it gives neither aid nor comfort to The Enemy. This book reveals no state secrets nor does it make public any classified documents that may cause embarrassment to the United States of America or its commander in chief. No hidden messages to terrorists are contained within. This is a good Christian book, written by a patriotic American who knows that we will crush him should he ever step out of line. If you have purchased this book we are required to notify you per Section 29A of the USA Patriot Act that your name has now been entered into a database of potential suspects should the need to declare martial law ever arise, which we are sure will never happen. Being on this list of names also qualifies you for the grand prize drawing where ten lucky winners will receive all new Formica kitchen counters, compliments of Kitchen Magic. If you are indeed a bona fide terrorist and have purchased this copy in a bookstore, or obtained it at a library in the hopes of using the information embedded on these pages, rest assured that we already know who you are. This page you are fingering right now is made of a top-secret linen paper that registers an automatic fingerprint and beams it to our central command in Kissimmee, Florida. Do not attempt to tear this page out of the book—IT IS TOO LATE. Do not attempt to run because we've got a lock on you right now, you dirty no good evil-doer . . . FREEZE! DROP THE BOOK! HANDS IN THE AIR! YOU HAVE A RIGHT TO . . . SCREW IT! YOU DON'T HAVE ANY RIGHTS!! YOU NO LONGER EXIST! AND TO THINK IF YOU HAD ONLY APPRECIATED OUR WAY OF LIFE YOU COULD HAVE HAD YOUR OWN STAIN-RESISTANT FORMICA COUNTERS!

—Tom Ridge, Secretary of the Homeland
—George W. Bush, Commander in Chief of the Fatherland

ALSO BY MICHAEL MOORE

Stupid White Men

Downsize This!

Adventures in a TV Nation
(with Kathleen Glynn)

Michael Moore

WARNER BOOKS

An AOL Time Warner Company

Warner Books, Inc., 1271 Avenue of the Americas,
New York, NY 10020

Visit our Web site at www.twbookmark.com.

An AOL Time Warner Company

Printed in the United States of America

First Printing: October 2003
10 9 8 7 6 5 4 3 2 1

Library of Congress Control Number: 2003109314
ISBN: 0-446-53223-1

for Rachel Corrie
*   will I ever have her courage*
*   will I let her death be in vain*

*   for Ardeth Platte, Carol Gilbert*
*   will I go sit in their cell*
*   they would come sit in mine*

*   for Ann Sparanese*
*   one simple act, a voice was saved*
*   are there a million more of her*
*   to save us all*

Contents

Introduction

I love listening to people's stories about where they were and what they were doing on the morning of 9/11, especially the stories from the ones who, through luck or fate, were allowed to live.

For instance, there's this guy who had just returned the day before from his honeymoon. That night, on September 10, his new bride thought she'd make him her special homemade burrito. The burrito was horrible, like eating tar stripped off the center line of the Major Deegan expressway. But love ignores all of that and what counts is the gesture, not the digestion. He told her how grateful he was and how much he loved her. And he asked for another.

The next morning, September 11, 2001, he's on the subway from Brooklyn to his job on one of the top floors of the World Trade Center. The subway might have been heading to Manhattan, but the burrito was heading south, and I don't mean the Jersey shore. He starts to get sick, real sick, and decides to get off just one stop before the World Trade Center. He runs up the subway stairs in a desperate search for facilities. But this is New York and that was not to be. And thus, on the corner of Park Row and Broadway, he became a poster boy for Depends.

Embarrassed and humiliated—but feeling much better!—he flagged down a gypsy cab and offered him a hundred dollars to take him home ($9 for the ride, and $91 toward the price of a new car).

When the man got home, he ran inside to take a shower and to put on a new set of clothes so he could get back to Manhattan. Coming out of the shower he flipped on the TV and, as he stood there, he watched the plane slam right into the floor where he worked, where he would have been *right now* had his loving wife not made him that wonderful—that absolutely perfectly incredible amazing . . . He broke down and began to cry.

My own 9/11 story wasn't so close a call. I was asleep in Santa Monica. The phone rang around 6:30 a.m. and it was my mother-in-law. "New York is under attack!" is what I heard her say through my half-awake ear. I wanted to say, "Yeah so what's new—and it's 6:30 in the morning!"

"New York is at war," she continued. This made no sense other than, again, it always feels like war in New York. "Turn on the TV," she said. And so I did. I woke up my wife and as the television faded on there were the towers, on fire. We tried to call our daughter back home in New York, no luck, then tried to call our friend Joanne (who works near the World Trade Center), no luck, and then we just sat there stunned. We didn't leave the bed or the TV until five that afternoon when we finally found out that our daughter and Joanne were okay.

But a line producer we had just worked with, Bill Weems, was not okay. As the networks started to run a scroll along the bottom of the TV with the names of those who were on the planes, along came Bill's name on that screen. My last memory of him was the two of us horsing around at a funeral home where we were shooting a piece about the tobacco industry. Put two guys with a dark sense of humor around a bunch of undertakers and you've got what we would call nirvana. Three months later he was dead and—how do they say it?—"life as we knew it changed forever."

Really? Did it? How has it changed? Is there enough distance from that tragic day to ask that question and find an intelligent answer? Things certainly changed for Bill's wife and his seven-year-old daughter. There's the crime, right there, to have her daddy taken from her at such a young age. And life changed for the loved ones of the other

3,000 who were murdered. They will never lose the sorrow they feel. They are told that they "must move on." Move on to where? Those of us who have lost someone (and I guess that's eventually everyone) know that while life does "move on," the sock in the gut, the sorrow in the heart, will never leave, so ways must be found to embrace it and make it work for you and the living.

Somehow we all work our way through our own personal losses and we get up the next morning and the morning after that and fix the kids' breakfast and do another load of laundry and pay the bills and . . .

Meanwhile, in faraway Washington, D.C., life is changing, too. Taking advantage of our grief, and our fear that "it" may happen again, an appointed president uses the dead of 9/11 as a convenient cover, a justification, for permanently altering our American way of life. Is that why they died, so that George W. Bush can turn the country into Texas? We've already conducted two wars since 9/11, and an upcoming third or a fourth is not all that unlikely. If this is allowed to continue, then all we will have accomplished is to dishonor those 3,000-plus dead. I know Bill Weems didn't die so he could be used as an excuse to bomb innocents overseas. If his death, his life, is to have a greater meaning from this moment forward, it is to make sure that no one else like him will have to lose his or her life in this insane, violent world, a world we now seem hell-bent on running any way we damn well please.

I'm lucky, I guess, that I even get to write these words you are reading. Not just because I get to live in the *most wonderfulest country in the whole wide world!*, but because after 9/11, my former publisher, Regan Books (a division of HarperCollins which is a division of the News Corp which owns Fox News and it's all owned by Rupert Murdoch), was trying its hardest to make sure my career as an author would come to an early end.

The first 50,000 copies of *Stupid White Men* came off the printing press the day before 9/11, but when the tragedy struck the next morning, the trucks that would carry them to the nation's bookstores never left the loading dock. The publisher then held the books hostage for five long months—not simply out of good taste and respect (which I might have been able to understand), but out of a desire to censor me and the things I wanted to say. They insisted I rewrite up to 50 percent of the book and that I remove sections that they found offensive to our leader, Mr. Bush.

I refused to change a word. A standoff ensued until a librarian in New Jersey heard me talking about the phone call I had just received from the Murdoch publisher telling me that it looked as if they had no choice, thanks to my stubbornness, but to "pulp" and recycle all 50,000 copies of my book that were gathering dust in a warehouse in Scranton, Pennsylvania. I also was told by others not to expect much in the way of a book career after this, as word would spread that I was considered "trouble," a royal pain in the ass who wouldn't play ball.

This librarian, Ann Sparanese, a woman I did not know, sent out an e-mail to a list of librarians, telling them that my book was being banned. Her letter shot around the Internet and, within days, letters from angry librarians were flooding Regan Books. I got a call from the Murdoch police.

"What did you tell the librarians?"

"Huh? I don't know any librarians."

"Yes you do! You told them about what we are doing with your book and now . . . *we're getting hate mail from librarians!*"

"Hmm," I replied, "I guess that's one terrorist group you don't want to mess with."

Fearing there would soon be a crazed mob of wild librarians storming down Fifth Avenue and surrounding the HarperCollins building, refusing to leave until either my book was liberated from the Scranton warehouse or Murdoch himself was drawn and quartered (though I would have settled for making Bill O'Reilly wear his underwear on his head for a week), the News Corp surrendered. They dumped my book in some bookstores with no advertising, no reviews, and the offer of a three-city tour: Arlington! Denver! Somewhere in New Jersey! In other words, the book was sent to the gallows for a quick and painless death. It's too bad you wouldn't listen to us, one Murdoch operative told me, we were only trying to help you. The country is behind George W. Bush and it is intellectually dishonest of you not to rewrite your book and admit that he has done a good job since 9/11. You are out of touch with the American people, and your book will now suffer as a result of it.

I was so out of touch with my fellow Americans that, within hours after the book's release, it went to number one on Amazon—and within five days it had gone to its ninth printing. It's in its fifty-second printing as I write this.

The worst thing to tell a free people in a country that's still mostly free is that they are not allowed to read something. That I was able to be heard—and that my book would go on to be the number-one selling nonfiction hardcover book of the year in the United States—screams volumes about this great country. The people will not be intimidated and they will not be bullied by those in charge. The American people may look like they don't know what's going on half the time, and they may spend too much time picking out different-colored covers for their cell phones, but when push comes to shove, they'll rise to the occasion and be there for what is right.

So here I am now with this new book at none other than AOLTIMEWARNER and Warner Books. I know, I know, when will I learn my lesson? But here's the good news. During the entire time I've been writing this book, AOL has been trying to *get rid of Warner Books*. Why would a media company want to get rid of its book division? What did Warner Books do to upset the gods of AOL? I figure if AOL wants to dump these guys, they *have* to be okay. Plus, the other Warner folks in this tangled web—Warner Bros. Pictures—are the people who distributed my first film, *Roger & Me*. They were good and decent and they never threatened to "pulp it."

Okay, I'm rationalizing. Six media companies own everything. Break up these monopolies for the good of the country! The free flow of news and information in a democracy must not be in the hands of just a few rich men.

Yet, I have to say, they seem to be behind me here 100 percent. 1000 percent!! Not once have they said I was "trouble."

But then, it's not me they really need to worry about.

It's the librarians.

And you.

Michael Moore
Somewhere over Greenland
August 15, 2003

DUDE, WHERE'S MY COUNTRY?

CHAPTER

1

7 Questions for George of Arabia

AT FIRST, it seemed like a small plane had accidentally flown into the north tower of the World Trade Center. It was 8:46 a.m. on September 11, 2001, and as the news leaked out across America, no one stopped what they were doing. It was a freaky occurrence to be sure, but most of the country carried on with getting itself to work or school or back to sleep.[1]

Seventeen minutes later, reports came in that, now, a second plane had hit the World Trade Center. Suddenly the collective thinking of a nation shifted, in one fell swoop, to one single thought: *"This is no accident!"*

---

1. A NOTE ABOUT NOTES IN THIS BOOK: For all other chapters, I have placed sources and notes in the back of the book so as not to interrupt the reading flow. But this chapter contains so many serious questions, facts and charges, I thought it best to include them right here on the pages. Many of these source articles will be posted on my Web site, *www.michaelmoore.com* where you can read them in full.

TV sets everywhere were flipped on. It was unlike anything you had ever seen. Your brain, now confronted with an event for which it had no prior reference, was scanning itself trying to figure out what it all meant, and in particular, what it all meant for your own personal survival, whether you were watching from your rooftop in Tribeca or on CNN in Topeka.

You were in a daze, paralyzed in front of screen or a radio, then you called everyone you knew, 290 million Americans all asking each other the same question: *What the hell is going on????*

This was the first of many questions that arose about the tragedy of September 11. Now, I'm not into conspiracy theories, except the ones that are true or involve dentists. I believe that all dentists must have gotten together at some point and decided that the real money was in root canals and full sets of X-rays every time you go in. No other mammal in the animal kingdom has to go through this.

The questions I have about September 11 are not about how the terrorists got past our defense system, or how they were able to live in this country and never be detected, or how all Bulgarians who worked at the WTC got a secret communiqué to not show up to work that day, or how the towers came down so easily when they were supposedly built to withstand earthquakes, tsunamis, and truck bombs in their parking garage.

These were all questions that a special commission investigating September 11 was supposed to answer. But the very formation of that commission was opposed by the Bush administration and the Republicans in Congress.[2] Reluctantly, they finally agreed—but then they sought to block the investigative body from doing its job by stonewalling them on the evidence that they sought.[3]

2. Ken Guggenheim, "Advocates for 9/11 commission blame White House after deal collapses," The Associated Press, October 11, 2001.
3. Joe Conason, "Can Bush Handle Panel's Questions?" *The New York Observer*, April 7, 2003.

Why wouldn't the Bush people want to find out the truth? What were they afraid of? That the American people would learn that they screwed up, that they were asleep at the wheel when it came to terrorist threats, that they belligerently ignored the warnings of the outgoing Clinton officials about Osama bin Laden[4] simply because they hated Clinton (SEX! BAD!)?

The American people are a forgiving lot. They didn't hold it against Franklin Roosevelt when Pearl Harbor was bombed. They didn't shun John F. Kennedy over the Bay of Pigs fiasco. And they still don't care that Bill Clinton had those forty-seven people mysteriously murdered. So why, after this monumental breakdown of national security, does George W. Bush not come clean, or, at the very least, stop prohibiting the truth from coming out?

Perhaps it's because George & Co. have a lot more to hide beyond why they didn't scramble the fighter jets fast enough on the morning of September 11. And maybe we, the people, are afraid to know the whole truth because it could take us down roads where we don't want to go, roads that end with a sinking feeling because now we know too much about the people who run this country.

Though I myself was filled with the healthy skepticism that is required for a citizen in a democracy, I also shared the basic mind-set held by most Americans in the fall of 2001: Osama did it, and whoever helped him with it must be tracked down and brought to justice. I hoped that this was what Bush was doing.

And then one night in November 2001, as I lay in bed, half asleep reading *The New Yorker* magazine, in an article by investigative journalist Jane Mayer, I stumbled across a paragraph that made me sit up and read it again, because I couldn't believe what it said. It read:

---

4. Michael Elliot, et al., "They had a plan," *Time* magazine, August 12, 2002.

Around two dozen other American-based members of the bin Laden family, most of them here to study in colleges and prep schools, were said to be in the United States at the time of the attacks. *The New York Times* reported that they were quickly called together by officials from the Saudi Embassy, which feared that they might become the victims of American reprisals. With approval from the FBI, according to a Saudi official, the bin Ladens flew by private jet from Los Angeles to Orlando, then on to Washington, and finally to Boston. Once the FAA permitted overseas flights, the jet flew to Europe. United States officials apparently needed little persuasion from the Saudi ambassador in Washington, Prince Bandar bin Sultan, that the extended bin Laden family included no material witnesses.[5]

What? How had I missed this story in the news? I got up and went back through *The New York Times*, and there I found this headline: "Fearing Harm, Bin Laden Kin Fled From U.S." The story began:

> In the first days after the terror attacks on New York and Washington, Saudi Arabia supervised the urgent evacuation of 24 members of Osama bin Laden's extended family from the United States . . .[6]

So, with the approval of the FBI and the help of the Saudi government—and even though fifteen of the nineteen hijackers had been Saudi citizens—the relatives of the number one suspect in the terror attacks were allowed not only to just up and leave the country, *but they were assisted by* our own authorities! According to

---

5. Jane Mayer, "The House of bin Laden: A family's, and a nation's, divided loyalties," *The New Yorker*, November 12, 2001.
6. Patrick E. Tyler, "Fearing harm, bin Laden kin fled from US," *The New York Times*, September 30, 2001.

The London Times, "The departure of so many Saudis worried U.S. investigators, who feared that some might have information about the hijackings. FBI agents insisted on checking passports, including the royal family's."

That's all the FBI could do? Check some passports, ask a few brief questions, like, "Did you pack your own bags?" and "Have your bags been in your possession since you packed them?" Then, these potential material witnesses were sent off with a bon voyage and a kiss goodbye. As Jane Mayer wrote in *The New Yorker*:

> When I asked a senior United States intelligence officer whether anyone had considered detaining members of the family, he replied, "That's called taking hostages. We don't do that."

Was he serious? I was dumbstruck. Had I read this correctly? Why wasn't this being reported more widely? What else had happened? What else was going on that we weren't being told or, if we were, why weren't we paying attention? Wouldn't the rest of America—and the rest of the world—like to know the whole truth?

I got out a big-ass legal pad and started making a list of all the questions that just didn't add up. Of course, I was never good at math, so to help me add it all up, and analyze what it all meant, I figured I needed the help of, say, a graduate of the Harvard Business School.[7]

So, George W., how about giving me a hand? Seeing how most of the questions involve you personally, you are probably the best individual to help me—and the nation—sort through what I've dug up.

---

7. In 1975, George received a master of business administration degree from Harvard Business School, according to his White House biography.

I have seven questions for you, Mr. Bush, and if you would be so kind, I would like you to answer them. I ask them on behalf of the 3,000 who died that September day, and I ask them on behalf of the American people. I know you share the same sorrow we all feel, and I would hope that you (or the people you know who may have accidentally contributed to this tragedy) would not be so reticent with the truth. We seek no revenge against you. We want only to know what happened, and what can be done to bring the murderers to justice, so we can prevent any future attacks on our citizens. I know you want the same, so please help me out with these seven questions . . .

Question #1: Is it true that the bin Ladens have had business relations with you and your family off and on for the past 25 years?

Mr. Bush, in 1977, when your father told you it was time to get a real job, he set you up with your first oil company, something you called "Arbusto" (Spanish for "shrub").[8] A year later, you received financing from a man named James A. Bath.[9] He was an old buddy of yours from your days (the ones when you weren't AWOL[10]) in the Texas Air National Guard.[11] He had been hired by Salem bin Laden—Osama's brother—to invest the bin Ladens' money in var-

---

8. Mike Allen, "For Bush, a slippery situation," *The Washington Post*, June 23, 2000.

9. Thomas Petzinger Jr., et al., "Family Ties: How oil firm linked to a son of Bush won Bahrain Drilling Pact—Harken Energy had a web of Mideast connections; in the background: BCCI—entrée at the White House," *The Wall Street Journal*, December 6, 1991.

10. Walter V. Robinson, "Military Record: Questions Remain on Bush's Service as Guard Pilot," *The Boston Globe*, October 31, 2000; Ellen Gamerman, "Bush's past catching up on road to White House," *The Baltimore Sun*, November 4, 2000.

11. Jonathan Beaty, "A Mysterious Mover of Money and Planes," *Time* magazine, October 28, 1991.

ious Texas ventures. Some $50,000—or 5 percent of control of Arbusto—came from Mr. Bath.[12]

Was he acting on behalf of the bin Ladens?

Most Americans might be surprised to learn that you and your father have known the bin Ladens for a long time. What exactly is the extent of this relationship, Mr. Bush? Are you close personal friends, or simply on-again, off-again business associates? Salem bin Laden first started coming to Texas in 1973 and later bought some land, built himself a house, and created Bin Laden Aviation at the San Antonio airfield.[13]

The bin Ladens are one of the wealthiest families in Saudi Arabia. Their huge construction firm virtually built the country, from the roads and power plants, to the skyscrapers and government buildings. They built some of the airstrips America used in your dad's Gulf War, and they renovated the holy sites at Mecca and Medina.[14] Billionaires many times over, they soon began investing in other ventures around the world, including in the United States. They have extensive business dealings with Citigroup, General Electric, Merrill Lynch, Goldman Sachs, and the Fremont Group— a spin-off of energy giant Bechtel. According to *The New Yorker*, the bin Laden family also owns a part of Microsoft and the airline and defense giant Boeing.[15] They have donated $2 million to your alma mater, Harvard University, $300,000 more to Tufts Univer-

---

12. Jerry Urban, "Feds investigate entrepreneur allegedly tied to Saudis," *Houston Chronicle*, June 4, 1992; Mike Ward, "Bin Laden relatives have ties to Texas," *Austin American-Statesman*, November 9, 2001.

13. Mike Ward, "Bin Laden relatives have ties to Texas," *Austin American-Statesman*, November 9, 2001; Suzanne Hoholik & Travis E. Poling, "Bin Laden brother ran business, was well-liked in Central Texas," *San Antonio Express-News*, August 22, 1998.

14. Susan Sevareid, "Attacks hurt bin Laden conglomerate," The Associated Press, October 7, 2001; Richard Beeston, "Outcast who brought shame on family," *The London Times*, September 15, 2001.

15. Jane Mayer, "The House of bin Laden: A family's, and a nation's, divided loyalties," *The New Yorker*, November 12, 2001; Michael Moss, et al., "Bin Laden family, with deep western ties, strives to re-establish a name," *The New York Times*, October 28, 2001.

sity, and tens of thousands more to the Middle East Policy Council, a think tank headed by a former U.S. ambassador to Saudi Arabia, Charles Freeman.[16] In addition to the property they own in Texas, they also have real estate in Florida and Massachusetts.[17] In short, they have their hands deep in our pants.

Unfortunately, as you know, Mr. Bush, Salem bin Laden died in a plane crash in Texas in 1988 (his father, Mohammad, also died in a plane crash in 1967).[18] Salem's brothers—there are around 50 of them, including Osama—continued to run the family companies and investments.

After leaving office, your father became a highly paid consultant for a company known as the Carlyle Group. One of the investors in the Carlyle Group was none other than the bin Laden family. The bin Ladens put a minimum of $2 million into the Carlyle Group.[19]

Until 1994, you headed a company called CaterAir, which was owned by the Carlyle Group. The same year you left the soon-to-be-bankrupt CaterAir, you became governor and quickly oversaw the University of Texas—a state institution—make an investment of $10 million in the Carlyle Group.[20] The bin Laden family had also gotten on the Carlyle gravy train in 1994.[21]

The Carlyle Group is one of the nation's largest defense contrac-

----

16. "The bin Laden business empire," *St. Petersburg Times*, September 23, 2001; Anne E. Kornblut & Aaron Zitner, "Terror figure's family has benign ties in US," *The Boston Globe*, August 26, 1998; Marcella Bombardieri, "In Cambridge, a bin Laden breaks family silence," *The Boston Globe*, October 7, 2001.

17. Michael Dobbs & John Ward Anderson, "A Fugitive's Splintered Family Tree," *The Washington Post*, September 30, 2001.

18. Mitch Frank, "A Wealthy Clan and Its Renegade," *Time* magazine, October 8, 2001; "18 die in holiday weekend plane crashes," United Press International, May 31, 1988.

19. Kurt Eichenwald, "Bin Laden Family Liquidates Holdings with Carlyle Group," *The New York Times*, October 26, 2001.

20. Joe Conason, "Notes on a native son," *Harper's Magazine*, February 1, 2000.

21. Kurt Eichenwald, "Bin Laden Family Liquidates Holdings with Carlyle Group," *The New York Times*, October 26, 2001.

tors, among their many other lines of work. They don't actually build weapons themselves. Rather, they buy up failing defense companies, turn them around by making them profitable, and then sell them for huge sums of money.

The people who run the Carlyle Group are a Who's Who of past movers and shakers, everyone from Ronald Reagan's defense secretary, Frank Carlucci, to your dad's secretary of state, James Baker, to former British Prime Minister John Major.[22] Carlucci, the head of Carlyle, also happens to sit on the board of directors of the Middle East Policy Council along with a representative of the bin Laden family business.[23]

After September 11, *The Washington Post* and *The Wall Street Journal* both ran stories pointing out this strange coincidence. Your first response, Mr. Bush, was to ignore it, hoping, I guess, that the story would just go away. Your father and his buddies at Carlyle did not renounce the bin Laden investment. Your army of pundits went into spin control. They said, we can't paint these bin Ladens with the same brush we use for Osama. They have disowned Osama! They have nothing to do with him! They hate and despise what he has done! These are the *good* bin Ladens.

And then the video footage came out. It showed a number of those "good" bin Ladens—including Osama's mother, a sister and two brothers—with Osama at his son's wedding just six and a half months before September 11.[24] It has been reported in *The New Yorker* that not only has the family *not* cut ties to Osama, but they have continued to fund him as they have been doing for years. It was no secret to the CIA that Osama bin Laden had access to his family fortune (his share is estimated to be at least $30

---

22. www.carlylegroup.com.

23. Middle East Policy Council's board of directors. http://www.mepc.org/public%5Fasp/about/board.asp.

24. Al Jazeera; Washington Foreign Press Center Briefing with Richard Boucher, Assistant Secretary of State for Public Affairs, February 28, 2001; "Bin Laden full of praise for attack on USS *Cole* at son's wedding," *Agence France Presse*, March 1, 2001.

million[25]), and the bin Ladens, as well as other Saudis, kept Osama and his group, al Qaeda, well funded.[26]

Mr. Bush, weeks went by after the attacks on New York and the Pentagon, yet your father and his friends at the Carlyle Group refused to buckle in their support for the bin Laden empire.

Finally, nearly two months after the attacks, with more and more people questioning the propriety of the Bush family being in bed with the bin Ladens, your father and the Carlyle Group were pressured into giving the bin Ladens their millions back and asked them to leave the company as investors.[27]

Why did this take so long?

To make matters worse, it turned out that one of bin Laden's brothers—Shafiq—was actually at a Carlyle Group business conference in Washington, D.C., the morning of September 11. The day before, at the same conference, your father and Shafiq had been chatting it up with all the other ex-government Carlyle bigwigs.[28]

Mr. Bush, what is going on here?

You've gotten a free ride from the media, though they know everything I have just written to be the truth (and, in fact, I have taken it from the very same mainstream news sources they work for). They seem unwilling or afraid to ask you a simple question: WHAT IS GOING ON HERE?

In case you don't understand just how bizarre the media's silence is regarding the Bush–bin Laden connections, let me draw an

---

25. Borzou Daraghi, "Financing Terror," *Money*, November 2001.

26. Jane Mayer, "The House of bin Laden," *The New Yorker*, November 12, 2001.

27. Daniel Golden, et al., "Bin Laden family is tied to US group," *The Wall Street Journal*, September 27, 2001; Michael Dobbs & John Ward Anderson, "A Fugitive's Splintered Family Tree," *The Washington Post*, September 30, 2001; Kurt Eichenwald, "Bin Laden family liquidates holdings with Carlyle Group," *The New York Times*, October 26, 2001.

28. Dan Briody, *The Iron Triangle: Inside the Secret World of The Carlyle Group*; Greg Schneider, "Connections and then some," *The Washington Post*, March 16, 2003.

analogy to how the press or Congress may have handled something like this if the same shoe had been on the Clinton foot. If, after the terrorist attack on the Federal Building in Oklahoma City, it was revealed that President Bill Clinton and his family had financial dealings with Timothy McVeigh's family, what do you think your Republican Party and the media would have done with that one? Do you think at least a couple of questions might have been asked, like, "What is THAT all about?" Be honest, you know the answer. They would have asked more than a couple of questions. They would have skinned Clinton alive and thrown what was left of his carcass in Gitmo.

So, what *is* this all about, Mr. Bush? We have a right to know.

Question #2: What is the "special relationship" between the Bushes and the Saudi royal family?

Mr. Bush, the bin Ladens are not the only Saudis with whom you and your family have a close personal relationship. The entire royal family seems to be indebted to you—or is it the other way around?

The number-one supplier of oil to the U.S. is the nation of Saudi Arabia, possessor of the largest-known reserves of oil in the world. When Saddam Hussein invaded Kuwait in 1990, it was really the Saudis next door who felt threatened, and it was your father, George Bush I, who came to their rescue. The Saudis have never forgotten this and, according to a March 2003 article in *The New Yorker*, some members of the royal family consider your family to be part of *their* extended family. Haifa, wife of Prince Bandar, the Saudi ambassador to the United States, says that your mother and father "are like my mother and father. I know if ever I needed anything I could go to them."[29] And as Robert Baer—who was a case

---

29. Elsa Walsh, "The Prince: How the Saudi Ambassador became Washington's indispensable operator," *The New Yorker*, March 24, 2003.

officer in the CIA's Directorate of Operations from 1967 to 1997—revealed in his book *Sleeping with the Devil*, your dad even has a special name for the Saudi prince—he calls him "Bandar Bush."[30]

This relationship, as you know (but have never revealed to the American people), was forged over many years. Through his stints in the CIA and as vice president and president, your father learned that whenever the dirty work needed to be done, the United States could always turn to Saudi Arabia. When White House aide Oliver North needed money to buy arms for Iran in the Iran-Contra Affair, it was the Saudis who provided the $30 million in secret cash.[31] When the CIA needed funds to help destroy the Italian Communist Party in 1985 and finance its opponents in elections, it was your good friends the Saudis who happily put $10 million in an Italian bank.[32] This was all while dad was V.P., and he was having the Saudi ambassador over for frequent lunches.[33]

It is no surprise then that the Saudi ambassador is the only diplomat in Washington who receives his own personal State Department security detail, compliments of the U.S. taxpayers. Robert Baer reported that Prince Bandar donated $1 million to the George Bush Presidential Library and Museum in Texas and a million dollars more to Barbara Bush's literacy program.[34]

Even though Poppy was defeated by Clinton in 1992, the ties remained just as strong. Your father's Carlyle Group did a lot of business with the Saudis when it came to weapons procurement. The Saudis spent more than $170 billion on armaments in the 1990s, and a chunk of the business went through the Carlyle

---

30. Robert Baer, *Sleeping with the Devil*, Crown, 2003.
31. James Rupert, "US-Saudi relations were built on oil, security—and secrecy," *The Washington Post*, August 9, 1990.
32. Robert G. Kaiser & David Ottaway, "Oil for security fueled close ties," *The Washington Post*, February 11, 2002.
33. Elsa Walsh, "The Prince: How the Saudi Ambassador became Washington's indispensable operator," *The New Yorker*, March 24, 2003.
34. Robert Baer, *Sleeping with the Devil*, Crown, 2003.

Group.[35] Your dad has met with the Saudi royals on many occasions and has traveled to the Arabian peninsula at least twice since leaving office and stayed in the royal palaces of the House of Saud, both times on behalf of the Carlyle Group.[36] Prince Bandar is also an investor in the Carlyle Group,[37] and he attended your mother's seventy-fifth birthday party in Kennebunkport.[38] It has been a fruitful relationship all around.

When there was all that nasty stress surrounding the hanging chads in the Florida ballot boxes in the late fall of 2000, your close friend Prince Bandar was there for your family, offering his support. He took your father on a pheasant hunting trip to England, to help take his mind off all the chaos, while the royal family's lawyer—*your* lawyer, James Baker—went to Florida to direct the battle for the ballots. (Baker's firm would later represent the Saudi royals in the lawsuits against them by the families of the September 11 victims.)[39]

To be fair, Mr. Bush, it's not just your family members who are the recipients of the Saudis' largesse. A major chunk of the American economy is built on Saudi money. They have a trillion dollars invested in our stock market and another trillion dollars sitting in our banks.[40] If one day they chose to suddenly remove that money, our corporations and financial institutions would be sent into a tailspin, causing an economic crisis the likes of which has never

35. Tim Shorrock, "Crony capitalism goes global," *The Nation*, April 1, 2002; Warren Richey, "New snags in US-Saudi ties play to bin Laden," *Christian Science Monitor*, October 29, 2001.

36. Oliver Burkeman, "The winners: The Ex-President's Club," *The Guardian*, October 31, 2001; Leslie Wayne, "Elder Bush in big GOP cast toiling for top equity firm," *The New York Times*, March 5, 2001.

37. Robert Kaiser, "Enormous wealth spilled into American coffers," *The Washington Post*, February 11, 2002.

38. David Sharp, "Former President pulls off secret birthday bash," The Associated Press, June 11, 2000.

39. Elsa Walsh, "The Prince: How the Saudi Ambassador became Washington's indispensable operator," *The New Yorker*, March 24, 2003; Michael Isikoff and Mark Hosenball, "A legal counterattack," *Newsweek*, April 16, 2003.

40. Robert Baer, *Sleeping with the Devil*, Crown, 2003.

been seen. That threat looms every day over our heads, and it is something no one ever wants to talk about. Couple that with the fact that the one and a half million barrels of oil[41] we need *daily* from the Saudis also could vanish on a mere royal whim, and we begin to see how not only you, but all of us, are dependent on the House of Saud. George, is this good for our national security, our homeland security? Who is it good for? You? Pops?

Not us.

Here's what I don't get: Why have you and your father chosen to align yourselves with a country that is considered by most human rights groups to be among the worst and most brutal dictatorships in the world?

Amnesty International had this to say in its 2003 report on Saudi Arabia:

> Gross human rights violations continued and were exacerbated by the government policy of "combating terrorism" in the wake of the 11 September 2001 attacks in the USA. The violations were perpetuated by the strictly secretive criminal justice system and the prohibition of political parties, trade unions and independent human rights organizations. Hundreds of suspected religious activists and critics of the state were arrested, and the legal status of most of those held from previous years remained shrouded in secrecy. Women continued to suffer severe discrimination. Torture and ill-treatment remained rife.[42]

In 2000, 125 people were publicly beheaded, many of them in the city of Riyadh at a place popularly known as "Chop-Chop Square."[43]

---

41. Department of Energy, Energy Information Administration, "Table 4.10: United States—Oil Imports, 1991–2002 (Million Barrels per Day)."

42. *Amnesty International Report 2003*, "Saudi Arabia," www.amnesty.org.

43. "Saudi beheaded for shooting compatriot to death," The Associated Press, November 13, 2001; Robert Baer, *Sleeping with the Devil*, Crown, 2003.

After meeting with the Saudi crown prince in April 2002, you happily told us that the two of you had "established a strong personal bond" and that you "spent a lot of time alone."[44] Were you trying to reassure us? Or just flaunt your friendship with a group of rulers who rival the Taliban in their suppression of human rights? Why the double standard?

Question #3: Who attacked the United States on September 11—a guy on dialysis from a cave in Afghanistan, or your friends, Saudi Arabia?

I'm sorry, Mr. Bush, but something doesn't make sense.

You got us all repeating by rote that it was Osama bin Laden who was responsible for the attack on the United States on September 11. Even I was doing it. But then I started hearing strange stories about Osama's kidneys.

It turns out that there have been reports on Osama's health problems for years. For example, in 2000 The Associated Press reported, ". . . a Western intelligence official said [Osama] is suffering from kidney and liver disease. Bin Laden has kidney failure and 'his liver is going,' the official said. . . . He said bin Laden's followers were trying to find a kidney dialysis machine for their ailing leader."[45]

After September 11, these reports escalated. I was watching *Hardball with Chris Matthews* one night on MSNBC, and one of the guests—a Taliban expert—said, ". . . Osama bin Laden appears to need dialysis treatment for his kidney problem, so he's got to be close to some dialysis. He really can't travel far."[46]

---

44. Elisabeth Bumiller, "Saudi tells Bush US must temper backing of Israel," *The New York Times*, April 26, 2002.

45. Kathy Gannon, "Bin Laden reportedly ailing," The Associated Press, March 25, 2000.

46. *Hardball with Chris Matthews*, MSNBC, November 19, 2001; interview with Michael Griffin, author *Reaping the Whirlwind: The Taliban Movement in Afghanistan* (Pluto, May 2001). For more on Osama's history with dialysis, see John F. Burns, "Pakistanis say bin Laden may be dead of disease," *The New York Times*, January 19, 2002.

Did he just say "dialysis"? The world's biggest monster, the most sinister, evil man on all of planet Earth—and he can't even piss in a pot without help? I don't know about you, but if I'm told to be seriously frightened by an evildoer, especially the top evildoer, I want that evildoer to have all his bodily functions working at 110 percent! I want him strong, scary, and omnipresent—and the possessor of two working kidneys. How am I supposed to be supporting all these Homeland Security measures when the lead bad guy is flat out on a table somewhere hooked up to a kidney machine?

Suddenly, I don't know who or what to trust. I started to ask other questions. How could a guy sitting in a cave in Afghanistan, hooked up to dialysis, have directed and overseen the actions of nineteen terrorists for two years in the United States and then plotted so perfectly the hijacking of four planes and then guaranteed that three of them would end up precisely on their targets? How did Osama do this? I mean, I can't get this computer to stop crashing every time I type the word "gingivitis." I can't get a cell signal from here to Queens! And he's supposed to have pulled off all of September 11 from his little cave, 10,000 miles away? What was he doing, then, when we started the bombing over there? Was he running from cave to cave in Afghanistan with his tubes and dialysis machine trailing behind him? Or, um, maybe there was a dialysis machine in every third cave in Afghanistan. Yeah, that's it! A real modern country, Afghanistan! It has about fifteen miles of railroad track. And lots of dialysis machines, I guess.

None of this is to say that Osama isn't a baddie or even that he didn't have something to do with the attacks. But it seems that maybe a few journalists might want to ask a few commonsense questions, like how could he have really pulled this off while his skin was turning green and he was living in a country with no Kinko's, no FedEx, no ATMs. How did he organize, communicate, control and supervise this kind of massive attack? With two cans and a string?

Yet, we're told by you to believe it. The headlines blared it the first day and they blare it the same way now two years later: "Terrorists Attack United States." *Terrorists.* I have wondered about this word for some time, so, George, let me ask you a question: If fifteen of the nineteen hijackers had been North Korean, and they killed 3,000 people, do you think the headline the next day might read, "NORTH KOREA ATTACKS UNITED STATES"?

Of course it would. Or if it had been fifteen Iranians or fifteen Libyans or fifteen Cubans, I think the conventional wisdom would have been, "IRAN (or LIBYA or CUBA) ATTACKS AMERICA!"

Yet, when it comes to September 11, have you ever seen the headline, have you ever heard a newscaster, has one of your appointees ever uttered these words: "Saudi Arabia attacked the United States"?

Of course you haven't. And so the question must—must—be asked: *WHY NOT?* Why, when Congress releases its own investigation into September 11, you, Mr. Bush, censor out twenty-eight pages that deal with the Saudis' role in the attack? What is behind your apparent refusal to look at the one country that seems to be producing the "terrorists" that have killed our citizens?

I would like to throw out a possibility here: What if September 11 was not a "terrorist" attack but, rather, a *military attack* against the United States? What if the nineteen were well-trained soldiers, the elite of the elite, unquestioning in their duty to obey their commander's orders? That they lived in this country for nearly two years and were not discovered—that takes a certain amount of discipline, the discipline of a soldier, not the erratic behavior of some wild-eyed terrorist.

George, apparently you were a pilot once—how hard is it to hit a five-story building at more than 500 miles an hour? The Pentagon is only five stories high. At 500 miles an hour, had the pilots been off by just a hair, they'd have been in the river. You do not get this skilled at learning how to fly jumbo jets by being taught on a video game machine at some dipshit flight training school in Arizona. You learn to do this in the air force. Someone's air force.

The Saudi Air Force?

What if these weren't wacko terrorists, but military pilots who signed on to a suicide mission? What if they were doing this at the behest of either the Saudi government or certain disgruntled members of the Saudi royal family? The House of Saud, according to Robert Baer's book, is full of them, and the royal family—and the country—is in incredible turmoil. There is much dissension over how things are being run, and with the king incapacitated by a stroke he suffered in 1995, his brothers and numerous sons have been in a serious power struggle. Some favor cutting off all ties to the West. Some want the country to go the more fundamentalist route.[47] After all, this was Osama's originally stated goal. His first beef wasn't with America, it was with the way Saudi Arabia was being run—by Muslims who weren't *true* Muslims. There are now thousands of princes in the royal family, and many observers have commented that Saudi Arabia is on the brink of civil war, or perhaps a people's revolution. You can only behead so many of your citizens and then, before long, they lose their heads and go crazy and overthrow your ass. That is what is on the "To Do" list for many Saudi citizens these days, and the royals are circling the wagons.

A 1999 article in the political journal *Foreign Affairs* pretty much spelled out why: "Like Pakistan, Saudi Arabia would like to leave bin Laden in Afghanistan. His arrest and trial in the United States could be highly embarrassing, exposing his continuing relationship with sympathetic members of the ruling elites and intelligence services of both countries."[48]

So, did certain factions within the Saudi royal family execute the attack on September 11? Were these pilots trained by the Saudis? One thing we do know: Nearly all the hijackers were Saudis and they were apparently able to enter the United States legally, thanks,

---

47. Robert Baer, "The fall of the House of Saud," *The Atlantic Monthly*, May 2003.

48. Ahmed Rashid, "The Taliban: Exporting Extremism," *Foreign Affairs*, November 1999.

in part, to the special arrangement set up by our State Department and the Saudi government that allowed Saudis to get quickie visas without going through the normal vetting process.[49]

Mr. Bush, why have the Saudis received red-carpet treatment? Sure, we need their oil. And, yes, they received the same kissy-face welcome from all the presidents before you.

But why have you blocked attempts to dig deeper into the Saudi connections? Why do you refuse to say, "Saudi Arabia attacked the United States!"?

Mr. Bush, does this have anything to do with your family's close personal relationship with the ruling family of Saudi Arabia? I would like to think that's not possible. But what is your explanation? That it was just some nut in a cave (who just happened to be on dialysis)? And, after you couldn't find this nut, why did you try to convince us that *Saddam Hussein* had something to do with September 11 and al Qaeda, when you were specifically told by your intelligence people that there was **no** connection?

Why are you so busy protecting the Saudis when you should be protecting us?

Question #4: Why did you allow a private Saudi jet to fly around the U.S. in the days after September 11 and pick up members of the bin Laden family and then fly them out of the country without a proper investigation by the FBI?

Mr. Bush, not that this is personal or anything, but I was stranded in Los Angeles on the morning of September 11. I scrambled to find a rental car, and then drove 3,000 miles to get back home—all because traveling by air was forbidden in the days following the attack.

---

49. Susan Schmidt & Bill Miller, "Homeland Security Department to oversee visa program," *The Washington Post*, August 6, 2002.

Yet, members of the bin Laden family were allowed to fly in private jets, crisscrossing America as they prepared to leave the country—can you explain that to me?

Private jets, under the supervision of the Saudi government—and with your approval—were allowed to fly around the skies of America and pick up twenty-four members of the bin Laden family and take them first to a "secret assembly point in Texas." They then flew to Washington, D.C., and then on to Boston. Finally, on September 18, they were all flown to Paris, out of the reach of any U.S. officials. They never went through any serious interrogation, other than a few questions that the FBI asked them and a request to check each of their passports before leaving.[50] One FBI agent I spoke to told me that the FBI was "furious" that they were not allowed to keep the bin Ladens in the country to conduct a real investigation—the kind police like to do when they are trying to track down a murderer. Usually, the police like to talk to the family members of the suspect to learn what they know, who they know, how they might help capture the fugitive.

None of the normal procedures were followed.

This is mind-boggling. Here you have two dozen bin Ladens on American soil, Mr. Bush, and you come up with some lame excuse that you were worried about "their safety." Might it have been possible that at least one of the twenty-four bin Ladens would have possibly known *something*? Or maybe just one of them could have been "convinced" to help track Osama down?

Nope. None of that. So while thousands were stranded and could not fly, if you could prove you were a close relative of the biggest mass murderer in U.S. history, you got a free tip to gay Paree!

---

50. Jane Mayer, "The House of bin Laden," *The New Yorker* November 12, 2001; Patrick E. Tyler, "Fearing harm, bin Laden kin fled from US," *The New York Times*, September 30, 2001; Kevin Cullen, "Bin Laden kin flown back to Saudi Arabia," *The Boston Globe*, September 20, 2001; Katty Kay, "How FBI helped bin Laden family flee US," *The London Times*, October 1, 2001.

Of course, the bin Ladens have been your business associates. Why wouldn't you do a little favor for some old family friends? But, to use the Clinton analogy again, imagine, in the hours after the Oklahoma City bombing, Bill Clinton suddenly started worrying about the "safety" of the McVeigh family up in Buffalo—and then arranged a free trip for them out of the country. What would you and the Republicans have said about that? Suddenly, a stain on a blue dress probably wouldn't have been the top priority for a witch hunt, would it?

With all that was happening in the days after September 11, how did you find the time to even begin *thinking* about protecting people named bin Laden? I'm amazed at your ability to multi-task.

As if bin Ladens Over America ("Air Laden?") wasn't enough, *The Tampa Tribune* reported that the authorities also found the time to help even more Saudis. Apparently, another Saudi jet, this one a private Lear jet (arranged by a private hangar owned by defense contractor Raytheon, which also happens to be a hefty GOP donor), was allowed to fly from Tampa on September 13 (during the air-travel lockdown) to Lexington, Kentucky, to drop off some members of the Saudi royal family to be with other Saudi royals who had been in Kentucky looking at horses. Two bodyguards for the Tampa Bay Buccaneers were hired to travel along on the flight and they told their story to the *Tribune* about how the pilot revealed to them upon returning to Tampa that he had still another run to make to Louisiana.[51]

Why, Mr. Bush, was this allowed to happen?

A frightened nation struggled to get through those days after September 11. Yet, in the sky above us, the bin Ladens and Saudi royals jetted home.

I think we deserve an explanation.

---

51. Kathy Steele, "Phantom flight from Florida," *The Tampa Tribune*, October 5, 2001.

Question #5: Why are you protecting the "Second Amendment rights" of potential terrorists?

Mr. Bush, in the days after September 11, the FBI began running a check to see if any of the 186 "suspects" the feds had rounded up in the first five days after the attack had purchased any guns in the months leading up to September 11. Using the instant background check files for gun purchases created under the Brady Bill, the FBI immediately found two of the suspects had indeed purchased weapons.[52]

When your attorney general, John Ashcroft, heard about this, he immediately shut the search down. He told the FBI that the background check files could not be used for such a search and these files were only to be used at the time of a purchase of a gun, not to find out information on law-abiding gun-toting citizens.[53]

So, the FBI was prohibited by Ashcroft from doing any further investigation as to whether those detained—because they were possible associates of the hijackers—had procured any weapons in the ninety days leading up to that fateful day. Why? Because even though all their other rights had been thrown out the window, your administration *insisted* that they still had one constitutional right that you were willing to protect: their sacred Second Amendment rights to bear arms and for the government not to know about it.

Mr. Bush, you can't be serious! Is your administration so gun nutty and in the pocket of the National Rifle Association that, even though you have not given a nanosecond of thought to protecting the rights of any of the Arab-Americans you have arrested, detained, and harassed in the past two years, when it comes to their GUN rights, then all of a sudden you are the biggest defender of constitutional rights and civil liberties that the nation has ever seen?

---

52. Fox Butterfield, "Justice Dept. bars use of gun checks in terror inquiry," *The New York Times*, December 6, 2001.
53. Ibid.

Do you realize that when most Americans figure out you have protected potential terrorists by stymying a legitimate police investigation, they are going to run you and Dick and Reverend John out of Dodge with their own six-shooters of ballot boxes a-blazing?

I guess none of this should come as a surprise, considering what Mr. Ashcroft was up to in the summer of 2001. Instead of protecting the country from events like the one that was about to take place, the attorney general was busy trying to dismantle the National Instant Criminal Background Check System. He said that the government should not be keeping a database on gun owners and wanted the law changed so that the files were kept for only twenty-four hours![54]

The Senate (and the public) did not find out about Ashcroft's orders to stop the search for the terrorists' gun files until December 2001, when Ashcroft not only proudly admitted to doing this in front of the Senate Judiciary Committee, but went on to attack anyone who would question his actions to protect the hijackers' gun rights. He told the panel that critics of his anti-terror practices were "providing ammunition to America's enemies. . . . To those who scare peace-loving people with phantoms of 'lost liberty,' my message is this: Your tactics only aid terrorists."

But who was the one aiding the terrorists, Mr. Bush? An attorney general who won't let the FBI do its job? An attorney general who won't let the police thoroughly investigate what the terrorists were up to, including the purchasing of weapons?

At that same Senate hearing, Mr. Ashcroft held up what he said was an al Qaeda training manual.

"In this manual," he warned, "al Qaeda terrorists are told how to use America's freedom as a weapon against us."

On this point he was correct. One of the freedoms al Qaeda apparently really likes is our Second Amendment.

---

54. Cheryl W. Thompson, "Senators challenge Ashcroft on Gun Issue," *The Washington Post*, July 27, 2001.

Another al Qaeda pamphlet that was originally found in terrorist safe houses in Afghanistan heaps praise on the United States.
Obviously, Ashcroft missed all of the beautiful irony.

Here's what this al Qaeda training manual says:

• In some countries of the world, especially the USA, firearms
training is available to the general public. One should try to join a
shooting club if possible and make regular visits to the firing
range. There are many firearms courses available to the public in
the USA, ranging from one day to two weeks or more.

• Useful courses to learn are sniping, general shooting, and other
rifle courses. Handgun courses are useful but only after you have
mastered rifles.

• In other countries, e.g. some states of the USA and South
Africa, it is perfectly legal for members of the public to own certain
types of firearms. If you live in such a country, obtain an assault rifle legally, preferably an AK-47 or variations, learn how to use it
properly and go and practice in the areas allowed for such training.

• Respect the laws of the country you are in and avoid dealing
in illegal firearms. One can learn to operate many arms legally, so
there is no need to spend years in prison for dealing in small, illegal
firearms. Learn the most you can according to your circumstances
and leave the rest to when you actually go for jihad.

So, Mr. Bush, al Qaeda is apparently plotting to use one of our
"freedoms"—the right to bear arms—against us.

I truly love how you have rounded up hundreds of people, grab-
bing them off the streets without notice, throwing them in prison
cells, unable to contact lawyers or family and then, for the most
part, shipping them out of the country on mere immigration
charges. You can waive their Fourth Amendment protection from
unlawful search and seizure, their Sixth Amendment rights to an

open trial by a jury of their peers and the right to counsel, and their First Amendment rights to speak, assemble, dissent and practice their religion. You believe you have the right to just trash all these rights, but when it comes to the Second Amendment right to own an AK-47—oh no! THAT right they can have—and you will defend their right to have it, even after they've flown a plane into a building and killed a bunch of people.

When this story first broke, you naturally got worried that it wouldn't spin the right way to the public (the vast majority of whom want *stronger* gun laws), so you trotted out a Justice Department spokeswoman to explain to us that the decision had been reached by "senior Justice officials" after they had done an exhaustive study of "the law." Among those spinmeisters was Mr. Viet Dinh—the assistant attorney general for legal policy. Dinh's justification for blocking the background checks? According to *The New York Times*, "Mr. Dinh ruled that these checks were improper, reasoning that they would violate *the privacy of these foreigners*" (my emphasis).

Yes, when it comes to guns, finally the rights of foreigners count for something.

But in July 2002, the truth came out and the General Accounting Office released the Justice Department's *actual* legal opinion on the matter, dated October 1, 2001, a report that your attorney general had apparently suppressed. What did it say? That the Justice Department's legal advisers had ruled that—get this—*there was nothing wrong with using the gun background files to check if a suspected terrorist had purchased a gun.* Did you read that, Mr. Bush? I'll underline it and put it in bigger type so you can read it nice and slow and easy:

There's nothing wrong with looking to see if a suspected terrorist bought a gun.

Nothing wrong! How shocking! Who else, other than you and John Ashcroft, would think that it's a crime to find out if alleged terrorists were buying guns? (The GAO also reported that 97 percent of illegally purchased guns that were initially approved and then taken back once their mistake was realized would not have been detected if the gun check records had been destroyed in twenty-four hours rather than ninety days.)

Your administration talks of the "phantoms of lost liberty"? Tell that to the men and women who were thrown in jails, not because they were terrorists, but because they were Muslims. And tell me why you think you have the right to find out what books a suspected terrorist is reading, but not what guns he might be packing.

Who, Mr. Bush, is really aiding the terrorists here?[55]

Question #6: Were you aware that while you were governor of Texas, the Taliban traveled to Texas to meet with your oil and gas company friends?

Mr. Bush, I don't know what compelled me to type in some key words one night on the BBC Web site, but there I was, punching in the words "Taliban" (the British spell it "Taleban") and "Texas," and lo and behold, look what popped up on my computer: a BBC story from December of 1997:

"Taleban to Texas for Pipeline Talks."

---

55. Fox Butterfield, "Justice Dept. bars use of gun checks in terror inquiry," *The New York Times*, December 6, 2001; Neil A. Lewis, "Ashcroft defends antiterror plan; says criticism may aid US foes," *The New York Times*, December 7, 2001; Peter Slevin, "Ashcroft blocks FBI access to gun records," *The Washington Post*, December 7, 2001; Violence Policy Center (www.vpc.org), "Firearms training for Jihad in America"; Fox Butterfield, "Ashcroft's words clash with staff on checks," *The New York Times*, July 24, 2002.

The Taliban, as you know, were invited to come to Texas while you were governor of the state. According to the BBC, the Taliban went there to meet with Unocal, the huge oil and energy giant, to discuss Unocal's desire to build a natural gas pipeline running from Turkmenistan through Taliban-controlled Afghanistan and into Pakistan.[56]

Mr. Bush, what was this all about?

According to London's *Telegraph Online*, your oil company friends rolled out the red carpet for some of the world's most notorious, murderous thugs and showed them a real good, down-home, Texas time.

First, the Taliban leaders spent a few days in Sugarland, Texas, enjoying the pleasures of Western extravagance. The oilmen put the brutal bastards up in a five-star hotel, took them to the zoo and, of course, to the NASA space center.[57]

"Houston, we have a problem" apparently never crossed your mind, even though the Taliban were perhaps the most repressive fundamentalist regime on the planet. If the reverse had happened and they were hosting you in Kabul, the entertainment would have been the hanging of women who didn't keep themselves covered from head to toe. Now, that would have been some barbecue, huh?

After Texas, the Taliban dictators moseyed on over to Washington, D.C., where they met with Karl Inderfurth, assistant secretary of state for South Asian affairs. Then they went to Omaha, where the University of Nebraska eventually created a special training program for Afghanis to teach them how to build pipelines—all paid for by your friends at Unocal. During one of their visits there, in May 1998, two Taliban members—this time in the U.S. sponsored by Clinton's State Department—took in some more sites, in-

---

56. "Taleban to Texas for pipeline talks," *BBC World Service*, December 3, 1997, http://news.bbc.co.uk/1/hi/world/west—asia/36735.stm.

57. Caroline Lees, "Oil barons court Taliban in Texas," *The Telegraph (Online)*, December 14, 1997.

cluding the Badlands National Park, the Crazy Horse Memorial, Gerald Ford's birthplace, and Mount Rushmore.[58]

Yes, it was an amazing amount of hospitality, a fine example of American good will and our big, generous hearts. Or our love of money and cheap energy. Heck, if the price is right, we'll give anyone a chance!

As you know, in the former Soviet republics east of the Caspian Sea, there's hundreds of billions of dollars worth of natural gas and oil just waiting to be tapped. Everyone was trying to get in on the rush, and the U.S. government was more than eager to help them. Even President Clinton was all for the idea of the Unocal pipeline.[59]

The trick to getting our hands on all this booty was in beating the Russians to it—and we had to find a way to access it without having to build a pipeline through hostile Iran.

So, while Unocal came up with the idea of running a pipeline through Afghanistan, Enron had been working on their own plan— to bring gas from Turkmenistan and pipe it under the Caspian Sea and into Turkey. The U.S. government actually paid for Enron's feasibility study.[60] Enron was also busy with neighboring Uzbekistan, where it was trying to strike deals to develop natural gas fields there. In late 1996, Unocal had begun looking into including Uzbekistan in its pipeline deal heading through Afghanistan and into Pakistan.[61]

And then you, Mr. Bush, decided to get in on the action. You

---

58. Caroline Lees, "Oil barons court Taliban in Texas," *The Telegraph*, December 14, 1997; Barbara Crossette, "US, Iran relations show signs of thaw," *The New York Times*, December 15, 1997; "Taleban in Texas for talks on gas pipeline," *BBC News*, December 4, 1997; Kenneth Freed & Jena Janovy, "UNO partner pulls out of Afghanistan project," *Omaha World Herald*, June 6, 1998.

59. Ed Vulliamy, "US women fight Taliban oil deal," *The Guardian*, January 12, 1998; Dan Morgan, et al., "Women's fury toward Taliban stalls pipeline," *The Washington Post*, January 11, 1998.

60. "Trans-Caspian gas line receives go-ahead," *Europe Energy*, February 26, 1999.

61. Justin Weir, "Natural resources," *Institutional Investor International*, April 1997; Gerald Karey, "Unocal's Uzbekistan deal adds to Central Asia plan," *Platt's Oilgram News*, November 5, 1996.

met personally with Uzbekistan's ambassador on behalf of Enron. Enron chairman Ken Lay ended a letter to you prior to the meeting with this little bon mot:

"I know you and Ambassador Safaev will have a productive meeting which will result in a friendship between Texas and Uzbekistan.—Sincerely, Ken"[62]

What role exactly did you play in the Unocal meetings with the Taliban? I'm guessing you knew that the leaders of a foreign country were visiting your state and meeting with people who were donors to your campaign. So why exactly were brutal dictators being wined and dined in your state when you seem to be so against brutal dictators?

Of course, to be fair, you weren't the only one trying to help others make a buck from what is believed to be the world's last vast untapped reserves of oil and gas. There was the Clinton White House, Henry Kissinger and another former secretary of state, Alexander Haig, all of them willing to lend a hand.[63]

And, of course, there was Dick Cheney. Cheney was then the CEO of the giant oil services company, Halliburton. When not building jails in Guantanamo Bay, ignoring massive human rights violations in order to do business with Burma, and working deals with Libya, Iran and Saddam Hussein's Iraq (which Halliburton did happily in the nineties), Halliburton built (and still builds) oil and gas pipelines.[64] In 1998, your future co-president, Mr. Cheney, had this to say about the situation in that part of the world: "I can't think of a time when we've had a region emerge as suddenly

---

62. Letter from Kenneth L. Lay to Governor George W. Bush, April 3, 1997.

63. David B. Ottaway & Dan Morgan, "In drawing a route, bad blood flows," *The Washington Post*, October 5, 1998; Daniel Southerland, "Haig involved in plans to build gas pipeline across Iran," *Houston Chronicle*, January 22, 1995.

64. Jeremy Kahn, "Will Halliburton clean up?" *Fortune*, April 14, 2003; Peter Waldman, "A pipeline project in Myanmar puts Cheney in Spotlight," *The Wall Street Journal*, October 27, 2000; Colum Lynch, "Firm's Iraq deals greater than Cheney has said," *The Washington Post*, June 23, 2001.

to become as strategically significant as the Caspian. It's almost as if the opportunities have arisen overnight." And in a talk to the Cato Institute the same year, he revealed this information about Halliburton: "About 70 to 75 percent of our business is energy related, serving customers like Unocal, Exxon, Shell, Chevron, and many other major oil companies around the world. As a result, we oftentimes find ourselves operating in some very difficult places. The good Lord didn't see fit to put oil and gas only where there are democratically elected regimes friendly to the United States. Occasionally we have to operate in places where, all things considered, one would not normally choose to go. But, we go where the business is."[65]

Yes, there certainly was business in Afghanistan. After the Soviets were repelled in their occupation of Afghanistan by U.S.-backed mujahedeen fighters like Osama bin Laden, the U.S. quickly forgot about Afghanistan and let chaos take over.[66] The country plunged into civil war. When the Taliban rose to power in the mid-nineties, they were met with absolute glee in Washington.

Initially, the Taliban were thought to be following the U.S.-approved Saudi Arabian model of good government—stronghand oppression while giving the West what it needed. This made them a country we could play ball with. Quickly, however, their murderous ways came to light and American political leaders began to back off.[67]

But not the oil companies. Unocal stuck it out and plunged on with their pipeline deal with the Taliban, teaming up with Saudi-owned Delta Oil. Delta is headed by a man named Mohammed

---

65. Tyler Marshall, "High stakes in the Caspian," *Los Angeles Times*, February 23, 1998; Richard B. Cheney, "Defending liberty in a global economy," speech delivered to the Collateral Damage Conference at the Cato Institute, June 23, 1998.

66. Peter Gorrie, "US underestimated bin Laden at first," *Toronto Star*, September 22, 2001.

67. Ahmed Rashid, *Taliban: Militant Islam, Oil, and Fundamentalism in Central Asia*, March 2001.

Hussein Al-Amoudi, who has been investigated for ties to Osama bin Laden.[68] It didn't seem to bother either party that Osama bin Laden had taken up residence in Afghanistan, with the Taliban's blessing, in 1996—the same year he first issued his call for "Holy War" against the United States.[69]

That kill-all-the-Americans jihad talk didn't bother your close friends at Enron, either. In addition to their plan to pipe the Caspian's natural gas all the way to the Mediterranean, Ken Lay and his associates were also hard at work on another great scam. They were building a giant, natural gas-powered energy plant in Dabhol, India. The Dabhol plant, like everything else Enron cooked up (including your campaign!), was a titanic rip-off.[70] And who better to screw the indigent people of India than the same company that screwed its own American employees and customers?

But, George, I'm curious about something else here. Can you tell me if it was just coincidence that Enron and Unocal were in the same region, one building a natural gas power plant, and the other building a natural gas pipeline? Was there something else going on here?

See, this is how it looks to me—and please George, feel free to tell me if I am wrong: Unocal would pay off the Taliban to build their pipeline through Afghanistan and into Pakistan. They were then planning to build an extension on that pipeline that would run into India and stop at New Delhi. At the same time, Enron was planning to build a pipeline from Dabhol to New Delhi where, of course, it could meet up with the Turkmen pipeline, bringing Unocal and En-

---

68. Jack Meyers, et al., "Saudi clans working with US oil firms may be tied to bin Laden," *Boston Herald*, December 10, 2001.

69. Robert Fisk, "Saudi calls for jihad against US 'crusader,'" *The Independent*, September 2, 1996; Tim McGirk, et al., "The Taliban allow a top 'sponsor' of terrorism to stay in Afghanistan," *Time* magazine, December 16, 1996.

70. Claudia Kolker, "The Fall of Enron: Dead Enron power plant affecting environment, economy, and livelihoods in India," *Houston Chronicle*, August 4, 2002.

ron together.[71] An alternate Unocal plan had the pipeline terminating at the Arabian Sea in Pakistan, where the gas could be exported.[72] Enron's Dabhol plant would have been a quick tanker ride away.

But then Osama blew up two American embassies in Africa, and that was enough for President Clinton to decide he no longer wanted anything to do with Afghanistan. He responded to bin Laden by firing missiles into a Sudanese aspirin factory and a deserted al Qaeda training camp in Afghanistan.[73]

I guess one thing you and every other business student learned in school is that once your country bombs the country you're trying to do business with, the deal is pretty much off. So, two days later, Unocal suspended their involvement with the Taliban to build the pipeline in Afghanistan, and pulled out of the deal completely three months later.[74] Suddenly, the Taliban were out billions of dollars, money they desperately needed to fund their regime and to protect bin Laden.

I'm not certain, but I would guess, Mr. Bush, that the Taliban were mighty pissed off at Unocal and the Americans for going back on such a lucrative deal. One thing I do know about those crazy Taliban, they hold some mean grudges.

But one thing was clear to your friends at Enron and Unocal and Halliburton, Mr. Bush—the Taliban and Osama bin Laden really screwed business up with these two terrorist acts, and Clinton shut the deal down. So, as long as the Taliban were around and

---

71. "Turkmen-Pakistani export gas pipeline marks progress," *Oil & Gas Journal*, November 3, 1997; "Gulf gas rides to the rescue," *Middle East Economic Digest*, January 16, 1998.

72. Unocal press release, "Unocal, Delta sign MOU with Gazprom and Turkmenrusgaz for natural gas pipeline project," August 13, 1996.

73. James Astill, "Strike one: In 1998, America destroyed Osama bin Laden's 'chemical weapons' factory in Sudan. It turned out that the factory made medicine," *The Guardian*, October 2, 2001.

74. "Unocal Statement: Suspension of activities related to proposed natural gas pipeline across Afghanistan," press release, August 21, 1998; "Unocal Statement on withdrawal from the proposed Central Asia Gas (CentGas) pipeline project," press release, December 10, 1998.

giving a home to Osama, that pipeline would never be built. What would be the solution?

A new president wouldn't hurt.

Clinton was never going to let Unocal, Halliburton and Enron be in business with these terrorists.

So Enron became one of the biggest contributors to your campaign to unseat the Clinton/Gore axis. Cheney, hired to pick your vice president, ended up picking himself.[75] Then he picked a bunch of your dad's friends for the other top spots and you said okay. Then you got appointed president by the Supreme Court.

And then . . .

You weren't in office a month when the Taliban came a-knocking on your door. They still wanted those billions from the pipeline deal. Six days after Cheney set up his secret Energy Task Force, the *London Times* reported that the Taliban were offering to work out a deal with the new administration that would have involved kicking Osama out of Afghanistan, and had conveyed this to you.[76] Everyone was looking for a little quid pro quo, and it just so happened that you'd installed Zalmay Khalilzad, a former Unocal consultant, in your administration. Khalilzad, now a member of Condoleezza Rice's National Security Council, had attended a dinner for the Taliban during the Unocal meetings in Texas.[77] In October 1996, he had told *Time* magazine that the Taliban "are not into exporting revolution. Nor are they hostile to the U.S."[78]

---

75. Alison Mitchell, "Bush is reported set to name Cheney as partner on ticket," *The New York Times*, July 25, 2000.

76. Zahid Hussain, "Taleban offers US deal to deport bin Laden," *London Times*, February 5, 2001; Joseph Kahn & David E. Sanger, "President offers plan to promote oil exploration," *The New York Times*, January 30, 2001; Eric Schmitt, "Cheney assembles formidable team," *The New York Times*, February 3, 2001.

77. Joe Stephens & David B. Ottaway, "Afghan roots keep adviser firmly in the inner circle," *The Washington Post*, November 23, 2001.

78. Christopher Ogden, "Good News/Bad News in the Great Game," *Time* magazine, October 14, 1996.

To sweeten the pot, the Taliban had recently joined America's "War on Drugs." As Afghanistan was responsible for 75 percent of the world's poppy crop (the prime ingredient of heroin), this was good news to you. The Taliban banned all poppy cultivation and, after an international delegation traveled to the country and declared it poppy-free, you wasted no time in granting $43 million in "humanitarian" aid to the ravaged country. The aid was to be distributed by international organizations. This is the kind of aid that our government has almost always refused to give to places like Cuba and a host of other countries in the past. But, suddenly the Taliban were "okay."[79]

Of course, the Taliban still had huge stockpiles of heroin sitting around in warehouses, which they continued to sell. If you pretty much control the market for an in-demand substance, and then you drastically cut the availability of that product, even a failed businessman like you, George, could see what would happen. Prices will go up, up, up! As *Foreign Policy In Focus* has reported, that meant a kilo of heroin went from $44 to $700. And that's all pure profit in your evil, freedom-hating pocket if you're the Taliban.[80]

According to various reports, representatives of your administration met with the Taliban or conveyed messages to them during the summer of 2001. What were those messages, Mr. Bush? Were you discussing their offer to hand over bin Laden? Were you threatening them with a use of force? Were you talking to them about a pipeline? Did you and your administration, as one former CIA op-

79. Preston Mendenhall, "Afghanistan's cash crop wilts," MSNBC.com, May 23, 2001; Robin Wright, "U.S. pledges $43 million to ease Afghanistan famine," *Los Angeles Times*, May 18, 2001.
80. Molly Moore, "Iran fighting a losing drug war; armed villagers struggle to seal Afghanistan border," *The Washington Post*, July 18, 2001; Jerry Seper, "Cash flow for Taliban eyed as reason for opium surge," *The Washington Times*, October 3, 2001; "What is the role of drugs/heroin in Afghanistan conflict," *Foreign Policy In Focus*, December 5, 2001.

erative suggested to *The Washington Post*, foul up a chance to get bin Laden into American custody?[81] Whatever the case, the talks continued until just days before September 11. There would be no pipeline. The Taliban were out the loot, and the companies who supported you had now lost millions themselves on all the prep that went into this lucrative pipeline. What was going to happen next?

Well, we know what happened. Two planes took down the World Trade Center and another one crashed into the Pentagon. A fourth plane went down in Pennsylvania. And you decided to protect our freedom by taking some of our freedoms away. Then we swooped into Afghanistan and sent the Taliban and their al Qaeda buddies running—which was a hell of a lot easier than catching them. Most of the big shots escaped.

Oh, and we turned Afghanistan over to Unocal. The new American ambassador to Afghanistan? Unocal consultant and National Security Council member Zalmay Khalilzad. And the newly American-installed leader of Afghanistan? Former Unocal staffer Hamid Karzai.[82]

On December 27, 2001, Turkmenistan, Afghanistan and Pakistan signed a pipeline deal.[83] The gas will eventually flow from the Caspian Sea region and all of your friends will be happy.

81. Michael Elliott, et al., "They had a plan; Long before 9/11, the White House debated taking the fight to al-Qaeda," *Time* magazine, August 12, 2002; Chris Mondics, "US courted, castigated Taliban," *The Philadelphia Inquirer*, October 21, 2001; George Arney, "US 'planned attack on Taleban'" *BBC News*, September 18, 2001; David Leigh, "Attack and Counter Attack," *The Guardian*, September 26, 2001; Jonathan Steele, et al., "Threat of US strikes passed to Taliban weeks before NY attack," *The Guardian*, September 22, 2001; "US tells Taliban: End bin Laden aid," *The Chicago Tribune*, August 3, 2001; Barton Gellman, "A strategy's cautious evolution," *The Washington Post*, January 20, 2002; David B. Ottaway & Joe Stephens, "Diplomats met with Taliban on bin Laden; some contend US missed its chance," *The Washington Post*, October 29, 2001.

82. Ilene R. Prusher, et al., "Afghan power brokers," *The Christian Science Monitor*, June 10, 2002.

83. Balia Bukharbayeva, "$5 billion gas pipeline planned in Afghanistan," The Associated Press, December 28, 2002.

Something here just doesn't smell right, Mr. Bush. But it can't be the natural gas. *Natural* gas is odorless.

Question #7: What exactly was that look on your face in the Florida classroom on the morning of September 11 when your chief of staff told you, "America is under attack"?

On the afternoon of September 10, you flew down to Florida. Staying in an upscale Sarasota resort, you had dinner with brother Jeb, and then went to sleep.[84]

In the morning, you took a jog on the golf course and then headed to Booker Elementary to read to little children. You left the resort between 8:30 a.m. and 8:40 a.m., a good ten to twenty minutes after the FAA knew they had hijacked planes in the air. No one bothered to tell you.[85]

You arrived at the school after the first plane had hit the north tower in New York City. Three months later you told a third-grader at a "town hall" meeting in Orlando that you were "sitting outside the classroom waiting to go in, and I saw an airplane hit the tower—the TV was obviously on, and I used to fly myself, and I said, well, there's one terrible pilot. I said, it must have been a horrible accident. But I was whisked off there, I didn't have much time to think about it . . ."[86]

---

84. Tom Bayles, "The day before everything changed, President Bush touched locals' lives," *Sarasota Herald-Tribune*, September 10, 2002.
85. "Transcript American Airlines Flight 11," *The New York Times*, October 16, 2001; Dan Balz & Bob Woodward, "America's chaotic road to war," *The Washington Post*, January 27, 2002; Alan Levin, et al., "Part I: Terror attacks brought drastic decision: clear the skies," *USA Today*, August 12, 2002.
86. "President meets with displaced workers in town hall meeting," Official White House transcript, December 4, 2001.

You repeated that same story a month later at another "town hall" gathering in California.[87] The only problem with the story is that you *didn't* see the first plane hit the tower—*no one* saw it live on TV, as the tape wasn't aired until the next day.[88] But that's okay, we all were confused that morning.

You entered the classroom around 9 a.m.[89] and the second plane hit the south tower at 9:03 a.m.[90] Just a few minutes later, as you were sitting in front of the class of kids, listening to them read, your chief of staff, Andrew Card, entered the room and whispered in your ear. Card apparently was telling you about the second plane and the part about us being "under attack."[91]

And it was at that very moment that your face went into a distant glaze, not quite a blank look, but one that seemed partially paralyzed. No emotion was shown. And then . . . you just sat there. You sat there for another *seven minutes* or so doing *nothing*. It was, to say the least, weird. Creepy. You just stayed there in your little kid's chair and listened to children read, listening peacefully for five or six minutes.[92] You didn't look worried, you didn't excuse yourself, you weren't rushed from the room by your advisors or the Secret Service.

George, what were you thinking? WHAT was going on inside

---

87. "President holds town hall forum on economy in California," Official White House transcript, January 5, 2002. Here, Bush stated, "first of all, when we walked into the classroom, I had seen this plane fly into the first building. There was a TV set on. And you know, I thought it was pilot error and I was amazed that anybody could make such a terrible mistake. And something was wrong with the plane, or—anyway, I'm sitting there . . ."

88. Stephanie Schorow, "What did Bush see and when did he see it?" *Boston Herald*, October 22, 2002.

89. William Langley, "Revealed: What really went on during Bush's 'missing hours,'" *London Telegraph*, December 16, 2001.

90. "September 11, 2001: Basic Facts," United States State Department, August 15, 2002.

91. David E. Sanger & Don Van Natta, Jr., "In four days, a national crisis changes Bush's Presidency," *The New York Times*, September 16, 2001.

92. Ibid.

your head? What did that look on your face mean? Of all the questions I've asked you, it is *this* one that has me totally stumped.

Were you thinking you should have taken reports the CIA had given you the month before more seriously? You had been told al Qaeda was planning attacks *in* the United States and that planes would possibly be used. There had been previous intelligence reports talking of al Qaeda's interest in attacking the Pentagon.[93] Were you saying to yourself at that moment, "Well, thank God they didn't fly into the Pentagon!"?

Or were you just scared shitless? It's okay if you were, we all were. Nothing wrong with that. Except, you have taken on the mantle of commander in chief and that means you have to command when we are under attack, not just sit frozen in a chair.

Or maybe you were just thinking, "I did not want this job in the first place! This was supposed to be Jeb's job; he was the chosen one! Why me? Why me, Daddy?" Hey, we understand. And we don't blame you. You looked like a lost puppy who just wanted to go home. Suddenly, this was not the party you thought it would be, and you were no longer the CEO/President; you were now expected to be the Warrior/President. And we know what happened the last time you were expected to perform in a military uniform.

Or . . . maybe, just maybe, you were sitting there in that classroom chair thinking about your Saudi friends—both the royals and the bin Ladens. People you knew all too well that might have been up to no good. Would questions be asked? Would suspicions arise? Would the Democrats have the guts to dig into your family's past with these people (no, don't worry, never a chance of that!)? Would the truth ever come out?

Within the hour you were on a plane—not back to Washington, D.C., to lead the nation in its defense and comfort a frightened cit-

---

93. Bob Woodward and Dan Eggen, "Aug. memo focused on attacks in US," *The Washington Post*, May 18, 2002.

izenry, not even to nearby MacDill Air Force Base in Tampa where the army's central command is located.[94] No, you *ran*—first to Louisiana, and then halfway across the country to Nebraska to go into hiding underground.[95] How reassuring that was for the rest of us! For weeks afterward you and your people pushed the phony story that it was for your own safety because you yourself were the intended target of al Qaeda.

Of course, the problem with that story is that any dunderhead knew that if hijacked planes are being used as missiles, the last place you wanna be is up there flying around in the air in a big target called Air Force One.

Maybe someday we will learn what that was all about. To me and millions of others, it just looked chickenshit. And I guess by late afternoon you figured it looked like that, too, and you knew you had better hightail it back to the White House where you could look presidential.[96] From the moment your chopper landed on the south lawn that evening, your "presidency" was something no one would or should dare question again.

Two nights later, according to a *New Yorker* article written by Elsa Walsh, you went out on the Truman Balcony of the White House to relax and smoke a cigar. It had been a horrific forty-eight hours, and you needed to wind down. In that private moment, you asked one close friend to join you. As he came in the White House the two of you embraced, and then you took him out to the balcony where he had a drink that you offered him. The two of you then lit up your cigars and stared out across the Ellipse toward the Washington Monument. You told him that "if we can't get them [any al Qaeda operatives who may have been involved in the attack] to cooperate, we'll hand them over to you." It was an offer

---

94. "Timeline in terrorist attacks on Sept. 11, 2001," *The Washington Post*, September 12, 2001.
95. Ibid.
96. Ibid.

that I am sure he appreciated. After all, he was your good friend "Bandar Bush," the prince from Saudi Arabia.[97]

As the smoke from the ashes still billowed through the air over Manhattan and Arlington, the smoke from the Saudi prince's cigar wafted through the balmy night air of Washington, D.C., with you, George W. Bush, by his side.

These are my seven questions, Mr. Bush—seven questions that I believe you should answer. The 3,000 dead and their surviving loved ones deserve no less, and a nation of millions is sooner or later going to want to know the truth and demand you come clean, or leave.

---

97. Elsa Walsh, "How the Saudi Ambassador became Washington's indispensable operator," *The New Yorker*, March 24, 2003.

CHAPTER

2

Home of the Whopper

WHAT IS the worst lie a president can tell?

"I did not have sexual relations with that woman, Miss Lewinsky."

Or . . .

"He has weapons of mass destruction—the world's deadliest weapons—which pose a direct threat to the United States, our citizens and our friends and allies."

One of those lies got a president impeached. The other lie not only got the liar who told it the war he wanted, but also resulted in huge business deals for his friends and virtually assures him a landslide victory in the next election.

Sure, we've been lied to before. Lots of lies: big lies, little lies,

lies that brought us down in the eyes of the world. "I am not a crook" was a lie, and it sent Richard Nixon packing. "Read my lips: No new taxes" wasn't so much a lie as a broken promise, but it nonetheless cost the first Bush his presidency. "Ketchup is a vegetable" was technically not a lie, but it was a good example of the Reagan administration's whacked view of the world.

Other presidents lied about Vietnam, lied about Korea, lied about the Indians, lied about all men being equal (as they kept their personal slaves chained up in the backyard). Boatloads of lies for hundreds of years. And, when caught in their lies, they were disgraced, punished, or removed. Sometimes.

Maybe the reason Bush is still here is that he proved the old adage that if you tell a lie long enough and often enough, sooner or later it becomes the truth.

As the lies that led us into the Iraq War started to unravel and be exposed, the Bush administration went into survival mode with their only defensive maneuver: Keep repeating the lie over and over and over again until the American people are so worn down they'll scream "uncle!" and start believing it.

But nothing can hide this indisputable fact: There is no worse lie than one told to scare mothers and fathers enough to send their children off to fight a war that did not need to be fought *because there never was any real threat at all*. To falsely tell a nation's citizens that their lives are in jeopardy just so you can settle your own personal score ("He tried to kill my daddy!") or to make your rich friends even richer, well, in a more just world, there would be a special prison cell in Joliet reserved for that type of liar.

George W. Bush has turned the White House into the Home of the Whopper, telling one lie after another, all in pursuit of getting his dirty little war. It worked.

I like Whoppers. Flame-broiled, juicy, chock-full of onions and lettuce and loads of secret ingredients. They're big, too; bigger than a Big Mac. You don't even need to say "biggie size it, please" because it's already so damn BIG. But I know Whoppers are bad for me, so I've given them up.

George W. Bush likes whoppers, too. His are HUGE. Texas-sized. They're cooked up by a whole crew of people, and then he delivers them. And the American people gobble them up. One whopper after another. Big, juicy ones. And they go down nice and easy! The more the people eat, the more they want, and the more they think like Mr. Bush. They begin to believe everything he says because his whoppers are just so irresistibly *good*.

Bush's whoppers are available in all shapes and sizes and con-figurations. Allow me to present to you the tasty menu the Whopper-in-Chief served up special just for you. I'll call them "The Iraq War Combo Meals":

#1 The Original Whopper: "Iraq has nuclear weapons!"

There is no greater way to scare a population than to say there is a madman on the loose and he has (or is building) nuclear weapons. Nuclear weapons he intends to use on *you*.

George W. Bush laid the groundwork for scaring us silly early on. In his speech to the United Nations in September 2002, Bush said with a straight face that "Saddam Hussein has defied all these efforts and continues to develop weapons of mass destruction. The first time we may be completely certain he has a nuclear weapons [sic] is when, God forbid, he uses one."

Soon after, on October 7, Bush told a crowd in Cincinnati, "If the Iraqi regime is able to produce, buy or steal an amount of highly enriched uranium a little larger than a single softball, it could have a nuclear weapon in less than a year. . . . Facing clear evidence of peril, we cannot wait for the final proof—the smoking gun—that could come in the form of a mushroom cloud."

How to sway the American public from its initial reluctance to go to war with Iraq? Just say "mushroom cloud" and—BOOM!—watch those poll numbers turn around!

In addition to uranium from Africa, Bush said the Iraqis had "attempted to purchase high-strength aluminum tubes and other equipment needed for gas centrifuges, which are used to enrich uranium for nuclear weapons."

Frightening stuff. Imagine how much more frightening if it was actually true. Joseph Wilson, a senior American diplomat with more than 20 years of experience, including positions in Africa and Iraq, was sent to Niger in 2002 on a CIA-directed mission to investigate the British claims that Iraq had tried to buy "yellow-cake uranium" from Niger. He concluded that the allegations were false. Later, Wilson said:

> Based on my experience with the administration in the months leading up to the war, I have little choice but to conclude that some of the intelligence related to Iraq's nuclear weapons program was twisted to exaggerate the threat. . . . [The CIA] asked if I would travel to Niger to check out the story. . . . In early March, I arrived [back] in Washington and submitted a detailed briefing to the CIA. . . . There should be at least four documents in the United States government archives confirming my mission.

(In July 2003, Wilson also had this to say: "It really comes down to the administration misrepresenting the facts on an issue that was a fundamental justification for going to war. It begs the question, **what else are they lying about?**")

The White House ignored Wilson's report and instead kept the hoax alive. When the administration persisted with the fabricated story, one official, according to *The New York Times*, said, "People winced and thought, why are you repeating this trash?"

The documents from Niger were so badly faked that the Niger

foreign minister who "signed" one of them was no longer in the government—in fact, he had been, unbeknownst to the British or American liars who made up the story, out of office for more than a decade.

The aluminum tubes "discovery" also turned out to be a fictitious threat. On January 27, 2003—the day before Bush's State of the Union address—the head of the International Atomic Energy Agency, Mohamed ElBaradei, told the U.N. Security Council that two months of inspections in Iraq had produced *no* evidence of prohibited activities at former Iraqi nuclear sites. In addition, ElBaradei said, the aluminum tubes "unless modified, would not be suitable for manufacturing centrifuges."

According to reports in *The Washington Post, Newsweek*, and other publications, the assertion that the tubes could be used for nuclear weapons production had already been questioned by U.S. and British intelligence officials. U.N. inspectors said they had found proof that Iraq planned to use the tubes to build small rockets, not nuclear weapons. And the Iraqis were not trying to buy the equipment in secret—their purchase order was accessible on the Internet.

But Mr. Bush didn't let facts stand in the way of his tough-talking State of the Union address to almost sixty-two million viewers on January 28, 2003: ". . . Saddam Hussein recently sought significant quantities of uranium from Africa," he stated. "Imagine those nineteen hijackers with other weapons and other plans—this time armed by Saddam Hussein. It would take one vial, one canister, one crate slipped into this country to bring a day of horror like none we have ever known. We will do everything in our power to make sure that that day never comes."

On March 16, Co-President Dick Cheney appeared on *Meet the Press* and told the nation that Hussein has "been absolutely devoted to trying to acquire nuclear weapons. And we believe **he has, in fact, reconstituted nuclear weapons.**"

Three days later, we went to war.

*   *   *

In the spring and summer of 2003, criticism of the administration's reliance on lies about Iraq's nuclear capabilities heated up to the point that even President Bush could no longer ignore it or put a stop to the questions just by acting cranky. First, he tried to make CIA Director George Tenet the sacrificial lamb. "[The] CIA approved the president's State of the Union address before it was delivered," Tenet was ordered to say in July. "I am responsible for the approval process in my agency. And . . . the President had every reason to believe that the text presented to him was sound. These sixteen words [regarding the African uranium] should never have been included in the text written for the president." But then came the memos from October that showed that Tenet's CIA *did* tell the White House not to make such a bogus claim. While the White House initially took this advice, they repeatedly disregarded it afterwards, most notably in the State of the Union. The next scapegoat became Condoleezza Rice's deputy, Stephen Hadley, who said it was *he* who approved the language in Bush's January address. This looked so lame that finally Bush, in a rare press conference on July 30, said that he and he alone is responsible for any words that come out of his mouth. That *those* words even need to be said should make an entire nation wonder whether this guy should be the leader of the free world or flippin' Whoppers at the Waco Burger King.

#2 Whopper with Cheese: "Iraq has chemical and biological weapons!"

In his October 7, 2002, address from Cincinnati, George W. Bush offered up this freshly cooked whopper: "Some ask how urgent this danger is to America and the world. The danger is already significant, and it only grows worse with time. If we know Saddam Hussein has dangerous weapons today—and we do—does it make any sense for the world to wait to confront him as he grows even stronger and develops even more dangerous weapons?" Then, just a few months later, Bush added the cheese: "We have sources that tell us that Saddam Hussein recently authorized Iraqi field commanders to use chemical weapons—the very weapons the dictator tells us he does not have."

Who wouldn't want to bomb that bastard Saddam after hearing that? Then Secretary of State Colin Powell went even further—he said that the Iraqis weren't just concocting chemical weapons, they were doing it *on wheels!*

"One of the most worrisome things that emerges from the thick intelligence file we have on Iraq's biological weapons is the existence of mobile production facilities used to make biological agents," Powell told the United Nations. "We know that Iraq has at least seven of these mobile, biological agent factories."

He went on with such specifics that . . . *it had to be true!*

> . . . A missile brigade outside Baghdad was dispersing rocket launchers and warheads containing biological warfare agents . . . most of the launchers and warheads had been hidden in large groves of palm trees and were to be moved every one to four weeks to escape detection.
>
> Our conservative estimate is that Iraq today has a stockpile of between 100 and 500 tons of chemical weapons agents. That is enough agent to fill 16,000 battlefield rockets.

But after invading Iraq, the U.S. Army couldn't find a *single* one of these "mobile labs." After all, with so many palm trees to hide them under, who could blame our army for not uncovering them? We couldn't find any of the chemical or biological weapons either, even though on March 30, 2003, Secretary of Defense Donald Rumsfeld had said on ABC's *This Week*, "We know where they are. They're in the area around Tikrit and Baghdad and east, west, south, and north somewhat." Oh, okay, that's clear! Now we'll find them! Thank you Madhatter!

Finally, on June 5, 2003, George W. Bush declared: "We recently found two mobile biological weapons facilities, which were capable of producing biological agents. This is the man who spent decades hiding tools of mass murder. He knew the inspectors were looking for them."

That whopper lasted about a day. An official British investigation into the "two trailers" found in northern Iraq concluded "they are *not* mobile germ warfare labs, as was claimed by Tony Blair and George Bush, but were for the production of hydrogen to fill artillery balloons, as the Iraqis have continued to insist."

That was it. Tanks to fill up balloons! Weapons of mass balloonery! It was more than a little embarrassing for the American commanders in the field. Lt. Gen. James Conway, commander of the First Marine Expeditionary Force in Iraq, said, "It was a surprise to me then—it remains a surprise to me now—that we have not uncovered weapons, as you say, in some of the forward dispersal sites. . . . Believe me, it's not for lack of trying. . . . We've been to virtually every ammunition supply point between the Kuwaiti border and Baghdad, *but they're simply not there.*"

There never were any chemical or biological weapons—other than the ones we gave Saddam in the 1980s, the ones he used on the Kurds and the ones he used on the Iranians after we supplied him with the satellite photos so he could locate the Iranian troop movements. We knew why he wanted those photos and, less than a year after the U.N. reported the gassing of the Iranians, we reinstated full diplomatic relations with his regime.

It's only when you lift this whopper up off its bun a bit that you see that, yes, this guy did have weapons of mass destruction at one point—*courtesy of the USA and our allies.* Here is the list from a 1994 U.S. Senate Report of the chemical agents we allowed U.S. corporations to sell to Saddam Hussein between 1985 and 1990. We gave Saddam:

- **Bacillus Anthracis:** Anthrax is an often fatal infectious disease due to ingestion of spores. It begins abruptly with high fever, difficulty in breathing, and chest pain. The disease eventually results in septicemia (blood poisoning), and the mortality rate is high. Once septicemia is advanced, antibiotic therapy may prove useless, probably because the exotoxins remain, despite the death of the bacteria.

- **Clostridium Botulinum:** A bacterial source of botulinum toxin, which causes vomiting, constipation, thirst, general weakness, headache, fever, dizziness, double vision, dilation of the pupils, and paralysis of the muscles involving swallowing. It is often fatal.

- **Histoplasma Capsulatum:** Causes a disease superficially resembling tuberculosis that may cause pneumonia, enlargement of the liver and spleen, anemia, an influenzalike illness, and an acute inflammatory skin disease marked by tender red nodules, usually on the shins. Reactivated infection usually involves the lungs, the brain, spinal membranes, heart, peritoneum, and the adrenals.

- **Brucella Melitensis:** A bacteria that can cause chronic fatigue, loss of appetite, profuse sweating when at rest, pain in joints and muscles, insomnia, nausea, and damage to major organs.

- **Clostridium Perfringens:** A highly toxic bacteria that causes gas gangrene. The bacteria produce toxins that move along muscle bundles in the body, killing cells and producing necrotic tissue that is then favorable for further growth of the bacteria itself. Eventually, these toxins and bacteria enter the bloodstream and cause a systemic illness.

In addition, several shipments of Escherichia coli (E. coli) and genetic materials, as well as human and bacterial DNA, were shipped directly to the Iraq Atomic Energy Commission.

Records of U.S. corporate sales of biological material to Iraq before 1985 were "not available." The Senate report also noted, "These exported biological materials were not attenuated or weakened and were capable of reproduction." The first two, anthrax and botulinum, were the cornerstone of Iraq's biological weapons program, all of it made wonderfully possible by the United States of America.

As William Blum reported in *The Progressive*, "The report noted further that U.S. exports to Iraq included the precursors to chemical-warfare agents, plans for chemical and biological warfare production facilities, and chemical-warhead filling equipment."

There are numerous other biological materials that could be used in biological weapons that were sent to Iraq during the 1980s and documented in the 1994 Senate Report and through the Centers for Disease Control.

All of the above came from American companies, and were sent with the *permission* of the United States government during the Reagan/Bush years. Some of the companies include American Type Culture Collection, Alcolac International, Matrix-Churchill Corp., Sullaire Corp., Pure Aire, and Gorman-Rupp.

American companies also were responsible for delivering to Iraq "dual-use" technologies, including high-powered computers, lasers, and other items instrumental to the making of nuclear weapons and their components. As *L.A. Weekly* reported in 2003, Senate hearings and government records reveal that these companies included:

- **Hewlett-Packard**—Worked with Iraq from 1985 to 1990, supplying computers for an arm of the Iraqi government working on the scud and nuclear programs. HP also sent computers to two government agencies that oversaw the nuclear and chemical weapons programs. Other sales included radar components and cryptographic equipment.
- **AT&T**—In 2000 was paid to optimize the products of another company, Huawei. Between 2000 and 2001, Iraq was paying Huawei to spiff up their air defense systems.
- **Bechtel**—From 1988 to 1990, it was helping the Iraqis build a giant petrochemical plant, hand in hand with an Iraqi company known for its military ties.

- **Caterpillar**—Helped Iraq with construction of their nuclear program in the 1980s through the sale of $10 million worth of tractors.
- **DuPont**—In 1989, sold $30,000 worth of specially engineered oil to Iraq which was used in their nuclear program.
- **Kodak**—Also in 1989, sold $172,000 in equipment that was used in Iraq's missile programs.
- **Hughes Helicopter**—Sold sixty helicopters to Iraq in 1983, which the Iraqis modified for military use.

In all, from 1985 to 1990, the Department of Commerce approved the sale of $1.5 billion worth of dual-use technologies, from chemical and biological components to computers and equipment for conventional and nuclear weapons systems. In the same period $308 million worth of aircraft, helicopters and associated parts were also transferred to Iraq.

But America was doing far more than just handing Saddam Hussein the stepping-stones for chemical, biological and nuclear weapons. The Reagan/Bush White House was also hard at work securing even more military might for the Iraqi dictator.

In August 2002, senior military officers revealed to *The New York Times* an even broader view of America's aid. Our boys in D.C. thought it would be a grand idea to give the Iraqis intelligence information and battle-planning advice in the war against Iran, knowing full well that Iraq had used and would continue to use chemical weapons in these battles.

You see, the administration had made the decision that Iraq could not lose the Iran-Iraq war, and that they would do everything they could "legally" do to ensure that madman Saddam Hussein was victorious. Reagan went so far as to sign a national security directive backing this promise up.

In a 1995 sworn affidavit, the directive's co-author and a member of Reagan's National Security Council, Howard Teicher, revealed even more about America's involvement:

CIA Director Casey personally spearheaded the effort to ensure that Iraq had sufficient military weapons, ammunition and vehicles to avoid losing the Iran-Iraq war. Pursuant to the secured *[National Security Directive]*, the United States actively supported the Iraqi war effort by supplying the Iraqis with billions of dollars of credits, by providing U.S. military intelligence and advice to the Iraqis, and by closely monitoring third-country arms sales to Iraq to make sure that Iraq had the military weaponry required.

One of those "third-country arms sales" was of particular interest. Imagine our shock when it was discovered that our good despotic friends the Saudis had "accidentally" transferred 300 American-made MK-84 2,000-pound bombs to Iraq. For the most part, though, Reagan's handlers were smart enough to funnel weapons untraceably through other countries.

It wasn't just his handlers who were getting involved. Reagan and Bush I decided to personally get their hands dirty. According to Teicher's affidavit:

[I]n 1986, President Reagan sent a secret message to Saddam Hussein telling him that Iraq should step up its air war and bombing of Iran. **This message was delivered by Vice President Bush** who communicated it to Egyptian President Mubarak, who in turn passed the message to Saddam Hussein.

Even after Saddam used his weapons of mass destruction to gas his own people—an event Bush and his buddies are so totally offended by now, a decade and a half too late—the Reagan administration was unfazed. The United States Congress tried to put economic sanctions on Hussein's country, but the White House quashed the idea. Their reasons? According to declassified State Department documents, economic sanctions might hurt America's chances at contracts for "massive postwar reconstruction" once the Iran-Iraq war finally came to a close.

Weapons of mass destruction? Oh yeah, he had them at one time. All we had to do was check the receipts and count the profits as they rolled into the bank account of the campaign backers of Reagan and Bush.

#3 Whopper with Bacon: "Iraq has ties to Osama bin Laden and al Qaeda!"

As if having the atomic bomb, nerve gas and the bubonic plague in a bottle wasn't enough, suddenly Saddam Hussein was in cahoots with the Mother of All Terrorists himself, Osama bin Laden! I'm sure you had the same reaction I did when you heard: "How much worse can it get? When can we get rid of this Saddam guy?"

Just hours after the attacks on September 11, U.S. Secretary of Defense Donald Rumsfeld had already figured out who was responsible, or at least, who he wanted to punish. According to CBS News, Rumsfeld wanted as much information as possible about the attacks, and told his fact-finding team to "go massive. . . . Sweep it all up. Things related and not." He already had intelligence indicating a connection to Osama (whom he called "Usama"), but he wanted more because he had other goals in mind. He wanted intelligence "good enough to hit S.H. [Saddam Hussein] at the same time. Not only U.B.L."

W.A.B.O.B.S!

I say Osama, you say Usama . . . and Rumsfeld just says the magic word "Saddam" and before you know it, everyone else was saying it, too! Ret. Gen. Wesley Clark has said that he received phone calls on September 11 and in the weeks after from people at "think tanks" and from people within the White House telling him to use his position as a pundit for CNN to "connect" September 11 to Saddam Hussein. He said he'd do it if someone could show him the proof. No one could.

During the buildup to war in the fall of 2002, Bush and members of his administration kept repeating the claim, keeping it uncluttered by specifics (also known as "facts") so it stayed nice and simple and easy to remember. Bush circled the country at campaign stops for Republican congressional candidates, inseminating the minds of the American people with the bogus Saddam/Osama connection on a continuous loop. Check out just one week's worth of serial lying:

"This [Hussein] is a person who can't stand America. This is a person who has had contacts with al Qaeda."

—*George W. Bush, Alamogordo, New Mexico, October 28, 2002*

"He's a threat to America and he's a threat to our friends. He's even more of a threat now that we've learned that he's anxious to have, once again, to develop a nuclear weapon. He's got connections with al Qaeda."

—*George W. Bush, Denver, Colorado, October 28, 2002*

"This is a man who cannot stand what we stand for. He hates the fact, like al Qaeda does, that we love freedom. See, they can't stand that. This is a guy who has had connections with these shadowy terrorist networks."

—*George W. Bush, Aberdeen, South Dakota, October 31, 2002*

"That's the nature of this man. We know he's got ties with al Qaeda."

—*George W. Bush, Portsmouth, New Hampshire, November 1, 2002*

"We know that he's had connections with al Qaeda."

—*George W. Bush, Tampa, Florida, November 2, 2002*

"This is a man who has had contacts with al Qaeda. This is a man who poses a serious threat in many forms, but catch this form: He's the kind of guy that would love nothing more than to train terrorists and provide arms to terrorists so they could attack his worst enemy and leave no fingerprints. This guy is a threat to the world."

—*George W. Bush, St. Paul, Minnesota, November 3, 2002*

"This is a man who can't stand America and what we believe in. This is a man who hates some of our closest allies. This is a man who has had al Qaeda connections."

—*George W. Bush, St. Louis, Missouri, November 4, 2002*

"This is the kind of guy we're dealing with. This is a man who hates America, he hates our friends, he can't stand what we believe in. He's had contacts with al Qaeda."

—*George W. Bush, Bentonville, Arkansas, November 4, 2002*

"This is a man who cannot stand America, he cannot stand what we stand for, he can't stand some of our closest friends and allies. This is a man who has got connections with al Qaeda."

—*George W. Bush, Dallas, Texas, November 4, 2002*

Just in case we missed the point, Bush continued to hammer it home in his State of the Union address on January 28, 2003: "Evidence from intelligence sources, secret communications, and statements by people now in custody reveal that Saddam Hussein aids and protects terrorists, including members of al Qaeda," Bush insisted.

Immediately following the address, a CBS online poll found that support for U.S. military action in Iraq increased.

A week later, on February 5, Bush's claims were echoed by Secretary of State Colin Powell in a lengthy address to the United Nations Security Council. After detailing what Powell said were Iraq's numerous failures to comply with weapons inspections, he moved on to the Saddam/Osama connection: "But what I want to bring to your attention today is the potentially much more sinister nexus between Iraq and the al Qaeda network, a nexus that combines classic terrorist organizations and modern methods of murder."

But the meat of the administration's "evidence" had already begun to turn rancid. During that same first week of February, a British intelligence report leaked to the BBC said there were no links between Saddam and Osama. The two evildoers had tried to form a friendship in the past, but it had turned out like a great episode of *Blind Date*—they *hated* each other. According to the report, Bin Laden's "aims are in ideological conflict with present-day Iraq."

On top of this, the al Qaeda poison and explosives factory Bush and his team claimed Saddam was harboring was located in northern Iraq—an area controlled by Kurds and patrolled by U.S. and British warplanes since the early nineties. The north of Iraq was out of Saddam's reach, but within our own. The base actually belonged to Ansar al Isalam, a militant fundamentalist group whose leader has branded Saddam Hussein an "enemy." A tour of the base by a large group of international journalists quickly revealed that no weapons were being manufactured there.

But none of that mattered. The president had said it—*it had to be true!* Yes, this whopper worked so well that, in the months leading up to the war in Iraq, polls showed that up to half of Americans said they believed that Saddam Hussein had ties to Osama bin Laden's network. Even before Bush had served up his 2003 State of the Union address, and Powell had presented the Saddam-Osama "evidence" to the U.N., a Knight-Ridder poll found that half of those questioned already incorrectly thought that one or more of the 9/11 hijackers held Iraqi citizenship. Bush didn't even have to say it.

The Bush administration had succeeded in perpetrating one of the biggest lies of all time, confusing Saddam with Osama in the minds of the American public. Once you sell the people on the notion that Saddam had a hand in the mass murder of nearly 3,000 people on American soil, well, even if the bogus weapons of mass destruction whopper didn't hold up, this would be enough to get the flags waving and the troops a-packin'.

Of course the problem with this whopper—other than it is a cynical, premeditated fabrication—is that Osama bin Laden considers Saddam to be an infidel. Hussein committed the sin of creating a secular Iraq instead of a Muslim state run by fanatical Muslim clerics. Under Saddam, Baghdad had churches, mosques and, yes, even a synagogue. Hussein had persecuted and killed thousands and thousands of Shiites in Iraq because of the threat they posed to his secular government.

In fact, the biggest reason Saddam and Osama don't like each other is the same reason the Bushes stopped liking Saddam: the invasion of Kuwait. Bush & Co. was pissed because Saddam was threatening the security of our oil in the Gulf, and Osama was pissed because it brought American troops to Saudi Arabia and the Muslim holy lands. That's bin Laden's biggest problem with us—and it's all because of Saddam!

Saddam and Osama were mortal enemies and they could not put their mutual hatred aside, even to join together to defeat the USA. Man, to not team up when it meant destroying the Great Satan Bush—THAT is a lot of hate!

#4 Whopper, Heavy on the Pickles and Onions: "Saddam Hussein is the world's most evil man!"

Okay, he was bad. Really bad. He gassed the Kurds, gassed the Iranians, tortured the Shiites, tortured the Sunnis, tortured countless others, and during the sanctions against Iraq, let his people starve and suffer all types of deprivation while he hoarded money and kept his many palaces well-stocked with provisions (and a petting zoo for his nutcase adult sons).

This is all gruesome stuff, and the world was right to condemn him and to support any efforts by the people of Iraq to have him removed.

But the United States never gave a rat's ass about how badly Saddam the Dictator treated his own people. We *never* care about that stuff. In fact, we like dictators! They help us get what we want and they do a great job of keeping their nations subservient to our galloping global corporate interests.

We have a long and proud history of propping up madmen and their regimes as long as it helps us rule the world. Obviously, there are our old pals the Saudis, and there's Saddam, and then there's these places where we proudly sowed our oats:

- **Cambodia**—After secretly extending the Vietnam War into Cambodia in the late sixties and then watching the already decimated country slip under the control of Pol Pot and his Khmer Rouge, the United States chose to support this madman for the simple reason that he offered opposition to the Vietnamese communists, who had just fought mighty America to total defeat. Then he took control and wiped out millions of his own people.

- **The Congo/Zaire**—The CIA got in bed with Mobutu Sese-Seku early, setting off years of horrific violence that continues today. Afraid of the nationalist leader Patrice Lumumba, America helped Mobutu to power, oversaw the assassination of Lumumba and then helped crush the resulting uprisings. Mobutu took dictatorial control, outlawed political activity, had people killed, and ruled the country until 1990, with the continued help of the United States (and, yes, also the dastardly French). With the approval of successive American governments he spread his fingers through the crises of his neighboring African countries.

• **Brazil**—Left-leaning, democratically elected President Joaõ Goulart wasn't what Washington had in mind for South America's largest country. Despite pledging his solidarity to the United States during the Cuban missile crisis, Goulart's days were numbered. Preferring friendly authoritarian rule to democracy, the United States pushed a coup on Brazil, which resulted in 15 years of terror, torture and killing.

• **Indonesia**—The Southeast Asian archipelago state is one of America's favorite allies, and also happens to be home to yet another repressive regime. It is also the world's most populous Muslim country. In 1965, yet another democratically elected president was overthrown with the help of the United States government, which installed in his place yet another military dictatorship. General Suharto headed a hard-line government that ruled the country for three decades. Around half a million people were killed in the years after Suharto took power, but that didn't stop the U.S. from approving, in advance, Indonesia's illegal annexation of East Timor in the seventies. About 200,000 more people died there.

Of course, there are many, many more examples, from dictators we supported to democratically elected governments we simply threw into chaos or got rid of altogether (Guatemala and Iran in the fifties and Chile in the seventies are further examples of how much we love freedom by helping to overthrow heads of state who were *chosen* by their own citizens).

These days, China, the world's biggest Saddam-o-rama, is our favorite dictatorship. The government imposes severe limits on media outlets, the Internet, workers' rights, religious freedom, and any attempts at independent thinking. Combined with a judicial system that totally ignores any rule of law and is festering with corruption, China is a perfect place for American companies to do business. There are more than 800 Kentucky Fried Chicken restaurants in

China, around 400 McDonald's and another 100 Pizza Huts. Kodak is quickly approaching a monopoly on film sales.

The many companies who have set up shop there are not only hawking their wares to the Chinese. The $103 billion trade imbalance between China and the United States is the largest deficit between two countries the world has ever seen. We import six times as much as we export, with Wal-Mart alone accounting for $12 billion worth of Chinese imports, making the All Sino-American company one of China's biggest trading partners—ahead of Russia and Great Britain.

There are plenty of other companies taking advantage of the state-controlled cheap labor in China, too, from General Motors to Boeing to . . . hell, just take off your pants and have a look at the label, or dismantle your television. Or take off your pants while you're dismantling your television. And while China makes a killing on exports, and American corporations make a killing on high-profit returns, the American economy flounders, and the Chinese people, well, they just wait for the government's mobile killing vans to pull around the corner, grab them, and put them out of their misery.

If the criteria for invading another country is "liberating the people from an oppressive regime," well then, we better hurry up and institute mandatory military service for every man and woman eighteen and older because—by God—we're going to be busy! Since we've already invaded Iraq to "free the Iraqis," we might as well continue with the other countries we've royally screwed. After that, maybe we can head back to Afghanistan, then on to Burma, Peru, Colombia, Sierra Leone, and end up somewhere that at least *sounds* nice, Côte d'Ivoire.

Before the Iraq War, when the public was being duped with the endless barrage of whoppers, the idea of "liberation of the Iraqi people" was always tacked on as an afterthought. It never took a front and center position in the justifications for why we had to go to war *right then*. Why? Obviously those who choose our wars don't care much about liberating people from oppressive regimes—if they did, we'd be kicking the shit out of half the world. No, they talk about "our security" and, even more important to them, "our interests." And we all know that "our interests" have never included the good life for anyone but us. We don't share the wealth—be it monetary or ideological—we just cover our own asses and enhance our own well-being. It's plain to see, and it's everywhere—from "welfare to work" to our exploitation of cheap labor to our historical love of dictators to our refusal to forgive Third World debt. Liberation sounds nice, but it ain't worth dying for, and it sure as hell isn't worth a dime of our money. Cheap gas, cheap clothes, cheap TVs? Yeah . . . that's more like it!

Even professional warmonger and Bush advisor Paul Wolfowitz came clean with the truth, in the Defense Department transcript of a May 2003 interview with *Vanity Fair*:

> The truth is that for reasons that have a lot to do with the U.S. government bureaucracy we settled on the one issue that everyone could agree on which was weapons of mass destruction as the core reason . . . [T]here have always been three fundamental concerns. One is weapons of mass destruction, the second is support for terrorism, the third is the criminal treatment of the Iraqi people. Actually I guess you could say there's a fourth overriding one which is the connection between the first two. . . .
>
> The third one by itself, as I think I said earlier, is a reason to help the Iraqis but it's not a reason to put American kids' lives at risk, certainly not on the scale we did it.

Not worth the risk? Then why did we do it?

Of course, Wolfowitz had deviated from the script. When no weapons of mass destruction were found and not a single al Qaeda guy showed up in the parts of Iraq under Saddam Hussein's control, and when that imminent threat Saddam posed to America's security couldn't be proven, the Bush administration and its many media puppets quickly tried to change their whopper order. "No, you see, we weren't there to find nuclear weapons, *we were there to free the people of Iraq!* Yes, um, that's the reason we bombed the place and sent 150,000 troops to invade!"

You know how sometimes they give you the wrong Whopper, when they've switched yours with someone else's? You then have to decide whether you're going to just go ahead and eat this other Whopper or take it back and get the one you ordered.

After the original "justifications" for war were exposed as lies, this new whopper gave pro-war Democrats and liberals a place to duck when they went looking for cover. How could they be so stupid as to believe Bush's claims regarding the weapons of mass destruction and the 9/11 connection? "Hey, we weren't stupid—look at all these mass graves we've uncovered. That's why we supported the war—to stop this brutality and oppression!" the Democrats cried.

That's right. Say it two more times, click your heels together and tell yourself there's no place like home, there's no place like home, there's no place like home. That's what we have brought to the Iraqis—a little piece of home. The American Way. Democracy. That's why we're there. That's what we'll give them.

Recently on *Nightline,* they were interviewing an Iraqi woman who is pro-American and teaches English. She said that things are so bad now since the American invasion, she sometimes wishes Saddam were still in power. Her sentiment seems widespread. Twenty years of living under a brutal dictator—and after only *ninety days* of living under the Americans—they want Saddam back! Jeez, how bad a houseguest have we been?

It seems that the crazy clerics are succeeding in filling the vacuum left by Saddam and now it's "meet the new boss, same as the old boss" time in Iraq. The Bush administration continually postpones turning control of the country over to the Iraqi people whom they've liberated. Why is that?

Because they know that if elections were held today, the people would democratically vote to stop having democracy and to give the country over to some rabid fundamentalist. Already women are living in fear for their lives if they don't "cover up," and anyone who sells alcohol or shows movies is facing execution. Woo hoo! Freedom! Democracy! Liberation!

I can't wait to see who we're going to free next around the world!

#5 Whopper with Freedom Fries (and *American* Cheese): "The French are not on our side and they may be our enemy!"

When you're into Tourette's lying, a number of things can happen. For instance, you're telling so many lies, you forget which lie you're telling, or which one you're supposed to be telling, or who you're telling it to, or if you've already told this person, or maybe you told it slightly differently before and you're trying your damnedest to make sure the stories match and then you have to get everybody who has joined you in the serial lying all on the same page and before you know it you're so jimmie-jammed up and spinning yourself into such a mess that your only recourse, your only way out, is to blame someone else.

Enter France.

When you need a scapegoat, when you need a worthy whipping boy, you really can't do better than the country of France. And that's who the Bush pundits went after, accusing the French of being an "Axis of Weasels." All this was done to distract the American public from the real rats who were in Washington.

France had decided not to support any rush to war in Iraq. It tried to convince the United States to let the weapons inspectors do their job. The French minister of foreign affairs, Dominique de Villepin, spoke eloquently at the United Nations as the war began:

> Make no mistake about it: the choice is indeed between two visions of the world. To those who choose to use force and think they can resolve the world's complexity through swift and preventive action, we offer in contrast determined action over time. For today, to ensure our security, all the dimensions of the problem must be taken into account: both the manifold crises and their many facets, including cultural and religious. Nothing lasting in international relations can be built therefore without dialogue and respect for the other, without exigency and abiding by principles, especially for the democracies that must set the example. To ignore this is to run the risk of misunderstanding, radicalization and spiraling violence. This is even more true in the Middle East, an area of fractures and ancient conflicts where stability must be a major objective for us.

During the first Gulf War, the United States had the support of an actual coalition of powerful allies. But when it came to Gulf War– The Sequel, most of those countries weren't so eager to sign up. Bush and his crack team of diplomats were left with a not-so-broad, not-so-daunting forty-nine-member "Coalition of the Willing." Most of these were countries (such as Tonga, Azerbaijan, and Palau) who always get picked last for United Nations volleyball games and will *NEVER* get invited to the Prom (not even by their desperate cousins). They're pathetically grateful to be asked for anything. (See Whopper #6.)

You'd think that if there was a serious threat of Saddam Hussein using his vast stockpile of weapons of mass destruction, or invading another nation, more countries would have quickly jumped into the fray to stop the madman, especially those countries much closer to Iraq.

The French, meanwhile, were taking it in the baguette. You

don't disobey the United States and get away with it! And you certainly don't tell everyone we're lying—*especially* when we are. Bush, his policy-makers, and all their little mouthpieces got busy attacking the Frenchies.

There was soft-spoken diplomat Colin Powell on PBS saying, "It was a very difficult period as we went through that second resolution vote and we didn't believe that France was playing a helpful role." When Powell was asked if France would suffer for not supporting America's stance on war, the secretary of state said simply, "Yes."

Donald Rumsfeld took a different approach—a more insulting one—in responding to a question about Europe's view of the war, "You're thinking of Europe as Germany and France. I don't. I think that's old Europe." (Rummy apparently prefers to think of Europe—or *Nouveau Europe*, as he calls it—as containing only such vital coalition members as Albania, Estonia, Hungary, Latvia and Slovakia.)

On the subject of French President Jacques Chirac, Bush told Tom Brokaw of NBC, "I doubt he'll be coming to the ranch any time soon." (Chirac was no doubt heartbroken at the prospect of missing a visit to Crawford, Texas.)

But it was an anonymous White House staffer who dealt the harshest punishment of all—accusing Democratic presidential hopeful (and decorated Vietnam veteran) Senator John Kerry of looking "French."

Representative Jim Saxton, R-New Jersey, proposed legislation in the House to keep French companies from getting U.S. financing for the reconstruction of Iraq. His colleague, Representative Ginny Brown-Waite, R-Florida, cooked up an even better way to really give the French the old "what for"—she introduced a bill to bring the bodies of World War II soldiers who had died and been buried in France back to the United States. "The remains of our brave heroes should be buried in patriotic soil," she explained, "not in a country that has turned its back on us."

An anti-tax group ran ads against two Republican U.S. senators who opposed Bush's tax cut. The ads pictured each senator standing next to a waving French flag with the message: "President Bush courageously led the forces of freedom but some so-called allies like France stood in the way. At home, President Bush has proposed bold job-creating tax cuts to boost the economy. But some so-called Republicans . . . stand in the way."

Fox News commentator Sean Hannity told his viewers, "If I had a trip planned to France this summer, I would have cancelled it. I'm going to tell you why. What Jacques Chirac did in our moment of need and how he undermined us and to the extent that he did it for his own selfish reasons, his duplicity is beyond forgiveness at this point. I'm sorry, I just—I would tell every American to stay away from France, go to Great Britain."

It wasn't long after being fed these French Whoppers that the American people took the bait. French wine was poured onto the street, and, at one New Jersey restaurant, down the toilet. French restaurants were shunned. Vacationers cancelled their plans to travel to France—with bookings down 30 percent. The Congressional dining room substituted "freedom" fries for french fries on its menu, following the lead of a North Carolina restaurant owner who was following the lead of a WWI-era effort to rename sauerkraut "liberty cabbage." Restaurants across the country followed suit, and as the president of the Fuddruckers restaurant chain put it, "Every guest who steps up to a counter at their local Fuddruckers and says, 'Give me freedom fries!' shows their true support for those who guard our most important freedoms, especially freedom from fear." (Not to mention freedom from facts: What we know as "French" fries originated in Belgium.)

More than 200 years ago, Patrick Henry voiced the battle cry of the American Revolution with "Give me liberty or give me death!" Today he could demonstrate his patriotic zeal by changing his takeout order.

A Lebanese-owned chain of stores in California's San Joaquin Valley, French Cleaners, had one of its stores tagged with anti-French graffiti and another burned to the ground. The French-owned Sofitel Hotel in Manhattan replaced the French flag flying outside with Old Glory. Fromage.com, a French cheese distributor, received hundreds of hostile e-mails.

In Las Vegas, an armored fighting vehicle, complete with two machine guns and a 76-millimeter cannon, was used to crush French yogurt, French bread, bottles of French wine, Perrier, Grey Goose vodka, photos of Chirac, a guide to Paris, and, best of all, photocopies of the French flag. The makers of British-owned French's Mustard didn't wait for a backlash; they put out a press release explaining that "the only thing French about French's Mustard is the name!"

Throughout the U.S., programs that matched visiting French students with American families were unable to find enough U.S. hosts for the first time in years.

One weasel who escaped this wrath was the White House pastry chef—a man who despite his Frenchness was entrusted with preparing our president's meals. Mocking your longtime allies by renaming food and wasting a lot of expensive wine is all fine and good, but George W. Bush still needs his *pain au chocolat*—it gives him fortitude, or "Freedom Strength."

Of course, it was easy to go after France. Too many of its citizens had been "rude" to us, and it had this history of always seeming to cave to despots. While it had brave Resistance fighters and many French citizens died during World War II, instead of fighting the Germans to the bitter end (like the Russians did), France decided to cooperate and collaborate, especially when it came to rounding up the Jews and Commies and sending them off to die in concentration camps.

Plus, the French had a history of not getting things quite right. Like the Maginot Line, a series of bunkers built along the French-German border before World War II to defend France from the invading Huns. The only problem was, they built the bunkers facing the wrong way and Germans were deep into France before you could say "garçon, more stinky cheese, please!"

Then there's the simple jealousy factor. Most Americans know the

French are more sophisticated, more intelligent, more well-read than the average American. We don't like to admit that it was the French who invented the movies, the automobile, the stethoscope, Braille, photography, and most important of all, the Etch A Sketch. They've brought us the Enlightenment, and The Enlightenment paved the way for the widespread acceptance of all the ideas and principles that America was founded on. Then when we find out that the French have to work only thirty-five hours a week and everyone gets at least four weeks paid vacation, all we can do is make snide remarks about their unions and how they're always shutting their country down.

So, France was the perfect country to pick on. And it was an entertaining distraction. If you're a cable news company, why spend priceless reporting time on investigating whether Iraq really does have weapons of mass destruction when you can do a story about how rotten the French are?

Yet, after the lies started to unravel, a few people started to reconsider what they had been told about the French and what they really did to us.

It turns out, it was more like what the French have done *for* us.

Most Americans can barely remember who won last year's Super Bowl, let alone the true story of how this country was founded.

We all know about the Tea Party and Paul Revere's midnight ride, but we like to forget that we could never have won the war without the French. Hell, we don't even want to think about the fact that Revere's father was . . . French (and it wasn't Revere—it was Rivoire!). But, it was the French and British war over Canada that really pushed the colonists over the edge. They were left to pay taxes on stamps and on tea to the crown to help the crown pay for a war the colonies had not gotten themselves into. When the colonial anger and frustration peaked and the colonies decided to break away, they knew perfectly well that they could not do it alone. They turned to the French, and the French gleefully agreed to aid in the humiliation of the British. They sent troops, ships, 90 percent of the gunpowder we used, and tens of millions of dollars.

The war ended at Yorktown with the British surrendering to Washington and the band playing "The World Turned Upside Down"—but the Brits were actually surrendering to the French. The Redcoats were boxed in by the French navy, and on that final day, there were more French troops in the ranks than colonists.

In fact, France has always been the best friend to the United States. Almost a third of France's direct foreign investment is in the United States. They are our fifth largest investor, and the French employ 650,000 people in the United States. The Universal Declaration of Human Rights was written by a committee chaired by Eleanor Roosevelt with Rene Cassin of France as the vice-chair. And, much like in Vietnam, we share a joint sordid history in Iraq where the Iraqi Petroleum Company—owned by U.S., British, Dutch and French oil giants—exploited Iraq's oil.

Still, Americans accused the French of all kinds of treachery when it came to Iraq. There were claims that the French were only opposing war to get economic benefits out of Saddam Hussein's Iraq. In fact, it was the Americans who were making a killing. In 2001, the U.S. was Iraq's leading trading partner, consuming more than 40 percent of Iraq's oil exports. That's $6 billion in trade with the Iraqi dictator. By contrast, 8 percent of Iraq's oil exports went to France in 2001.

Fox News led the charge of pinning Chirac to Saddam Hussein, showing old footage of the two men together. It didn't matter that the meeting had taken place in the 1970s. The media didn't bother to run (over and over again) the footage from when Saddam was presented with a key to the city of Detroit, or the film in the early 1980s, when Donald Rumsfeld went to visit Saddam in Baghdad to discuss the progress of the Iran-Iraq War. Those videos of Rumsfeld embracing Saddam apparently weren't worth running on a continuous loop. Or even once. Okay, maybe once. On *Oprah*. And when she showed Rumsfeld all lovey with Saddam, there was an audible gasp in her studio audience. Everyday, average Americans were shocked to see that the devil was actually *our* devil. Thank you, Oprah.

How soon we forgot that it was the French who led the United Nations Security Council on the day after September 11 to condemn the attacks and demand justice for the victims. Jacques Chirac was the *first* foreign leader to travel to America after the attacks to offer his support and condolences.

One of the signs of true friendship is when your friend feels comfortable enough to let you know when you're screwing up. That is the kind of friend you should *hope* for. That is the kind of friend France was being—until we took a piss on our best friend, biting into the whopper while freedom fried.

#6 Whopper Combo, Extra Lettuce: "This is not just the United States going to Iraq. It is a Coalition of the Willing!"

This is my favorite whopper because I can't stop laughing whenever I think about it.

In order to put some sort of international feel-good happy face on our invasion of Iraq, Bush stated that, hey, it's not just we who feel this way about Saddam: "Many nations, however, do have the resolve and fortitude to act against the threat to peace, and a broad coalition is now gathering to enforce the just demands of the world. The United Nations Security Council has not lived up to its responsibilities, so we will rise to ours."

Of course, it's always better sharing your whopper with friends. And the more the better. That way, everyone shares in the sacrifice equally. No one country will have to see only *its* young boys and girls die. No one country's citizens will have to bear the entire burden of billions of dollars to fight the war and then rebuild the country. No one country wants to see its cities and states go bankrupt, and run up billions of dollars in debt, just to remove one lousy dictator. So, let's create a coalition to share the load—what a lovely idea.

Only one problem: Hardly anybody wanted to join this "Coalition of the Willing." So just who were the motley crew of oddball nations that signed on to Bush's madness? Let's take a look at the list. It beings with . . .

Afghanistan.

Okay, stop right there. Afghanistan? What exactly was their contribution going to be? Horses? Ten sticks and a stone? Don't they have their own problems at the moment? Or did they have a warlord or two to spare to help us out in Iraq? I have asked the State Department to provide me with a list of the contributions that the nation of Afghanistan made to the war effort and so far no one has responded.

Batting next for the "Coalition of the Willing" is another heavy-hitter: Albania. Is this the same Albania where the main industry is survival farming, where there's one phone for every thirty people? Let's keep going . . .

Australia. Now that's a real country! Except the polls in Australia leading up to the war showed that its citizens, by a margin of 70 percent, opposed the war. So how did they get on the list? George W. Bush dangled the prospect of a free-trade agreement in front of Australian Prime Minister John Howard. If you can't join 'em, or they won't join you, bribe 'em.

Meanwhile Aussie neighbor New Zealand, who refused to join the coalition, was then—surprise!—shut out of trade talks.

Back to the "Willing": Azerbaijan (we're coming to get their oil next so they had no friggin' choice), Bulgaria (anytime you've got Bulgaria on your side, how can you lose? Plus I got to write "Bulgaria" twice in the same book!), Colombia (taking a break from that other war we're fighting there), the Czech Republic (how embarrassing! We were going to let you into NATO anyway!), Denmark (this alone should disqualify them from membership in Scandinavia—I never thought they belonged in it anyway. Let Finland in, where it belongs!), El Salvador (we didn't annex them for nothin'), Eritrea (where the hell is that?), Estonia (see, France, *some* Nazi collaborators love us!), Ethiopia (nothing like sending a squad of starving children to help!), Georgia, Hungary, Italy (that's the second real country, with 69 percent opposed to the war), Japan (no way! I don't believe this! Do the Japanese people, 70 percent of whom opposed the war, know they got put on this list?), South Korea, Latvia (more Nazi collaborators), Lithuania (even more collaborators!), Macedonia, the Netherlands (huh? Too much legalized drug use?), Nicaragua, the Philippines (maybe they should be spending their time routing out their own members of al Qaeda), Poland (didn't they hear that the pope said the war was wrong?), Palau . . .

Palau?

Palau is a group of North Pacific islands with 20,000 citizens, barely enough to fill Madison Square Garden. They do have—as *The Washington Post* pointed out—yummy tapioca and succulent coconuts but, unfortunately, no troops. Of course not having an army is no impediment to being in the Coalition of the Willing. Other army-less members include Iceland, Costa Rica, the Marshall Islands, the Solomon Islands, and Micronesia. But hey, we don't expect them to send their kids off to die! That's our job! We just want them to be *willing* to do it!

Wait! News flash! Poland *did* offer to send 200 troops! Thank you for your willingness!

And while Morocco also was short on military assistance, they did offer to send 2,000 monkeys to help detonate land mines in Iraq. But they didn't and, if you don't cough up the monkeys, you don't get to reap the benefits of being a member of the Coalition of the Willing. Anyways, the Coalition of the Willing doesn't need monkeys when it's already got a more advanced simian leading it.

But I'm getting out of order here. Let's see, that leaves Romania, Slovakia, Spain (only 13 percent of Spaniards were in favor of war, and that was only if it was a U.N.-supported invasion) and . . . hold the phone . . . Turkey. Turkish politicians refused $26 billion for the privilege of having U.S. troops based there. Maybe they were paying attention to polls that showed 95 percent of Turks opposed invading Iraq.

Bringing up the rear is the United Kingdom (*our bestest friend in the whole wide world!*) and Uzbekistan. In the United Kingdom, only 9 percent supported military action against Iraq if it meant the U.S. and the U.K. going it alone. The Brits were split evenly on who the "greatest threat to world peace" was, with Bush and Hussein each getting 45 percent of the vote. Why would Tony Blair involve himself in this? What did Bush promise him?

So there we have the Coalition of the Willing, representing about 20 percent of the world's population. But even that is deceptive, since most of the coalition members' citizens opposed the war in Iraq—making them the "Coalition of the Coerced." Or, more accurately, the "Coalition of the Coerced, Bribed and Intimidated."

For the record, here are a few of the many countries that wanted nothing to do with this fiasco, the "Coalition of the **Unwilling**":

Algeria, Argentina, Austria, Belgium, Brazil, Canada, Chile, China, Cuba, Egypt, Finland, France, Germany, Greece, India, Indonesia, Iran, Ireland, Israel, Jordan, Mexico, New Zealand, Nigeria, Norway, Pakistan, Russia, South Africa, Sweden, Switzerland, Syria, Thailand, United Arab Emirates, Venezuela, Vietnam, Yemen, Zambia, Zimbabwe—and 103 other countries.

Hey, who needs 'em? Chickens! Losers! Weasels!

#7 Junior Whopper Kids Meal: "We are doing everything possible so that no civilian lives are lost."

We learned a lot in the 1990s about how to fight a war and keep the Yank losses to the absolute minimum. That's what you get with a liberal in the White House. Clinton closed bases, reduced the number of troops, and funneled money into figuring out ways to bomb people from far away. No fuss, no muss. By the time Bill was finished we had one lean, mean, high-tech fightin' machine.

One of my favorite Clinton defense projects was the one located in Littleton, Colorado, up the road from Columbine High School. There, Lockheed Martin, the biggest arms-maker in the world, built rockets that carried into space the special new satellites that guided the missiles fired into Baghdad. When Bush unleashed a firestorm on Iraq's capital city (with a civilian population of five million) during Gulf War II, it couldn't have happened without those Lockheed rocket carriers. This precision-guided bombing began a whole new era of warfare. It was accurate almost to the inch, and it could be coordinated from the Army's central command in Tampa, Florida. The same satellites were used to bomb Afghanistan after September 11. And, between these two bombing campaigns, according to some estimates, 9,000 civilians were murdered. Three times as many civilians as died on September 11. And 8,985 more than died at Columbine High School.

The Pentagon brags about how perfect their guidance systems are now, and that in targeting only military installations, no civilians need die.

Tell that to the family of Razek al-Kazem al-Khafaji, who lost his wife, six children, his father, his mother, and two brothers in one attack.

"God take our revenge on America," he wailed to reporters amid the rubble and body parts.

Wow, what an ingrate!

Then there was the boy who lost his parents and his two arms when a U.S. missile struck his home. As tears streamed down his cheek, he begged reporters to help him find his arms.

Or the mother who began sobbing uncontrollably, then fainted as she watched as a young woman's torso, then a severed head— her daughter's—were pulled from a smoldering crater. The crater had been made by four U.S. bombs aimed at a restaurant that Saddam Hussein *"might"* have been in. Instead, the bombs obliterated three homes, killing fourteen people, including seven children and the woman's daughter.

You would think that Iraqis would be grateful to have their family members dismembered so that Americans might be safe from Saddam and his elusive weapons of mass destruction, and not carry on all fainty and teary like that.

One thing was clear though, for the second time since September 11, American officials were scratching their heads and wondering how another prime evildoer had gotten away.

While these same U.S. officials were killing Iraqi civilians, they left the counting to others. A British-American research group in London announced estimates of civilian deaths due to the war at between 6,806 and 7,797. That's a lot of accidents when you are talking about "precision-guided" weapons. Of course, the Pentagon doesn't like to talk about the search-and-destroy missions, or the cluster bombs.

Each 1,000-pound cluster bomb delivers 200 to 300 "bomblets," which in turn can spread hundreds of fragments over an area equivalent to several football fields. The bomblets, which can look like little toys to children, by the Pentagon's own estimates, fail to explode upon impact 5–20 percent of the time, and so they sit on the ground until some unsuspecting child picks one up.

Of course, just because the bleeding hearts at Human Rights Watch say that it's an "outrage" to use cluster bombs in urban areas where they remain dangerous for years doesn't mean we don't care about civilian casualties. No, we will make sure that our media doesn't disrespect the poor Iraqis by showing us disgusting images of maimed children at dinnertime. We promise only to show the bullet-ridden bodies of Saddam's sons, Uday and Qusay. Once, twice, a hundred times. That's all.

Because so many of our soldiers have been shot since Bush declared the war over, the soldiers have been understandably jumpy. Every civilian looks like a potential killer. Thus, innocent Iraqis have been shot by our soldiers. Like the ten women and children killed by U.S. soldiers when their van failed to stop at a checkpoint. They apparently thought they were heeding a U.S. order to evacuate TOWARD the checkpoint. Sorry about that, said Gen. Richard Meyers.

This kind of environment is never going to get better, not as long as we are the occupiers and they are the ones wondering where the electricity is.

#8 Whopper, Hold the Mayo: "We are there to protect the oil fields of Iraq!"

Um, this one's true.

#9 Double Whopper with Cheese and a Coke: "The American media has brought you the truth about Iraq!"

If you're going to sell a mess of Whoppers, you need a good advertising campaign. Corporations pay big money for that kind of marketing, but the Bush administration didn't have to spend a dime when the supposedly "liberal media" joined forces with the White House field office at Fox News to create a well-oiled, pro-war propaganda offensive that was almost impossible to avoid.

And it worked—even vegetarians were gobbling down these whoppers. Accompanied by round-the-clock patriotic, march-to-war music and flag-inspired graphics on the sorry-excuses-for-news channels, the images were relentless: Tearful farewells from proud families as brave soldiers headed overseas; heroic American girls rescued by daring American guys; smart bombs doing their brilliantly destructive work; grateful Iraqis toppling the Saddam statue; a united America standing by Our Resolute and Determined Leader.

Then there was the footage beamed directly to us from the harsh Iraqi desert, where reporters "embedded" with the ground troops were given great leeway to report without interference from the Pentagon (as we were supposed to believe). The result? Lots of up-close-and-personal stories about the hardships and dangers faced by our military—and virtually *nothing* examining why we had sent these fine young people into harm's way. And there was even less said about what was happening to the people of Iraq.

So unless you ignored U.S. news entirely and only watched the BBC or CBC or *Le Journal* from France (with its convenient English subtitles for an American audience too lazy and poorly educated to have learned another language), you could pretty quickly find yourself believing that all the sacrifice was for a valid cause.

And just what exactly was the reason for the war with Iraq? We were so thoroughly whopperized that polls showed that half of all Americans wrongly thought that Iraqis were on the September 11 planes, and, at one point, nearly half believed that the U.S. had found weapons of mass destruction in Iraq, when no such discovery had been made. One-quarter of those surveyed thought that Saddam had unleashed a chemical or biological attack against "coalition" forces, which also hadn't happened.

The widespread misconceptions were understandable. It was almost impossible to hear the perspective of anyone who questioned or opposed the Bush administration's rationale for rushing to war on American television.

The media watchdog group FAIR studied the evening newscasts of six U.S. television networks and news channels for three weeks, starting on March 20, 2003—the day after the U.S. bombing of Iraq began. The study examined the affiliations and views of more than 1,600 sources who appeared on-camera in stories about Iraq. The results were hardly a surprise:

• Viewers were *25 times* more likely to see a pro-war U.S. source than someone with an anti-war point of view.

- Military sources were featured twice as frequently as civilians.
- Only 4 percent of sources appearing during the three weeks were affiliated with universities, think tanks or non-governmental organizations.
- Of a total of 840 U.S. sources who were current or former government or military officials, only four were identified as opposing the war.
- The few appearances by people with anti-war viewpoints were consistently limited to one-sentence sound bites, usually from unidentified participants in on-the-street interviews. Not a single one of the six telecasts studied conducted a sit-down interview with anyone who opposed the war.

In some cases, journalists freely confessed to a startling lack of objectivity. The FAIR study quoted CBS News anchor Dan Rather during an appearance with Larry King on CNN: "Look, I'm an American. I never tried to kid anybody that I'm some internationalist or something. And when my country is at war, I want my country to win, whatever the definition of 'win' may be. Now, I can't and don't argue that that is coverage without a prejudice. About that I am prejudiced."

During the three-week study period, FAIR found only one "anti-war" sound bite on Rather's *CBS Evening News*. It was made by, um, me, at the Academy Awards, talking about the "fictitious war" waged by our "fictitious president."

Over at Fox News, Neil Cavuto had this to say on-air in response to a critic: "There is nothing wrong with taking sides here. . . . You see no difference between a government that oppresses people and one that does not, but I do."

MSNBC demonstrated its patriotism with "America's Bravest"— a billboard of photographs of military personnel fighting in the war, sent for display by their friends and families. And Brian Williams, of NBC and MSNBC, said this about the killing of Iraqi civilians: "Civilians used to be intentional military targets. The fire bombings of Dresden and Tokyo in World War II were meant to kill civilians and then terrorize survivors. Here we've seen the opposite happen."

(The Army recently signed a $470 million contract with Microsoft, which is co-owner of MSNBC along with NBC. NBC is in turn owned by General Electric, one of the nation's largest defense contractors. GE's military aircraft engine contracts run in the billions. But the FAIR study found that NBC actually featured more dissenting viewpoints about the war—a whopping *1 percent* more—than any of the other U.S. networks.)

Here are just a few more of the many whoppers provided by American networks and newspapers about the war in Iraq:

ABC reported on April 26, 2003, that "the U.S. military has found a weapons site 130 miles northwest of Baghdad that has initially tested positive for chemical agents. Among the materials there, fourteen fifty-five-gallon drums, at least a dozen missiles and 150 gas masks."

Turns out there were no chemical weapons at the site and the earlier reports were completely wrong. ABC did not run a correction or retraction.

The New York Times helped get the weapons of mass destruction ball rolling with this story on September 8, 2002, headlined "U.S. Says Hussein Intensifies Quest for A-Bomb Parts":

> More than a decade after Saddam Hussein agreed to give up weapons of mass destruction, Iraq has stepped up its quest for nuclear weapons and has embarked on a worldwide hunt for materials to make an atomic bomb, Bush administration officials said today. In the last 14 months, Iraq has sought to buy thousands of specially designed aluminum tubes, which American officials believe were intended as components of centrifuges to enrich uranium.

The story? Wrong.

* * *

The Washington Post brought us the riveting story of Pfc. Jessica Lynch, the young soldier who was rescued from an Iraqi hospital after being seriously injured during a battle in the Iraqi desert:

> Pfc. Jessica Lynch, rescued Tuesday from an Iraqi hospital, fought fiercely and shot several enemy soldiers . . . Lynch, a 19-year-old supply clerk, continued firing at the Iraqis even after she sustained multiple gunshot wounds and watched several other soldiers in her unit die around her in fighting March 23, one official said. . . . "She was fighting to the death," the official said. "She did not want to be taken alive."

The New York Times provided more dramatic details of the heroic rescue:

> Navy Special Operations forces, called Seals, extracted Private Lynch while being fired upon going in and coming back out. . . . Lynch [was] the first U.S. prisoner of war extracted from enemy hands since World War II and [it was] the first time a woman has ever been rescued . . .

It took some time, but the story soon became more complicated, as *The New York Times* reported two months later:

> It seems the plucky young private may not have fought like Rambo when her supply unit took a wrong turn into an Iraqi ambush. She may not have been shot and stabbed in that firefight, which may or may not have happened, and it seems likely now that she was not mistreated at an Iraqi hospital. Her heroic rescuers did not fight their way up the hospital halls; indeed the hospital staff may have been eager to hand her over.

Lynch was in fact given special medical care by the Iraqi hospital staff for her wounds, none of which was battle-related. An Iraqi nurse sang her to sleep at night, and she was given extra juice and cookies. The hospital staff had already tried to turn her over to U.S. authorities and were, in fact, waiting for them to arrive. Iraqi forces had already vacated the area.

While Lynch recovered in a U.S. hospital, television networks were tripping over themselves to get her exclusive story. CBS even offered her a package deal, with book, concert and TV movie prospects through CBS News, CBS Entertainment, MTV and Simon & Schuster—all under the corporate umbrella of the huge Viacom Corp.

No matter where the Jessica Lynch tale ends up being told, it's sure to be more *Survivor* than *The Real World*. I feel sorry for her, a young woman who volunteered to risk her life to defend the United States, and she ends up being used like this, sandwiched in a mess hall full of whoppers.

#10 Triple Whopper, Biggie Size: "We didn't lie. And we're not lying now to cover up the lies we told you before."

After a few in the media started to do their job and expose the lies of the Bush administration, after Bush struggled to find someone (anyone) to blame all the lying on, and after a majority of the American public said that they believe they were not told the whole truth about Iraq, Bush & Co. figured they had better come forward and put an end to this crisis once and for all.

So this is what they did: They biggie-sized the whoppers!

This strategy is called the pile-on effect—if you are caught in a lie, just keep denying it and keep lying no matter what.

Richard Pryor outlined this approach in his 1982 stand-up

routine, *Live on the Sunset Strip*. Pryor suggested that when a man is caught by his wife in bed with another woman, he should deny everything, even though his wife is standing right there witnessing him naked and in bed with the other woman. Just deny that you are in the middle of having sex, said Pryor, deny that there is even a woman in your bed: "Now are you going to believe me—or your lying eyes?"

One of the first whoppers about the whopper (the whopper squared) came last February when Collin Powell proclaimed, "My colleagues, every statement I make today is backed up by sources, solid sources. These are not assertions. What we are giving you are facts and conclusions based on solid intelligence."

Just days earlier, Powell apparently was not so sure. During a gathering of CIA officials reviewing the evidence against Saddam Hussein, Powell tossed the papers in the air and declared: "I'm not reading this. This is bullshit."

And he had good reason to distrust the "intelligence." A large chunk of Powell's background information had been lifted directly from sources easily located on the Internet, including a graduate student's paper based on twelve-year-old documents. Some sections had been outright plagiarized, to the extent that typos hadn't even been fixed. But Powell called all these whoppers "solid."

Then-White House spokesman Ari Fleischer gave it his spin: "The president's statement was based on the predicate of the yellowcake [uranium] from Niger. So given the fact that the report on the yellowcake did not turn out to be accurate, that is reflective of the president's broader statement."

Huh?

We'll leave the explaining to the Whoppermaster himself, George W. Bush: "I think the intelligence I get is darn good intelligence. And the speeches I have given were backed by good intelligence. And I am absolutely convinced today, like I was convinced when I gave the speeches, that Saddam Hussein developed a program of weapons of mass destruction."

Added Ari Fleischer: "The president has moved on. And I think, frankly, much of the country has moved on, as well."

Maybe in his country, but not in mine. Secretary of Defense Donald Rumsfeld quickly dished up some more whoppers on *Meet the Press*: "It turns out that it's technically correct what the president said ... But in the aggregate, do we believe that they had chemical and biological weapons and a nuclear program in progress? The answer is yes, I believe that."

Rumsfeld added: "And right before it, I said, as the president said, and right after it, I said as the president said. I was simply repeating what the president had said."

Are you following this? Before your head spins completely off your neck, let's turn to Condoleezza Rice to clear it all up for us. She had this to say to CNN's Wolf Blitzer. "Wolf, let me just start by saying, it is sixteen words, and it has become an enormously overblown issue ... Now, I think now that we're in Iraq and we are interviewing scientists and we are looking at the documents and we are finding, for instance, that he had somebody bury centrifuge parts in their yard ..."

That whopper had spoiled so badly that it got Blitzer's attention, and Rice was forced to admit that her "evidence" was twelve years old: "Before the first Gulf War—well, in 1991."

Undeterred, Rice also appeared that day on *Face the Nation,* where she insisted that "the president's State of the Union said something that was accurate. . . . We use a lot of data points. We give them to writers. They go to speeches, and then we rely on a clearance process ... And if you notice, the president's statement says 'in Africa.' It's not specific. It says he sought—it didn't say he received or he acquired. It's that he sought. And it cites the British document."

It just doesn't stop. Whoppers on top of whoppers. So many whoppers ... it could make a person sick.

So many whoppers, that even a witness to world-class lying, former Nixon aide John Dean was moved to comment: "It's important to recall that when Richard Nixon resigned, he was about to be impeached by the House of Representatives for misusing the CIA and FBI."

Why are there no consequences for telling all these whoppers? Why is George W. Bush still occupying our White House? Where are the articles of impeachment?

How many more whoppers will it take before Congress is full?

CHAPTER

Oil's Well That Ends Well

LAST NIGHT I had a dream. Actually I had a number of dreams. One had something to do with smearing Tofutti on a camel. Another involved me pushing around golfing great Fred Couples as he sat in my shopping cart while he recited sections of the Bhagavad Gita inside a Target store in Modesto, California. I know, I need help.

It was one of those nights when you have been out partying too hard and it's like once your head hits the pillow some sort of high-speed megachannel DirecTV comes on in your subconscious and you can't find the remote to turn it off. I had been out celebrating the killings of Uday and Qusay Hussein with friends and loved ones. You can never discount the importance of getting together with those close to you when your government is able to corner and gun down People We Don't Like. But one too many shots of tequila, with the whole bar chanting, "Uday! Uday! Uday!" as I chugged them down, was a bit too much, even for me. I hadn't partied this hard since the state of Texas executed that retard guy.

Anyway, back to my main dream. It was so real it felt like something right out of Scrooge. Suddenly, I was in the future. It was the year 2054, and it was the occasion of my one hundredth birthday. Either I had joined a health food co-op some years earlier or, for some reason, the world ran out of Ben & Jerry's because I was looking pretty good for a hundred.

In this dream I received a surprise visit from my great-grand-daughter, Anne Coulter Moore. I have no idea how she got that name and I was too frightened to ask. She told me she was doing an oral history project for her sixth-grade class at school and she wanted to ask me a few questions. But there were no lights, she had no computer, and the water she was drinking was not in a bottle. Here is how the conversation went, as best as I can recall . . .

ANNE COULTER MOORE: **Hi, Great-Grandpa! I brought you a candle. For some reason we got an extra one with our monthly ration. I figured there might not be enough light for the interview.**

MICHAEL MOORE: Thank you, Annie. Now if there is any way you could leave me that pencil you're using when you're done, I could burn it to keep me warm.

A: **Sorry, Great-Grandpa, but if I give it to you, then I will have nothing to write with for the rest of the year. Back in your day, didn't you have other things to use when you wrote something?**

M: Yes, we had pens and computers and we had little machines you could speak into and out would come the writing.

A: **What happened to those?**

M: Well, dear, it takes plastic to make them.

A: Oh, yes, plastic. Did everyone love plastic back then?

M: It was a magical substance, but it was made from oil.

A: I see. And ever since the oil dried up, we've had to use these pencils.

M: That's right. Boy, we all miss the oil, don't we?

A: **When you were young, were people really so stupid to think that there was enough oil to last forever? Or did they just not care about us.**

M: Of course we cared. But in my day, our leaders swore on a stack of Bibles there was plenty of oil, and, of course, we wanted to believe them because we were having so much fun.

A: **So, when you started to run out of oil, and you knew the end was near, what did you do?**

M: We tried to keep things under control by dominating those parts of the world where most of the remaining oil and natural gas was located. Many wars were fought. For the early wars, in Kuwait and Iraq, our leaders had to come up with excuses like, "this bad guy had bad weapons," or "these good people needed to be liberated." We liked that word "liberated."

But the fighting was never really for any of those reasons. It was always about the oil. We just couldn't speak plainly in those days.

The early wars didn't cost us a lot of lives, so it seemed everything would remain normal. But those wars only gave us a few more years of oil.

A: **I heard that when you were born there was so much oil that you switched to making *everything* out of it. And that most of these things would be used once and thrown** away. A couple of years ago Mom and Dad got scavenger permits for the dump. Mom said they struck it rich. They found a bunch of plastic bags that hadn't decomposed one bit. And inside them were lots of things made of plastic. You guys sure were smart to preserve all that stuff so neatly in those bags.

M: Well, thank you, but it was just a lucky accident. You're right that we made everything from oil by turning it into plastic. Furniture upholstery, grocery bags, toys, bottles, clothes, medicines, even baby diapers were made from oil. The list of what was made with oil and by-products of oil was endless: aspirin, cameras, golf balls, car batteries, carpet, fertilizers, eyeglasses, shampoo, glue, computers, cosmetics, detergents, telephones, food preservatives, footballs, insecticides, luggage, nail polish, toilet seats, panty hose, toothpaste, pillows, soft contact lenses, tires, pens, CDs, sneakers—you name it, and it came in some way from oil. Man, we were hooked on the stuff. We would take a drink from a plastic bottle and throw it away. We might burn a gallon of oil to drive to a store for a gallon of milk (which came in a plastic bottle, too). Every Christmas your grandmother would get presents mostly made of plastic under a plastic Christmas tree (but made to look real). And yes, it's true we even wrapped our garbage in plastic and tossed it out.

A: Where did people come up with the idea for BURNING oil? Why would you burn something you have only a little bit of? Did people burn diamonds back then, too?

M: No, people didn't burn diamonds. Diamonds were considered precious. Oil was considered precious, too, but no one cared. We just turned it into gasoline, lit a spark plug and burned the damned stuff any chance we could!

A: What was it like when you couldn't breathe because of the dirty air caused by burning what you called gasoline? Didn't that make you realize that anything that came from oil wasn't supposed to be burned? Maybe that smell was nature's way of trying to tell you, "Don't burn me!"

M: Ooh, ooh, that smell. It *was* nature's way of telling you something's wrong. What were we thinking? What were we singing?

A: Huh?

M: Never mind.

A: But it was poisoning you. And you didn't have breathing stations like we do now, so what did you do?

M: People would just have to suck it up and breathe it in. This caused millions of people to suffer and die. No one wanted to say it was air pollution from burning fossil fuels that was making it hard to breathe, so doctors said we had asthma or allergies. While you think of a ride in an automobile as something you do at a museum, in those days most people were "commuting" twenty, thirty, even forty miles to work and they hated the hours they spent trapped in their cars. It put them in really bad moods.

A: So you burned up all the precious oil while hating yourselves. Weird.

M: Hey, I didn't say we hated ourselves. We hated the commute, but lots of people thought it was worth it because they didn't want to live in cities that had lots of different people living in them.

A: What I don't get is if you were having all this fun, driving around and stuff, using up all our oil, why didn't you plan to switch over to another fuel before you ran out so you could keep having fun?

M: The American people were the kind of people who would get stuck on doing things one way and never want to change.

A: What's American?

M: Let's not get into that.

A: My sixth-grade teacher told us one of your leaders believed "hydrogen fuel cells" would replace gasoline cars, but they didn't. That was crazy! Today every kid knows that hydrogen is hard to get. Sure it's in H_2O, but it takes a lot of energy to break off the hydrogen—and a lot of energy was what you didn't have. Duh!

M: You're right, Anne, we were all hepped up on so much Prozac and cable television that we always believed what our leaders told us. We even believed them when they said that "hydrogen was the Second Coming—limitless, pollution-free energy that will soon replace oil!" We spent so much money on our military to make sure we had access to oil that our schools were falling apart, making everyone grow up dumb and dumber—and therefore, no one realized that hydrogen was *not even a fuel at all!* It got so bad, most college graduates didn't even know what "H_2O" stood for.

Soon things really got bad. We ran low on oil, and there wasn't any hydrogen to run our cars, so people got really mad. But it was too late. That's when the die-off began.

A: I know, the food ran out.

M: At the time, it seemed like a good idea to use oil to grow food. It does seem funny now that no one seemed to realize that the massive food production needed to keep so many people alive could not be sustained for very long.

That was probably our worst mistake of all. The artificial fertilizers, pesticides, and herbicides, not to mention all the tractors and agricultural equipment, depended on fossil fuels. When oil production peaked, the price of food went up in lockstep with the price of fossil fuels. The world's poor starved to death first. But, as soon as people realized what was happening, stores and warehouses were attacked, and being rich was little guarantee of having enough food to eat.

To make matters worse, when the die-off began, people could not afford to get to work, to heat their homes, to buy electricity. There were some experts who predicted world oil production would peak around 2015, and they were laughed at—but they were right. Fuel prices began escalating ever more sharply—but it was too late to plan for a smooth transformation to a different way to obtain energy. The catastrophe was upon us.

A: **Great-Grandpa, why are you pushing a golfer around in a shopping cart?**

M: Oh, sorry. That's from my other dream. Fred, get the #%&* out of here!

A: **I have a theory about what happened. I heard that your generation loved the sun and laid out in it all the time, just sleeping. I think that's why you used up all the cheap oil, so you could heat up the Earth, get rid of winter, and everybody could get really good tans and look cool.**

M: No, actually, we were scared to death of the sun. Most of us worked in buildings with the windows sealed tight, with machines to filter and clean our air and water. When we did venture outside we would slather ourselves in sun-block and put on dark sunglasses and hats to shield our heads. But as much as we hated the sun, we hated the cold even more. Everyone was moving to the hot states where it rarely snowed and then spent their days in air-conditioned homes and offices and rode around in air-conditioned automobiles. Of course this used even more gasoline, and that made the world even hotter, which made people turn up the air conditioning even more.

A: Why did they invent nuclear bombs if they wanted to kill everyone at once when they already had oil-based bombs? When they turned the nuclear bombs into nuclear power plants, didn't they know one might blow up and burn everyone?

M: A hundred years ago, we were told nuclear fission would produce electricity "too cheap to meter." Never happened. The second President Bush . . . or was it the third President Bush . . . well, definitely not the fourth President Bush . . . one of those damned Bushes stepped up nuclear plant production, but after a disgruntled nuke plant worker filled his pickup with fertilizer and detergent and smashed it into his place of employment, destroying a small town nearby, the program was quickly dropped.

A: Dad says in your day there were over six billion people in the world. Sometimes I get scared, but I try not to think about the time when so many people died of starvation and disease all over the world. In school, I heard there are now about a half a billion people in the world. It sounds like a lot to me. But I get a little worried sometimes that the die-off might still be going on. What do you think?

M: Don't worry. The die-off is over. You are safe now. Just keep digging up all that plastic and you'll be okay.

A: Great-Grandpa, how did you survive?

M: Your great-grandma and I were traveling overseas when the great die-off began. We were able to survive because, somewhere in the Big Oil Region, we found a cave with lots of food and cell phones and a FedEx box. I never would have believed someone could survive in a cave that long and not be detected. But we did, just like whoever used the cave before us. The only strange thing is, there was a dialysis machine in there. I kept thinking, naw, this couldn't be . . .

A: **Dad said he hoped you and Great-Grandma would move back in with us so we could all stay warmer. Even though I am mad at you for using up all the oil and not even saving a gallon for us, maybe it would be nicer to have family here when we snuggle under the family quilt when the temperature drops below zero and we can't get the neighbors to come over. Once it was so cold we had to get a couple of animals to sleep with us and, even though it was warmer, the stink was so bad I couldn't go to sleep. Mom said that you even sometimes heated the outdoors just so you could stand around without a jacket and sip drinks. Can you and Great-Grandma come stay with us?**

M: Why, yes, I would love to. But, I'm afraid at our age, we stink pretty bad, too.

A: **Mom said you were once famous for a few minutes for yelling about something during one of the Oil Wars. Now all we have is this old photo of you with your mouth open and pointing at something. And you're using two fingers! What were you angry about? Was it the oil?**

M: Um, well, Great-Grandma won't let me discuss this as long as she is alive. She got all dressed up that night and everything and she was so beautiful and . . . here, hand over that picture, little girl! I'm starting to hear boos in my head!

A: Sure. Here it is. Thanks, Great-Grandpa! Any last words? Your candle is almost gone.

M: Yes, you know, as I look back on it now, the ten years between 2005 and 2015 were the most critical time on this planet for our species. Many of us tried to warn everyone else of the danger of running out of oil, but few listened. There were good people, people who cared about each other, our children and the planet. We struggled, but not hard enough. The forces of selfish greed fought harder. They seemed bent on extinction, and almost succeeded. I'm sorry. We're sorry. Perhaps you can do better.

It was right around then, when I was getting all preachy and schmaltzy, that I awoke out of my dream in a cold sweat, mumbling something about an overdue dry cleaning bill in Toledo. I sat straight up in bed and then realized it was only a dream, that nothing as ridiculous as all that could ever happen, and so I laid back down and got all nice and cozy underneath the electric blanket and fell back asleep with sweet dreams of Tofutti dancing in my head . . .

CHAPTER

The United States of *BOO!*

THERE IS no terrorist threat.

You need to calm down, relax, listen very carefully, and repeat after me:

There is no terrorist threat.

There is no terrorist threat!

THERE . . . IS . . . NO . . . TERRORIST . . . THREAT!

Feel better? Not really, huh? I know, it's hard. Amazing how it didn't take long to pound that belief so deep into our psyche that the country, the world, is teeming with terrorists. Madmen are running amok on their evil mission to destroy every living American infidel!

Of course, it didn't help for us to watch the mass murder of 3,000 people, obliterated before our very eyes. That would tend to convince even the most cynical among us that there are people out there who don't like us and would like to see fewer of *us* in the world.

Why do they hate us? Our leader knew why, just days after September 11 when he addressed the nation: "They want us to stop flying and they want us to stop buying. But this great nation will not be intimidated by the evildoers."

Now, when I say there is no terrorist threat, I am not saying that there are no terrorists, or that there are no terrorist incidents, or that there won't be other terrorist incidents in the future. There ARE terrorists, they HAVE committed evil acts, and, tragically, they WILL commit acts of terror in the not-too-distant future. Of that I am sure.

But just because there are a few terrorists does not mean we are all in some exaggerated state of danger. Yet when they speak of terrorists, they speak of them as if they are in the *millions*, that they're *everywhere*, and they are never going away. Cheney has called this a "new normalcy," a condition that "will become permanent in American life." They only hope.

They call it a war on "terror." How exactly do you conduct a war on a noun? Wars are fought against countries, religions, and peoples. They are not fought against nouns or problems, and any time it has been attempted—the "war on drugs," the "war on poverty"—it fails.

Our leaders would have us believe this is a guerrilla war, fought by thousands of foreign terrorist-soldiers hidden on our soil. But this is *not* what is taking place, and it is time to do a reality check. Americans are rarely targets of international terrorism, and almost never on U.S. soil.

In the year 2000, your chance as an American of being killed in a terrorist attack in the United States was exactly *zero*. In 2002, your chance of dying in a terrorist incident was, again, **ZERO**. And in 2003, as of this writing, the total number of people to die in the United States from acts of terror? Zero. Even in the tragic year of 2001, your chance as an American of dying in an act of terrorism in this country was 1 **in 100,000**.

In 2001, you had a greater chance of dying from the flu or

pneumonia (1 in 4,500), from taking your own life (1 in 9,200), being a homicide victim (1 in 14,000), or riding in a car (1 in 6,500). But no one freaked out over the possibility of being killed every time you drove in your dangerous car to buy a heart-disease-inducing doughnut from a coughing teenager. The suicide rate alone means that YOU were a greater danger to yourself than any terrorist. All these causes of death were far greater than the terrorism, but there were no laws passed, no countries bombed, no emergency expenditures of billions of dollars per month, no National Guard units dispatched, no orange alerts and no non-stop tickers scrolling details across the bottom of CNN to send us in a panic over them. There was no response from the public but indifference and denial, or, at best, an acceptance that these tragedies were just part of life.

But when multiple deaths happen at the same time, with such viciousness, and on live TV, no rationalization with statistics like those above can undo the visceral response of witnessing actual horror as we did on September 11. We have come to believe that we are in harm's way, *that any of us anywhere in this vast country could die at any time.* Never mind that the chances of that happening are virtually *nil.* A mass psychosis has gripped the country; I'm part of it, you're part of it, and even high-ranking generals who now weep openly are part of it.

That's right, I'm caught up in it, too. I live part of the year in New York City and every day I'm there I wonder if today is the day when the other shoe will drop. I hear loud bangs outside my window, and I flinch. I see planes flying too low and I watch them with a suspicious eye. I check out everyone sitting near me when I fly and I always carry a weapon with me on the plane. That's right; I carry a weapon. A legal weapon. I have a baseball in my carry-on bag. It was a gift from Rudy Giuliani when we filmed *TV Nation* in New York. It's signed by all the 1994 New York Yankees. I figure I could get off a pretty good 50-mile-an-hour fastball if some motherfucker was trying to break down the cockpit door. (The baseball, when stuffed inside a long sock, works well, too; you give it a good swing and wham—a knockout wallop to the head!) Also, shoelaces, when wrapped between my hands, would make a nice strangling device once I get them around the bastard's neck. Whatever it takes, by any means necessary, I ain't goin' down without a fight.

See, I'm messed up, too. I guess knowing and having worked with someone who died on one of those planes will do that to you.

How did I get to this place, lil' ol' pacifist me? Hell, I'm scared, just like everyone else. Fear, the rational kind, is a critical part of our ability to survive. Sensing real danger and acting appropriately is an instinct that has served our species well throughout the millennia.

But *irrational* fear is a killer. It throws off our survival compass. It makes us reach for a gun when we hear a noise in the middle of the night (and you end up shooting your wife who was just on her way to the bathroom). It makes us not want to live near someone of another race. And it allows us to willingly give up the civil liberties we have enjoyed for more than 200 years, simply because our "leader" tells us there is a "terrorist threat."

Fear is so basic and yet so easy to manipulate that it has become both our best friend and our worst enemy. And when it is used as a weapon against us, it has the ability to destroy much of what we have come to love about life in the United States of America.

According to the Bush administration, and the stories they have planted in the media, the terrorists are *everywhere*. Each day seems to bring a new warning. A new alert! *A new threat!*

• *Watch out for model airplanes packed with explosives!* The FBI Law Enforcement Bulletin reported that they faced off "a terrorist threat" from an "unconventional weapon" in the form of "Satin [*sic*] gas." After the tiny canister was seized from a model airplane builder and flown to a special army base by hazardous materials support personnel in a special military aircraft, the modeling enthusiast admitted he labeled an empty canister "Satin [*sic*] gas" as a "joke."

Nonetheless, the government issued an alert to be on the lookout for model airplanes that could fly explosives into a building, and cable news channels presented experts in mid-July 2003 to warn us of the grave danger.

• *People might be lurking near train tracks preparing to derail trains!* The FBI issued a warning to law enforcement agencies throughout the U.S. about a possible attack against transportation systems, particularly railways, in October 2002. "Intelligence" officials said they had seen captured al Qaeda photos of train engines and railroad crossings. (Geez, I hope they haven't seen my Lionel setup in the basement!)

• *Beware of shoe bombs!* The FBI says the explosive the shoe bomber used, TATP, is presently undetectable in regular airport scanners, and explosives experts say it can be made in a basic lab by anyone with a college degree in chemistry. The last time I saw someone light their shoes on fire was at an ELO concert in 1978 at the IMA Auditorium in Flint. Some guy who had been drinking too much puked on his shoes and then someone next to him lit a match and dropped it and the guy's alcohol-laced puke ignited his Converse into a really cool blaze!

• *Look for suspicious people lingering near gas stations!* Now there's something we never see. But an alert Oklahoma pump attendant called authorities when a group pulled in with two vans and an equipment truck. Within minutes, police and FBI had surrounded, with guns drawn, the rock band Godspeed You! Black Emperor. Released after hours of questioning, singer Efrim Menuck told *Seattle Weekly*, "We're just lucky we're nice white kids from Canada."

• *Al Qaeda may be setting wildfires in the western U.S.!* The *Arizona Republic* reported that an FBI memo to law enforcement agencies alerted them that al Qaeda had developed a plan to set midsummer forest fires in Colorado, Montana, Utah and Wyoming, so that "once it was realized that the fires were terrorist acts, U.S. citizens would put pressure on the U.S. government to change its policies."

• *Terrorists are trading in sham consumer goods like fake Sony stereo equipment, fake Nikes, and Calvin Klein jeans!* Not long ago, an al Qaeda supporter sent a shipment of counterfeit perfume, shampoo and cologne from Dubai to Dublin. It's scary to think of all the damage that counterfeit perfume can do. Congress has extended this argument of "counterfeit goods" to "counterfeit drugs." How convenient to prevent access to cheap Canadian drugs by saying there's the possibility that terrorists will ship tainted drugs to us.

• *Especially keep an eye out for undercover al Qaeda agents with portable blow torches attempting to cut through the 21,736 wires holding up the Brooklyn Bridge!* The FBI nabbed a truck driver who had been casing the bridge and counting the wires. Best estimate is that you could cut through the wires in about a week, so be on alert!

• *Report any powdery substance you come across!* After receiving a suspicious powdery substance in the mail, a New Orleans woman called the authorities, and firefighters, postal officials, police officers and FBI agents quickly arrived to investigate. It turned out to be a free sample of laundry detergent. But that doesn't mean there aren't terrorists out there (even if the authorities suspect that the anthrax scare of 2001 was an inside job by someone who had access to the substance in the U.S. government or government-approved programs).

Boy, those terrorists sure are busy! Explosive model airplanes! Satin gas! Forest fires! Lions! Tigers! Bears! The boogeyman is coming to get me!! RUN FOR YOUR LIVES!

The only thing more amazing than this phony game of *BOO!* is our ability to fall for it. What happened to our basic common sense? You know, that reflex in your brain that used to make you scream *bullshit!* when confronted with such obvious nonsense? This is what happens when your fear radar is out of whack. You're so discombobulated you can't distinguish any longer between the real and unreal.

Why has our government gone to such absurd lengths to convince us our lives are in danger? The answer is nothing short of their feverish desire to rule the world, first by controlling us, and then, in turn, getting us to support their efforts to dominate the rest of the planet. Sounds crazy, huh? It reads more like a movie script, doesn't it? But Bush/Cheney/Ashcroft/Wall Street/Fortune 500 see this post-September-11-America-in-fear as *their moment*— a moment handed to them by fate, via the terrorists—to seize the reins and ram the USA down the throats of any people in the world who dare question who is number one. Who *is* number one? **I SAID, *WHO IS NUMBER ONE?*** That's right. Say it loud! Say it, for George and Dick and Johnny and Condi: **WE ARE NUMBER ONE! USA! USA! USA!**

They know that *real* Americans are not into dominating anyone, so they have to sell it to us in fancy packaging—and that package is FEAR. In order to properly scare us, they need a big, bad enemy. Once the Soviet Union disappeared, Bush Sr. couldn't figure it out. Before he knew it, Clinton had given him the boot. The right wing was out in the cold, but they had eight long years to plot their return.

To their rescue came a high-powered political think-tank, The Project for a New American Century (PNAC), which argued that America should have but one goal: an unchallengeable, military-imposed, U.S.-run world.

They took their first step on January 26, 1998, in an open letter to President Clinton. PNAC neoconservatives Paul Wolfowitz and William Kristol, along with Donald Rumsfeld and Richard Perle, warned that the policy of containing Iraq was "dangerously inadequate" and the aim of U.S. foreign policy must be "removing Saddam Hussein and his regime from power."

When Bush Jr. seized power in 2000, he turned the Pentagon over to this radical right-wing nut group. After September 11, Rumsfeld, Wolfowitz (now Rumsfeld's deputy secretary of defense), and the war crowd immediately pushed an attack on Iraq as one of the first actions in the new Permanent War Against Terror. Their next act: rush through a $400 BILLION defense budget, including $70 billion for new weapons.

Because of September 11, Wolfowitz and his right-wing hawk buddies had found the enemy they could sell to the public. Former Clinton CIA director James Woolsey joined in, declaring that World War IV had begun (the Cold War being "WWIII"). By this thinking, the "War on Terror" would be unilateral and without limits; it could last as long as the Cold War (fifty years) or longer, maybe forever. And if you don't believe me, maybe Donald Rumsfeld can convince you: "[I]t undoubtedly will prove to be a lot more like a cold war than a hot war," Rummy said. "If you think about it, in the Cold War it took fifty years, plus or minus. It did not involve major battles. It involved continuous pressure. . . . It strikes me that that might be a more appropriate way to think about what we are up against here."

Wow—a war without end. If you get the people to believe this, they'll let you do anything, just as long as it's in the name of protecting them. This is Bush's version of the old mafia protection racket. There's somebody out there who's gonna mess you up. Osama, he did it! Saddam, he did it! Those crazy ayatollahs, they might do it! North Korea, they could do it! Hello, PLO! We'll protect you, just give us all your money and all your rights. And keep your trap shut!

For the next year, leading up to the 2004 election, all you are going to hear from Bush is how there is a war going on, a war on terror, a war to liberate and rebuild Iraq, a war against Iranian clerics, a war against North Korean nuclear madmen, a war against Colombian drug lords, a war against extremism, a war against Communism in Cuba, a war against Hamas, a war against . . .

And to maintain the endless war, they need endless fear, a fear that can only be extended indefinitely by taking away our basic civil rights.

The right wing needs to keep this war, that war, going for as long as possible because it keeps people distracted. Everyone—except those who die in it—loves a good war, especially one you can win quickly. We, good. Them, bad. Them, dead. We win! Cue the cameras, the victorious POTUS is landing on the aircarrier!

This is how Bush intends to run his entire reelection campaign. "I won you a war. Then I won you another war. But there are more wars, and you need me to win them, too!" It'll be that old slogan, "You shouldn't change horses in the middle of the stream."

But this is no stream, folks. This will be a tidal wave that can swamp our democracy. Give these guys four more years, and do you think they will give up their megalomaniacal schemes peacefully to a duly elected Democrat or Green? How many of our freedoms and our children are we willing to sacrifice just so they can line their pockets with all the money that can be made from a terrified nation and a permanent war?

You are not going to be killed by a terrorist. We have seriously lost our sense of perspective. And it is being used against us, not by the terrorists, but by leaders seeking to terrorize us.

A great president once said that we have nothing to fear but fear itself. He encouraged and inspired a nation. Now we have nothing to fear but George W. Bush. It is my firm belief that Bush and his cronies (especially Attorney General John Ashcroft) have only one goal in mind: To scare the bejesus out of us so that whatever bill they want passed, whatever powers they want Congress to give them, we will happily hand it over.

Immediately after September 11, Bush was able to enact into law his USA PATRIOT Act (an actual acronym that stands for "Uniting and Strengthening America by Providing Appropriate Tools Required to Intercept and Obstruct Terrorism Act of 2001"). The Act gives the government unprecedented freedom to collect information with little regard to civil rights or privacy concerns. The Senate voted 98 to 1 in favor of the act. Wisconsin Democrat Russ Feingold was the only true patriot in the Senate that day, casting the sole dissenting vote, as he stood and spoke these eloquent words:

> There have been periods in our nation's history when civil liberties have taken a backseat to what appeared at the same time to be the legitimate exigencies of war. Our national consciousness still bears the stain and the scars of those events: The Alien and Sedition Acts, the suspension of habeas corpus during the Civil War, the internment of Japanese-Americans, German-Americans, and Italian-Americans during World War II, the blacklisting of supposed communist sympathizers during the McCarthy era, and the surveillance and harassment of antiwar protestors, including Dr. Martin Luther King Jr., during the Vietnam War. We must not allow these pieces of our past to become prologue.

The leaders of the Democratic Party, seeking to help the Republicans achieve a unanimous vote, did everything they could to keep Feingold "in line" but he resisted voting for the legislation (and suffered the wrath of Democratic party leader Tom Daschle on the Senate floor). Feingold told *Congressional Quarterly*: "I don't know if [dissenting] is dangerous or not, and frankly I don't care. . . . If the worst thing that ever happened to me was that I got thrown out of office for this, I'd be a pretty lucky guy, considering what we're up against here."

USA Patriot Act is really a gross misnomer. This law is anything but patriotic. The "Patriot" act is as un-American as *Mein Kampf*. The name is part of a masterful plan meant to camouflage a stench thicker than Florida swamp water.

You can always read the law yourself if you have several days and a gaggle of lawyers at your disposal. You see, this law is not like other laws that read, in clear language, "you can do this" or "you can't do that." The Patriot Act is mostly about amending existing laws. There are 342 pages where it never really says what it is doing but rather refers you to hundreds of other passages in other laws written over the past hundred years. So, in order to read the Patriot Act, you need to have all the other laws written in the past century in order to see what sentence or phrase the Patriot Act is changing. For instance, here is how Section 220 of the USA Patriot Act reads:

SEC. 220. NATIONWIDE SERVICE OF SEARCH WARRANTS FOR ELECTRONIC EVIDENCE.

(a) IN GENERAL—Chapter 121 of title 18, United States Code, is amended

(1) in section 2703, by striking 'under the Federal Rules of Criminal Procedure' every place it appears and inserting 'using the procedures described in the Federal Rules of Criminal Procedure by a court with jurisdiction over the offense under investigation'; and

(2) in section 2711—

(A) in paragraph (1), by striking 'and';

(B) in paragraph (2), by striking the period and inserting '; and'; and

(C) by inserting at the end the following:

(3) the term 'court of competent jurisdiction' has the meaning assigned by section 3127, and includes any Federal court within that definition, without geographic limitation.'

(b) CONFORMING AMENDMENT—Section 2703(d) of title 18, United States Code, is amended by striking 'described in section 3127(2)(A).'

Did you get all that?

*   *   *

That's why, when anyone has challenged them, the Justice Department folks throw up their hands and urge "the public to read the actual language of the act" for clarification. There is no way to humanly do this.

On October 11, just a month after September 11, the Senate passed a version of the bill that was less tolerable to civil rights advocates than the House version, to be voted on the next day.

The Bush administration did not like the protections contained in the House bill and, with the speaker of the house, worked through the night to strip it of all the civil rights protections the House Committees had voted for. It was finally submitted at 3:45 a.m. When Congress showed up a few hours later to vote on it, they thought they were voting on the language agreed to the previous day. Instead, they voted on the bill whose few protections were gutted by Attorney General John Ashcroft the night before. According to the American Civil Liberties Union, few members of Congress actually read the final version of the act. It was perhaps the most reckless and irresponsible action our Congress has ever taken.

Here's what this law does. Your government may now "trap and trace" all those countless e-mails you thought were private. If this continues, you might as well delete the word "CONFIDEN-TIAL" from your spellchecker. Also up for inspection: banking records, school records, the list of library books you or your nine-year-old checked out this year (or even how often you have logged onto the Internet at the library), and your consumer purchases. Think I'm exaggerating? Next time you are sitting in your doctor's waiting room or waiting in line at the bank, read their new privacy statements. Buried in the legalese you will find new warnings that your privacy protections do not cover the Big Brother provisions of our new Patriot Act.

There's more. Under the special "SNEAK AND PEEK" provision, agents may now come into your home and search through your stuff and—get this—never tell you they have been there!

One of the most important sections of our Bill of Rights is the Fourth Amendment. We all cherish our individual privacy and like living in a place that encourages the free flow of ideas. At the core of all this is PRIVACY. That's why under the United States Constitution, searching your home requires a warrant that is backed up with some proof there's a damn good reason to be doing so. But along comes the new order under Ashcroft that violates our dearly held notion of home and hearth. Ashcroft's law is no act of patriotism. Both my seventh-grade history teacher, Sister Mary Raymond, and our Founding Fellows (especially Jefferson) would not forgive me if I didn't point out that once you allow your rulers to snoop into your life and violate your "space," the notion of living in a free society is out the window.

Instead of showing probable cause in a regular court, Ashcroft's agents get their secret warrants from a secret court (the government's own Foreign Intelligence Surveillance Court, FISA, created in 1978), and the Feds can just show up, say the magical words "this is for intelligence purposes," and the secret court judges rubber stamp each and every request. In addition, newspapers reported that in 2002 more than 170 "emergency" warrants were issued, compared to forty-seven in the previous twenty-three years. Those so-called emergency warrants amount to no more than pieces of paper signed by Ashcroft, which allow FBI agents to conduct wiretaps and searches for seventy-two hours without any FISA court review.

Built into the secrecy of the USA Patriot Act is a gag order so that once the FBI collects your library records, no one may utter a word about the search under pain of prosecution. (Perhaps libraries could safely post regular weekly updates that read: "No FBI agents have spied here this week" and when the sign is missing, then you can assume the worst.) With no real threat of anyone monitoring their behavior, Bush/Cheney/Ashcroft et al. are allowed to freely graze on the landscape of our way of life.

The Patriot Act also allows the attorney general's office to demand and receive whatever information it wants from anyone just by issuing what is called a "national security letter." These have been flying out of Ashcroft's office so fast that no one—not even the House Judiciary Committee—knows how many have been sent. The Judiciary Committee demanded to know, but Ashcroft, citing his new powers, stonewalled them. With these national security letters, all the cops have to do is present one and presto—business, educational, Internet, consumer and other personal data are instantly turned over with no showing of probable cause or even a foreign intelligence need. The FBI can go after anyone—and Ashcroft refuses to reveal who they are going after—without even Congressional scrutiny.

That's not all. We now have the precedent of secret detention that might make banana republics envious. Some 5,000 young men, mostly students, have been "interviewed" by the FBI for no other reason than they may not be citizens or they are of Middle Eastern origin. Another 1,200 people were detained, and held indefinitely and secretly, most for no reason other than minor immigration violations that would have been ignored in the past. Of the Immigration and Naturalization Service detainees, 11 percent were imprisoned more than six months before being released or deported. About half were imprisoned for more than three months.

In a highly critical report, the Justice Department's own inspector general found that while imprisoned at the federal detention center in Brooklyn, detainees faced "a pattern of physical and verbal abuse" as well as "unduly harsh" detention policies, including 23-hours-per-day lockdown, 24-hours-per-day cell lighting, a communications blackout, and excessive handcuffing, leg irons and heavy chains. The report also criticized the FBI for making "little attempt to distinguish" between immigrants who had possible ties to terrorism and the vast majority who did not, including many swept up by chance.

It is un-American to incarcerate a large group of people when there is no credible reason to think they are dangerous.

Even worse, some detainees have been subjected to secret deportation proceedings. Soon after the September 11 attacks, immigration courts from coast to coast began conducting scores of hearings in secret, with court officials forbidden even to confirm that the cases existed.

Now, perhaps some of you are saying to yourselves, as card-carrying Americans, that you are safe from Bush's terror. Don't count on it. The Bush administration has never let the law limit its bigger goals. Bush maintains that he has the inherent power as commander in chief—i.e., without any basis in the laws of our country—to label *anyone* an *"enemy combatant,"* then lock them up and throw away the key. According to this novel approach—a wholesale violation of international law and everything this country stands for—an enemy combatant is a person with no legal rights whatsoever.

The USA Patriot Act and the enemy combatant designation are just a hint of what Bush has in store for us. Consider something called "Total Information Awareness," developed by the Pentagon. When some objected to the scary term "total," this got toned down to "Terrorist Information Awareness" (TIA). This program, first headed by Iran-Contra perp Adm. John Poindexter and run under the auspices of the Defense Advanced Research Projects Agency (DARPA), will have the capacity to search the records of every kind of transaction made by hundreds of millions of Americans. Every query run by the good admiral—for example, "give me the names of people who bought an optical mouse at CompUSA this week"—amounts to the government asking every person in the United States an intrusive and inappropriate question about his or her life. But these questions are not asked to your face—they take place in secret, as the government looks at data you may not even know has been collected about you, and gives you no opportunity to answer the questions yourself so you could perhaps explain errors or extenuating circumstances in the information that has been gathered about you.

Another brainchild of Poindexter and DARPA was the "Policy Analysis Market," which the government was to put up on a Web site. Apparently, Poindexter reasoned that commodity futures markets worked so well for Bush's buddies at Enron that he could adapt it to predicting terrorism. Individuals would be able to invest in hypothetical futures contracts involving the likelihood of such events as "an assassination of Yasser Arafat" or "the overthrow of Jordan's King Abdullah II." Other futures would be available based on the economic health, civil stability, and military involvement in Egypt, Iran, Iraq, Israel, Jordan, Saudi Arabia, Syria and Turkey. All oil-related countries. The proposed market lasted about one day after it was revealed to the Senate. Senators Wyden and Dorgan protested the Pentagon's $8 million request, and Wyden said, "Make-believe markets trading in possibilities that turn the stomach hardly seem like a sensible next step to take with taxpayer money in the war on terror." As a result of the uproar over this, Poindexter was asked to step down.

America has always stood for the principle that the government may not spy on its citizens unless there is probable cause to believe that a citizen is involved in wrongdoing. Even then, the spying must be approved by a judge. When we are being questioned lawfully, we have always had the constitutional right to refuse to answer any question. Those rights are out the window with programs like TIA.

There is usually very little in the way of an electronic or paper trail when it comes to terrorists. They pay cash and lay low. You and me, however, we leave trails everywhere—credit cards, cell phones, medical records, online; everything we do. Who is *really* being watched here?

Never mind that this was just another layer of bureaucracy created by the party that spends most of its time railing against the federal government and its layers of bureaucracy.

*   *   *

And then there are those who exist in some sort of terror limbo—
the prisoners of Guantanamo Bay. All of a sudden, we were really
excited to have Cuba right next door—what better place to put all
our newly captured evildoers? Six hundred and eighty people—including three children ages thirteen to sixteen—are incarcerated
there indefinitely. No charges, no sentence to serve, no lawyers, no
nothing. Is it any wonder there have been 28 suicide attempts
among those imprisoned there?

To date, there are already at least thirty-four documented cases
of FBI abuse under the Patriot Act—and at least another 966 individuals have filed formal complaints. Many of these people were
just minding their own business, or seeking to partake in our free
and open society. Consider these examples:

• John Clarke, an organizer with the Ontario Coalition Against
Poverty (OCAP), was detained at the American border by immi-
gration officials on his way to a speaking engagement at Michigan
State University. A State Department agent drove in from Detroit
and interrogated Clarke about his participation in anti-globaliza-
tion protests, about whether he "opposed the ideology of the
United States" and even about the whereabouts of Osama bin
Laden. The agent presented a State Department folder on OCAP
that included the name of a man with whom Clarke had stayed in
Chicago, and leaflets from Clarke's previous speaking engagements
in the U.S.

• A suburban New York judge asked Anissa Khoder, a U.S. citizen of Lebanese descent, if she was "a terrorist" when she appeared in court over parking tickets.

• In May 2002 six French journalists were stopped at Los
Angeles International Airport, interrogated and subjected to body

searches. They were detained for more than a day and expelled from the United States before they could reach their final destination: a video game trade show.

• At a high school in Vermont, a uniformed police officer entered teacher Tom Treece's classroom at 1:30 a.m. to photograph a student art project that depicted "President Bush with duct tape over his mouth" and the caption, "Put your duct tape to good use. Shut your mouth." Treece was removed from teaching his current-events class.

• A college student from North Carolina, A.J. Brown, was visited by two Secret Service agents who questioned her about her possession of "anti-American" material. Without inviting them in, Brown showed the agents what she assumed they came for: an anti-death-penalty poster showing Bush and a group of lynched bodies with the caption: "We hang on your every word."

• North Carolina Green Party activist Doug Stuber was detained and questioned while trying to fly to Prague, then told that no Greens were allowed to fly that day. His interrogators showed him a document from the Justice Department that showed that Greens were likely terrorists, and the Secret Service took a mug shot. Stuber was forced to turn back.

There are other incidents that, while they may not be the work of the Feds, they represent the chilling effect this has had on our society. Here are two examples:

• CBS fired a producer of *Hitler: The Rise of Evil* for statements he made comparing the mood of America to that in Germany when Hitler ascended to power.

• And, a twelfth-grade teacher at English High School in Lynn, Massachusetts, was forced to stop showing my film *Bowling for*

Columbine to her classes because the principal said the movie contains "anti-war messages."

As you can see, the effects of Bush's actions go far beyond issues
related to terrorism. There is an atmosphere that has been created
that people had better watch what they say or do, every day. (In fact,
no less an authority than White House spokesman Ari Fleischer
warned critics of the Bush administration—and specifically come-
dian Bill Maher—to "watch what they say, watch what they do.")

What really gets to me is the way this band of deceivers has
used September 11 as the excuse for *everything*. It's no longer
just to pass measures to protect us from a "terrorist threat."
September 11 is now *the* answer. It is the manna from heaven
the right has always prayed for. Want a new weapons system?
Have to have it! Why? Well . . . 9/11! Want to relax the pollution laws? It's a must! Why? 9/11! Want to outlaw abortion?
Absolutely! Why? 9/11! What does 9/11 have to do with abortion? Hey, why are you questioning the government? Someone
call the FBI!

To the rest of the world, it looks like we've gone mad. People in
most other countries have been living with acts of terrorism for
years, some for decades. What do they do? Well, they don't go crazy
with fear. The average German doesn't stock up on duct tape or stop
using the subway. They just learned to live with it. Shit happens.

But what do we do? We invent color-coded threat charts. We
frisk ninety-year-olds in wheelchairs. We attack the Bill of Rights.
Yeah, that'll show those terrorists! Let's dismantle our way of life
so they won't have to blow it up.

This makes no sense.

None of this is to say that certain rational precautions shouldn't
be taken to prevent those few acts of terror that do occur.

Perhaps George W. Bush should have made it a point to read the
reports the CIA sent him. On August 6, 2001, according to the
Washington Post, just weeks before September 11, Bush was given

a comprehensive report marked "URGENT" warning him that al Qaeda was planning a major attack on the U.S. (The full contents of the memo are not known because Bush has refused to release it, despite Condoleezza Rice saying repeatedly that there was nothing specific in the report. If there's nothing specific, then why can't they release it?) Worse, a 1999 report had already warned that al Qaeda was looking into using planes as missiles with the intention of crashing them into government buildings.

Why didn't Bush, with an intelligence memo in his hands warning that attacks were imminent, coupled with the reports passed along by the Clinton administration, alert the nation? Was he too busy taking his month-long vacation in Crawford, Texas? Bush failed to do his job and it may have cost 3,000 people their lives. That alone should be enough to haul him before an impeachment tribunal. Lying about sex, as far as I know, cost no one their life in the Clinton White House.

For instance, what if, during the late 1990s, the Republicans had let the FBI do its real job—protecting the lives of our citizens—instead of having them spend countless hours investigating the sex habits of the president or some rinky-dink land deal of the first lady's? At one point, more than 200 FBI agents were assigned to some portion of the witch hunt to get the Clintons. Two hundred agents who—maybe—should have been returning calls from flight schools in Texas that were worried they had strange guys not wanting to learn how to take off or land a plane. Two hundred FBI agents who should have been checking how terrorists got to stay in the country long after their visas expired. Two hundred FBI agents who should have been training airport security.

Two hundred FBI agents who should have been doing ANYTHING other than having their time wasted by vindictive, sex-obsessed, right-wing Republicans wanting to write a $50 million porn book about where the president kept his cigars.

There has been a lot of talk about what Bush might have done to prevent September 11 in the month before it happened. But no one is talking about an action *fourteen years before September 11* that almost certainly would have prevented the tragedy—at a cost of 50 cents more per airline ticket. In 1987, I went to work for a while in Ralph Nader's office in Washington, D.C. What was one of the projects Nader's Raiders were working on at that time? They were lobbying the government to make airline travel safer and pushing for all the airlines to install new cockpit doors that would be impenetrable. The airline industry objected loudly and refused to do a thing. Of course, had they listened to Nader then, would the nineteen hijackers have been able to get control of those planes? I can pretty much guarantee the 3,000 who died that September day would be alive today had Nader's group prevailed fourteen years earlier.

When we are talking about terrorists, we need to accept and admit that most acts of terror are inside jobs and most terrorists are homegrown. We must stop thinking that it is the foreigner, the stranger, who is out to harm us. That is rarely the case. We've learned a lot about this in modern times. We now know that when a person is killed, the vast majority of time the victim knows the murderer. Children are molested usually not by the mythical stranger in a trench coat, but rather by a family member, neighbor, or friendly clergy. Arsonists are far too often former firefighters, burglars are many times people who have been in or worked on your home. With all the security set up at New York's City Hall to protect it from some scary 9/11-style terrorists, it was a city councilman who walked his own killer around the metal detectors with the police's acquiescence. And when it has come to people hijacking and crashing airplanes, the only two times this happened before September 11, it was insiders—the airlines' own people—not madmen outsiders. Only airline employees had been responsible for such mass-murder hijacking until 9/11/01. (A disgruntled USAir employee did not have to walk through security and brought a gun on board in December 1987 and crashed a plane in California; and on November 16, 1999, an Egyptian airline employee took over the controls and crashed that plane into the Atlantic Ocean.)

It is crucial to stop thinking of the "terrorists" as masked, anonymous, and foreign. More likely, it's someone you know. You're having a drink with him right now.

I've always thought it was interesting that the mass murder of September 11 was allegedly committed by a multi-millionaire. We always say it was committed by a "terrorist" or by an "Islamic fundamentalist" or an "Arab," but we never define Osama by his rightful title: multi-millionaire. Why have we never read a headline saying, "3,000 Killed by Multi-Millionaire"? It would be a correct headline, would it not? No part of it is untrue—Osama bin Laden has assets totaling at least $30 million; he is a multi-millionaire. So why isn't that the way we see this person, as a rich fuck who kills people? Why didn't that become the reason for profiling potential terrorists? Instead of rounding up suspicious Arabs, why don't we say, "Oh my God, a multi-millionaire killed 3,000 people! Round up the multi-millionaires! Throw them all in jail! No charges! No trials! Deport the millionaires!!"

We need protection from our own multi-millionaire, corporate terrorists, the ones who rip off our old-age pensions, destroy the environment, deplete irreplaceable fossil fuels in the name of profit, deny us our right to universal health care, take peoples' jobs away whenever the mood hits them. What do you call a 19 percent increase in the homeless and the hungry from 2001 to 2002? Are these not acts of terrorism? Do they not cost lives? Is it not all part of a calculated plan to inflict pain on the poor and the working poor, just so that a few rich men can get even richer?

We have our own "terrorists" to deal with, and we need our entire focus returned to them so that we can one day live in a country where the people once again pick the president, a country where the wealthy learn that they have to pay for their actions. A free country, a safe country, a peaceful country that genuinely shares its riches with the less fortunate around the world, a country that believes in everyone getting a fair shake, and where fear is seen as the only thing we truly need to fear.

CHAPTER
5

How to Stop Terrorism? Stop Being Terrorists!

WELCOME TO Mike's Quick and Easy Guide to Preventing Future Terrorist Attacks.

Yes, that's right, there *will* be future terrorist attacks. How do I know this? Because that's what they tell us every bloody day!

I know I just said that there really is no terrorist threat, but in case I'm wrong, it probably isn't a bad idea to be prepared.

I have studied this matter thoroughly and, because I spend a good chunk of my year on Manhattan Island—the target of choice for international evildoers—I have made this study a top priority. Why? Because I want to live! Sorry to be so self-serving, but I've got a movie to make, I'm getting a new hybrid car, and I've just lost fifty pounds and I sure as hell better live so I can lose the other fifty!

Bush's program of homeland security is providing us with no security at all. If you want real security, I suggest you consider my ideas that will definitely make America a safer country:

1. **Catch Osama bin Laden.** Whoa, there's an original idea! I guess someone forgot to do this. Didn't they tell us that Osama was the mastermind of 9/11? Wouldn't that make him a mass murderer? With all the capabilities we have (like being able to read a license plate number from a spy satellite in outer space), why hasn't this man been caught? Who's his travel agent? My theory: He's back home in Saudi Arabia being protected by those who have been funding him and getting the medical help that he needs for his failing kidneys. Or he's in Newark. Or . . . he's right behind you, right now!! Run away! Run away!!!

2. **When staging a coup and overthrowing the democratically elected leader of another country, do it right.** Don't force the people of those countries to live under a U.S.-sponsored dictatorship as we did in Chile, Indonesia, and Guatemala. These regimes are set up primarily to allow U.S. corporations to run roughshod over their people. This type of behavior results in a certain unruly segment of the population just hating our guts. I know, I know, what a bunch of crybabies. Still, we're the ones who often end up suffering. The best way to help spread democracy may be for us to not undo the democratic decisions people in other countries make.

3. **Propping up existing dictators does not endear us to the people living under the rule of those dictators.** Our history of siding with the wrong guy is extensive. We've picked more losers than a television executive. Saddam and the Saudi royals are only the start of a long list. Those living under the boot of these despots know that *we're* responsible for their suffering.

4. **When attempting to prop up a Latin American dictator, try to do it without killing too many nuns or archbishops.** It

tends to give the natives, who are often very religious, a bad taste in their mouths, and some of them may get the weird desire to kill a few of us in return.

5. **When attempting to assassinate the president of Cuba, make sure you get the right kind of exploding cigars.** Failure to dispose of him properly, after we had just spent decades supporting his corrupt predecessors, gives the American position little credibility.

6. **It might be good to find out why hundreds of millions of people on three continents, stretching from Morocco on the Atlantic to the Philippines in the Pacific, are so pissed off about Israel.** Now, I'm not just talking about your everyday run-of-the-mill anti-Semites—you can find them on all seven continents, including Antarctica. No, I'm talking about a perceived notion that we Americans are supporting Israel in its oppression of the Palestinian people. Now, where did those Arabs come up with an idea like that? Maybe it was when that Palestinian child looked up in the air and saw an American Apache helicopter firing a missile into his baby sister's bedroom just before she was blown into a hundred bits. Touchy, touchy! Some people get upset over the pickiest things! Is that any reason to dance in the streets when the World Trade Center falls to the ground?

Of course, many Israeli children have died, too, at the hands of the Palestinians. You would think that would make every Israeli want to wipe out the Arab world. But the average Israeli does not have that response. Why? Because, in their hearts, they know they are wrong, and they know they would be doing just what the Palestinians are doing if the sandal were on the other foot.

Hey, here's a way to stop the suicide bombings—give the Palestinians a bunch of missile-firing Apache helicopters and let them and the Israelis go at each other head to head. Four billion dollars a year to Israel, four billion a year to the Palestinians—they can just blow each other up and leave the rest of us the hell alone.

7. **Five percent of the world's population (that's us) use up 25 percent of the entire world's energy resources, and the well-off 16 percent, mostly the U.S., Europe, and Japan, use up 80 percent of the world's goods.** To some, this seems to be a little greedy, and it's got to change. If there's not enough to go around because we're hogging everything, that will tend to get some people upset. They may say to themselves, "Hmmm, how come we are living on a dollar a day, and they aren't?" It's not like we *want* them to live on a dollar a day, and if we could we'd certainly give them another 50 cents a week, but God Blessed America and we can't help that.

8. **We need to offer the world a drink of water.** Right now, 1.3 billion people can't have a glass of clean water. 1.3 BIL-LION? That's a lot of thirsty people. I say, give them a friggin' drink! If that's all it'll take to stop them from coming over here to kill me, it seems a small price to pay.

There is no excuse, considering our wealth and technology, for not ensuring that everyone on this planet has safe, clean, and sanitary living conditions. What if we vowed to provide clean drinking water for everyone on Earth within the next five years? And then we did it! How would we be thought of then? Who would want to kill us? One cup of clean water, then maybe throw in some HBO and a Palm Pilot or two and, before you know it, they love us, they really love us! (And no, we don't do this by letting Bechtel or Nestlé go in, buy up water, and sell it back like they're already doing in many places.)

9. **People should be able to buy the products they are making.** The way it is now, Manuel in Monterey, who just built your new Ford, will never be able to buy that Ford for himself. That might make Manuel a bit edgy toward us. Or how about that worker in El Salvador who makes 24 cents for each $140 NBA jersey she produces? Or the factory workers in China who earn 12 cents an hour making those cute toys for Disney, or the workers making clothing for The Gap in Bangladesh, including pregnant women, who are routinely beaten and slapped for production mistakes?

America became well off when its workers were paid enough money to afford to buy the very houses and cars and stereos they built with their own hands. That made them happy, content, and not thinking thoughts of revolution or terrorism. The genius of Henry Ford was not only his invention of the assembly line; it was his idea that everyone should get five bucks a day (a bonanza in those times). By keeping the price of the Ford low enough, all his workers would be able to buy one.

Why have American corporations forgotten this lesson when they go abroad? It will be their doom. They say they are paying their overseas workers practically nothing so that the price of the products is kept low for American consumers. But the truth is they have moved these factories to foreign countries so they can pocket the profit. They made out handsomely when they produced things in the U.S.—Henry Ford and his contemporaries were rich men. But the new rich are not content to settle for mere wealth—they have an insatiable desire to make as much as is inhumanly possible. Enough is never enough for them. This gluttony will result in more of us losing our lives to angry terrorists from the Third World. Let's make the fat cats share their wealth with those who make their products for them overseas. It's a good way to keep the rest of us safe.

10. **No child must be a slave laborer.** You know how parents are—they want their kids in schools, not sweatshops. While you are sending your child to school with a banana in his lunch box, ten-year-olds in Ecuador are trotting off to work beside their parents at banana plantations where they earn . . . nothing! If anyone complains, the company fires the kids and expects the parents to make up the extra workload. Who do you think pays for this when this child becomes an angry adult?

11. **When we kill civilians we shouldn't call it "collateral damage."** When *they* kill civilians we call it terrorism. But we drop bombs on Iraq, and more than 6,000 Iraqi civilians are slaughtered. We then apologize for the "spillover." Al Qaeda bombs the World Trade Center and the Pentagon, 3,000 are slaughtered, and it's terrorism. But what right did we have to drop bombs on Iraq's civilian population? Were those civilians threatening any of our lives? I thought the only time you can take another's life is when they are about to take yours—or did I miss something somewhere?

Of course it's hard to not kill civilians when even your smart bombs go dumb—in Iraq about one in ten went off course, blowing up homes, markets, and bakeries instead of missile defense systems. Hell, some of the smart missiles didn't even hit IRAQ—they slammed into Iran, Turkey and Saudi Arabia. Sorry about that!

12. **When declaring your "MISSION ACCOMPLISHED," make sure it really is.** Otherwise, you might end up with a lot more dead soldiers. Kennedy, Johnson, and Nixon all said at

one time or another that the Vietnamese communists were on the run, defeated, or destroyed—and there was always a "light at the end of the tunnel." Some 58,000 dead American kids later—not to mention four million Vietnamese, Cambodians and Laotians—we finally figured out that the only way to "accomplish the mission" was to get the hell out of there. We've yet to apologize for our massacre. Something tells me that that "mission" has not been forgotten by the poor of the world.

13. **One sure-fire way to make us REALLY safe would be to destroy the weapons of mass destruction still in the hands of the nation that has killed more people with them than all other nuclear nations combined.** Yes, let's destroy *our* weapons of mass destruction, right here in the U.S.A. Then let's call in Hans Blix to verify we did the job. Only after we smash every atom bomb into depleted uranium ploughshares will we have the right to tell North Korea, India, Pakistan, Israel, and the rest that THEY don't need such weapons. Not only will we set a good example, but we'll save a lot of money, too. And we'll still have enough high-tech firepower to incinerate any people of our choosing, or out-gun any rogue nation.

14. **We must immediately disavow Bush's preemptive war policy.** We need to slam shut this insane Pandora's box Bush and Cheney have opened—the notion that it is ethical to kill people *in case* they want to attack us is not the way to relax the rest of the world when they see the Stars and Stripes.

15. **Stop acting like a thief who says "stick 'em up, hand over your weapons, and okay, now hand over your oil."** Just go straight for the oil and cut out the bullshit about nation building or democracy. Sure it would be wrong, but it would

be cheaper and more honest—and we wouldn't have to blow random civilians to smithereens.

16. **Stop terrorizing our own citizens with the Patriot Act.** And while you're at it, read *1984* by George Orwell and stop naming things in ways that remind us of totalitarian dictators. If you don't have time to read it, then here are my favorite passages to post on your refrigerator:

   "The two aims of the Party are to conquer the whole surface of the earth and to extinguish once and for all the possibility of independent thought."

   "All that was required of them was a primitive patriotism which could be appealed to whenever it was necessary to make them accept longer working hours or shorter rations."

   "They could be made to accept the most flagrant violations of reality, because they never fully grasped the enormity of what was demanded of them, and were not sufficiently interested in public events to notice what was happening."

   "The capitalists owned everything in the world, and everyone else was their slave. They owned all the land, all the houses, all the factories, and all the money. If anyone disobeyed them they could throw him into prison, or they could take his job away and starve him to death. When any ordinary person spoke to a capitalist he had to cringe and bow to him, and take off his cap and address him as 'Sir.' "

17. **Start bombing the hell out of people with WHITE skin.** I mean right now it looks like we're prejudiced or something, only attacking nations with dark-skinned, non-Christian people. When France and Germany pissed us off, we should have bombed them!

18. **And finally . . . let's set a good example.** Remember that les-
    son about treating people the way you would like to be
    treated? It still works! When you treat people well, 99.9 per-
    cent of the time they respond in kind. What if our entire for-
    eign policy was based on that novel concept? What if we
    were known as the country that sought first to help people
    instead of seeking first to exploit them for their labor or
    their natural resources? What if we were known as the
    country that shared its incredible wealth—shared it even to
    the point where it might mean that we go without some of
    the luxuries we're accustomed to? How would the poor and
    desperate around the globe feel toward us then? Wouldn't
    this reduce our chances of being victims of terrorist attacks?
    Wouldn't it be a better world to live in all around? Isn't it the
    right thing to do?

The fact is, the number of people willing to blow themselves up
to kill *you* is infinitely small. Yes, anyone prepared to die for their
cause may eventually pull it off, but those people exist everywhere—and they always have. The "War on Terror" should not be
a war on Afghanistan or Iraq or North Korea or Syria or Iran or
whatever place we'll end up invading. It should be a war on our
own dark impulses.

We all need to take a deep breath, and a step back. What would
it take for *you* to want to kill someone? What about 3,000 people?
Or four million? That's right—it would take something awful that
would have completely messed up your mind. Now, if you know
what breeds a terrorist, and you see that you and I are the ones
breeding them, doesn't it just make good common sense to stop
doing that?

I'm not saying that Osama, or whoever else, should just be free
to go on his way. In fact, that was the first point—*catch that bastard*! But what do you accomplish if you launch a war that scatters

al Qaeda members around the globe? And what message are you sending to Muslim people who have lived under oppressive governments that *you* have, at one time or another, helped to keep in power?

Yes, it's springtime in terror land, and we're germinating an entire region. Is this how to make the world safe?

The only true security comes from ensuring that all people, here and around the globe, are able to meet their basic needs and dream of a better life. At the very least, we have to make damn sure we are not the ones robbing them of that dream.

CHAPTER
6

Jesus W. Christ

HI. GOD HERE.

I hope you don't mind if I interrupt Mike's book with a few words from Me, your Almighty Creator, but hey, I'm God—who's going to stop Me?

You've probably heard My name bandied about quite a bit lately, and if there's one thing that really ticks Me off, it's bandying. Another thing that really puts Me in an ugly, Old Testament mood is people taking My name in vain. And there is one individual who invokes Me every chance he gets. He's passing himself off to you as My personal messenger. Remember, I see and hear *everything*, and here's some of what I've heard from this guy:

"I could not be governor if I did not believe in a divine plan that supercedes all human plans."

"I believe God wants me to be president."

"I feel the comfort and the power of knowing that literally millions of Americans I'm never going to meet . . . say my name to the Almighty every day and ask him to help me . . . My friend, Jiang Zemin in China, has about a billion and a half folks, and I don't think he can say that. And my friend, Vladimir Putin, I like him, but he can't say that."

Can you believe this nitwit? I actually like Putin and Jiang a lot. Do you think I keep making so many Chinese and Russians because I don't like them?

I have a confession to make: Sometimes I screw up. Not all of My creations are perfect. And, in the case of the human you know as George W. Bush, well, this is one that really got away from Me.

I'm not quite sure how it happened. I have a pretty strict inventory process and it's rare that something I create turns out to be a clunker. But when I screw up, I screw up big. Take Pompeii—I still don't know what the hell happened there. I was experimenting with a new mix of sulfur and dioxide and sugar-free cola and before I knew it—BOOM! At least it's good for the tourism (unlike Atlantis, which was *really* embarrassing). Then there's Bangladesh. I was trying to get the land and water levels just right but I miscalculated and couldn't quite make it fit. You know how when you're making the bed and after you've pulled everything into place and then there's always that one spot that just doesn't even itself out, so you kinda tuck it in under the mattress? That's Bangladesh. The whole damn thing is below sea level. All those floods were never meant to be a wrath-of-Me thing.

And, yes, I do wish I had given you all eyes in the back of your heads. Bad design flaw. Also, you're right—there are NOT enough hours in the day. When I created the heavens and the Earth, I should have rotated your axis a bit differently and given you at least an extra five hours of daylight to get all your errands done *and* get home in time to barbecue. Plus, who couldn't use two more hours of sleep each night? There are a few other things I'd also do differently: I'd never give any of you the brains to invent Astroturf. I would strike down Clear Channel with one awesome lightning bolt. I would knock some sense into Tony Blair's head. And I would smite the entire arena football league.

Believe Me, when I get to do it over again (after you all have blown up the world), I'll get it right.

But, for now, what do I do about this Bush fellow? I keep hearing him say that he is "acting" on My "behalf." Let's get one thing straight: This guy does NOT speak for Me or anyone else up here. I do My own talking, or when I'm tired, I send down a prophet or two to do the yammering for Me. Once I sent My Son, but that just stirred up a shitstorm which still hasn't died down. Things didn't go too well for Him and frankly, Our relationship is still a little strained over it. He's told Me in no uncertain terms that He is *never* going back to Earth, Second Coming or no Second Coming. "Send Gabriel," is all He ever says to Me when I broach the subject.

I'd hate to have to come down there Myself to straighten things out because, when I show up, it ain't a pretty sight. George W. Bush was not sent by Me on any kind of mission whatsoever. He was not sent to remove Saddam, he was not sent to fight some axis of evil, and he was not supposed to be president. I have no clue how that one even happened. First, I answered all of your prayers and removed his father from the presidency. Then, when his son showed up eight years later, I again answered all your prayers and that guy Gore got the most votes. Like you, I did not count on the interference of any other supreme beings or supreme courts. There was also the little problem of Lucifer rearing his ugly head in the form of someone who called herself "Katherine Harris." How many times have I told you that Beelzebub has many disguises (Jim Baker, Antonin Scalia) and works in tricky, deceitful ways?

In the beginning, I never really worried about this young Bush fellow because, in My divine plan, I created him to be one of your rich-kid party boys. In the Great Mix of the universe, I al-

low for all kinds of people—and I create between 200 and 300
party boys a day (even more during Spring Break). You need
them as much as you need the rocket scientists and cellists I send
you. These boys are crucial to keeping the party going—they get
people laughing; they line up the bands; they buy the drinks for
the underaged. Then, *after* the party, they occasionally have to
kill someone on the road because I need souls here on a steady,
rotating basis. That's the way it works and Little Georgie was doing just fine until that twelve-step program had to go and mess
him up.

Man, I hate those "anonymous" groups—AA, NA, OA, GA—
all of them invoking My name to sober up, stop eating, and quit
gambling. All of a sudden, no more sinners! That's NOT the way
it works. I need sinners sinning and then repenting and then sinning again and always in My clutches so I can get some penance
and good works out of them. When they stop sinning and start
"surrendering" themselves to a "higher power," then the whole
threat of hellfire and damnation that keeps them doing My will
goes out the window.

Well, that's what happened to this particular party boy. Before I
could whip up a plague of locusts, W. was off the divine plan. I
tried My best to make his life as miserable as possible. I saw to it
that every one of his business ventures failed. I made sure that his
baseball team sucked beyond belief. I even appeared to him in a
dream one night and convinced him to trade away Sammy Sosa,
and then, just to rub it in, I made Sosa a home-run king when he
went to his new team.

But nothing would defeat George W. So I put his father in the
White House, thinking, how could little Georgie survive this? It
drove brother Neil into the S&L scandal, and it forced brother
Marvin into hiding.

But it didn't faze George at all, and he found ways to use it for
his benefit. Before I knew it, he was governor of Texas and he was
deciding when people would die. THAT'S MY JOB! I don't know,

maybe I'm getting old, maybe I'm slowing down, but nothing I tried—not even making sure he lost the election—did the trick.

Soon, *he* was all-powerful and ruling the world. Many of you gave up on Me. The praying stopped and cursing began. Oh, yes, I have feelings, too. And it hurts. It really does. Who do I have to turn to in My time of need? The Holy Ghost? That Guy is useless, never around, never leaves a forwarding address.

So, for the few of you who still hold some faith in Me, let Me assure you of the following:

1. I am the Lord thy God and HE is the Son of George, not the Son of God. I will have him spending eternity parking cars in Hell's VIP lot as soon as I get my hands on him.

2. I did not order Bush to invade any countries. It is still wrong to kill other human beings unless they have a really big knife at your throat and all pleas for mercy and a warning shot have gone unheeded. Killing humans is My job, and boy, do I love it. You've all gotten Me so pissed off, I may just ax another 10,000 of you tonight!

3. I do not want school kids praying to Me in a classroom. Save it for the church and before bedtime—that's enough for the little tykes. You keep forcing them to pray to Me, they are going to hate My ass. Stop it!

4. An embryo is an embryo, a fetus is a fetus, and a baby is a baby. That's the way I set it up. When it *is* a baby, *then* it becomes a human being. You humans are difficult enough, I don't need more of you around any sooner than necessary. And while we're on the subject, I *really* don't care about your sex lives, as long as they're consenting and adult. Just keep it to yourselves, okay?

5. One more thing on the subject of creation: Let Me state once and for all that I did not invent and do not endorse "creationism."

It's a completely bogus concept, right up there with the New Hampshire primary and non-alcoholic beer. I'm an evolution guy, despite what the neanderthals claim in My name. Who do you think created science? Only a Higher Power could come up with something so complex and miraculous.

6. I do not approve of plaques and monuments with the Ten Commandments and other religious material being displayed in public buildings. My little-known Eleventh Commandment? Keep your religious convictions to your own damn selves.

7. As far as those other religions go, two points of clarification. One, there are never going to be seventy-two virgins waiting for you up here. We haven't had a virgin up here since Jesus' mother, and you're not getting anywhere near her. So save yourself the dynamite and blown-to-bits body parts because you aren't ever getting a room in My joint. And, two, there is no "Promised Land." That big truckload of sand I dumped in that horrid little strip between the Mediterranean and the River Jordan? NOBODY was supposed to live on it, let alone fight over it to the point where it may result in the end of the world. I did not give that land to the Israelites, I did not give that land to Mohammad, and if everyone keeps using Me as the landlord I'm going to settle the dispute once and for all, so knock it off.

8. And, finally, no more of this "God Bless America" crap. What makes you think you get to be blessed and no one else does? I don't play favorites. You don't hear anyone in Djibouti saying "God Bless Djibouti." I have never heard anyone utter the words "God Bless Botswana." They know better. Let's get this straight— God don't bless America, God don't bless anyone, God has got a tee time on the back nine and he doesn't have time to be interrupted with this patriotic mumbo jumbo. Go bless yourselves and quit using My name as a justification for feeling superior to everyone else. You aren't. You are actually among the dumbest people on the

planet. Don't think so? Name the president of Mexico. See? Ask anyone else in the world the name of the leader of the country next to theirs and they can tell you who it is. God bless America? More like God bleeps America.

Look, I'm asking for a little help here. I realize I should have put an end to this madness a few days after 9/11 when George W. said on the altar of the National Cathedral that it was his mission now to "rid the world of evil." People started to believe that he was going to do it. Well, you can't rid the world of "evil" because evil is necessary to define what is good. If there were no evil, there would be no Me. Evil is a necessary element for you humans, a way for Me to test you, challenge you, to give you the chance to decide with your free will whether you will chose evil or good.

You want to get rid of some evil? Why not start with eliminating a bit of the evil *you've* created. Letting people live on the street without a home is evil. Allowing millions of your children to go hungry, that is evil. Watching endless hours of reality television when you could be having really raunchy sex with someone you love, *that* is evil.

You wanna fight an evildoer? Go smack yourself around the room for an hour. Then go out and defeat the devil in the big white house.

That is your mission. Fail Me, and you'll be toast.

That is all. God has spoken.

Now back to the rest of this book . . .

CHAPTER
7

Horatio Alger Must Die

PERHAPS THE BIGGEST SUCCESS in the War on Terror has been its ability to distract the nation from the Corporate War on Us. In the two years since the attacks of 9/11, American businesses have been on a punch-drunk rampage that has left millions of average Americans with their savings gone, their pensions looted, their hopes for a comfortable future for their families diminished or extinguished. The business bandits (and their government accomplices) who have wrecked our economy have tried to blame it on the terrorists, they have tried to blame it on Clinton, and they have tried to blame it on us.

But, in fact, the wholesale destruction of our economic future is based solely on the greed of the corporate mujahedeen. There is a master plan, my friends, each company has one, and the sooner you can get over not wanting to believe it, or worrying that to believe it puts you in the ranks of the nutters who thrive on conspiracy theories, then the sooner we have a chance of stopping them. Their singular goal is to take enough control over our lives so that, in the end, we'll be pledging allegiance, not to a flag or some airy notions of freedom and democracy, but to the dictates of Citigroup, Exxon, Nike, GE, GM, P&G, and Philip Morris. It is their executives who now call the shots, and you can go vote and protest and cheat the IRS all you want to get back at them, but face it: *You* are no longer in charge. You know it and they know it, and all that remains is the day when it will be codified onto a piece of paper, the Declaration of the Corporate States of America.

"We hold these truths to be self-evident: that all men and women and their underaged children are created equally to serve the Corporation, to provide its labor without question, to accept whatever remuneration without complaint, and to consume its products without thought. In turn, the Corporation will provide for the common good, secure the defense of the nation, and receive the bulk of the taxes taken from the people . . ."

It doesn't really sound that absurd anymore, does it? The takeover has happened right under our noses. We've been force-fed some mighty powerful "drugs" to keep us quiet while we're being mugged by this lawless gang of CEOs. One of these drugs is called fear and the other is called Horatio Alger.

The fear drug works like this: You are repeatedly told that bad, scary people are going to kill you, so place all your trust in *us*, your corporate leaders, and we will protect you. But since we know what's best, don't question us if we want you to foot the bill for *our* tax cut, or if we decide to slash your health benefits or jack up the cost of buying a home. And if you don't shut up and toe the line and work your ass off, we will sack you—and then just try to find a new job in *this* economy, punk!

That shit is so scary, of course we do what we are told, mind our p's and q's in our dreary cubicles, and fly our little American flags to show that yes, boss, we *believe* in your War on Terror.

The other drug is nicer. It's first prescribed to us as children in the form of a fairy tale—but a fairy tale that can actually come true! It's the Horatio Alger myth. Alger was one of the most popular American writers of the late 1800s (one of his first books, for boys, was called *Ragged Dick*). Alger's stories featured characters from impoverished backgrounds who, through pluck and determination and hard work, were able to make huge successes of themselves in this land of boundless opportunity. The message was that anyone can make it in America, and make it *big*.

We're addicted to this happy rags-to-riches myth in this country. People elsewhere in other industrialized democracies are content to make a good enough living to pay their bills and raise their families. Few have a cutthroat desire to strike it rich. If they have a job that lets them go home after seven or eight hours of work and then gives them the standard four to eight weeks of paid vacation every year, they're relatively happy. And with their governments providing health care, good free schools, and a guaranteed pension to live well in old age, they're even happier.

Sure, some of them may fantasize about making a ton more money, but most people outside the U.S. don't live their lives based on fairy tales. They live in reality, where there are only going to be a few rich people, and you are not going to be one of them. So get used to it.

Of course, rich people in those countries are very careful not to upset the balance. Even though there are greedy bastards among them, they've got some limits placed on them. In the manufacturing sector, for example, British CEOs make twenty-four times as much as their average workers—the widest gap in Europe. German CEOs only make fifteen times more than their employees, while Swedish CEOs get thirteen times as much. But here in the U.S., the average CEO makes 411 times the salaries of their blue-collar workers. Wealthy Europeans pay up to 65 percent in taxes and they know better than to bitch too loud about it or the people will make them fork over even more.

In the United States, we are afraid to sock it to them. We hate to put our CEOs in prison when they break the law. We are more than happy to cut their taxes even as ours go up!

Why is this? Because we drank the Kool-Aid. We bought into the drug, the lie that we, too, could some day be rich. So we don't want to do anything that could harm us on that day *we* end up millionaires. The American carrot is dangled in front of us all our lives and we believe that we are almost within reach of making it.

It's so believable because we *have* seen it come true. A person who comes from nothing goes on to strike it rich. There are more millionaires now than ever before. This increase in the number of millionaires has served a very useful function for the rich because it means in every community there's at least one person prancing around as the rags-to-riches poster child, conveying the not-so-subtle message: "SEE! I MADE IT! YOU CAN, TOO!!"

It is this seductive myth that led so many millions of working people to become investors in the stock market in the 1990s. They saw how rich the rich got in the 1980s and thought, hey, this could happen to me!

The wealthy did everything they could to encourage this attitude. Understand that in 1980, only 20 percent of Americans owned a share of stock. Wall Street was the rich man's game and it was off-limits to the average Joe and Jane. And for good reason—the average person saw it for what it was, a game of risk, and when you are trying to save every dollar so you can send the kids to college, games of chance are not where you place your hard-earned money.

Near the end of the eighties, though, the rich were pretty much tapped out with their excess profits and could not figure out how to make the market keep growing. I don't know if it was the brainstorm of one genius at a brokerage firm or the smooth conspiracy of all the well heeled, but the game became, "Hey, let's convince the middle class to give us *their* money and *we* can get even richer!"

Suddenly, it seemed like everyone I knew jumped on the stock market bandwagon, putting their money in mutual funds or opening up 401(k)s. They let their unions invest all their pension money in stocks. Story after story ran in the media about how everyday, working people were going to be able to retire as near-millionaires! It was like a fever that infected everyone. No one wanted to be left behind. Workers immediately cashed their paychecks and called their broker to buy more stocks. Their broker! Ooh, it felt so good . . . after working your ass off all week at some miserable, thankless job, you could still feel that you were a step ahead, and a head above, because you had *your own personal broker!* Just like the rich man!

Soon, you didn't even want to be paid in cash. Pay me in stock! Put it in my 401(k)! Call my broker!

Then, each night, you'd pore over the stock charts in the newspaper as one of the all-finance-news-all-the-time cable channels blared in the background. You bought computer programs to map out your strategy. There were ups and downs but mostly ups, lots of ups, and you could hear yourself saying, "My stock's up 120 percent! My *worth* has tripled!" You eased the pain of daily living imagining the retirement villa you would buy some day or the sports car you could buy tomorrow if you wanted to cash out now. No, don't cash out! It's only going to go higher! Stay in for the long haul! Easy Street, here I come!

But it was a sham. It was all a ruse concocted by the corporate powers-that-be who never had any intention of letting you into their club. They just needed your money to take them to that next level, the one that insulates them from ever having to actually *work* for a living. They knew the Big Boom of the 1990s couldn't last, so they needed your money to artificially inflate the value of their companies so their stocks would reach such a phantasmal price that, when it was time to cash out, they would be set for life, no matter how bad the economy got.

And that's what happened. While the average sucker was listening to all the blowhards on CNBC tell him that he should buy even more stock, the ultrarich were quietly getting out of the market, selling off the stocks of their own company first. At the same time they were telling the public—and their own loyal employees—that they should invest even more in the company because forecasters were predicting even more growth, the executives were dumping their own stocks as fast as they could.

In September 2002, *Fortune* magazine released a staggering list of these corporate crooks who made off like bandits while their company's stock prices had dropped 75 percent or more between 1999 and 2002. They knew the downturn was coming, so these executives secretly cashed in while their own employees and common shareholders either bought up more stock ("Look, honey, we can get GM now really cheap!") or held on to their rapidly depleting "worth" in the hopes that it would bounce back ("It has to! It always has before! They say you have to be in the market for the long haul!").

At the top of the list of these evildoers was Qwest Communications. At its peak, Qwest shares traded at nearly $40. Three years later the same shares were worth $1. Over that period, Qwest's director, Phil Anschutz, and its former CEO, Joe Nacchio, and the other officers made off with $2.26 billion—simply by selling out before the price hit rock bottom. My corporate overlords here at AOL Time Warner stuffed their pockets with $1.79 billion. Bill Joy and Ed Zander and their friends at Sun Microsystems? $1.03 billion. Charles Schwab of, yes, Charles Schwab, took home just over $350 million all by himself. The list goes on and on and covers every sector of the economy.

With their man Bush in the White House and the economy pushed about as far as it could go, the market took a wallop. It was at first massaged with that old chestnut that "the market is cyclical—don't take your money out, folks, it will come back up, just as it always does." And so the average investor stayed in, listening to all the rotten advice. And the market kept going down, down, down— so low that you looked insane if you took your money out. It HAD to have bottomed out by now, so just hang tight. And then it just went down further, and before you knew it, your money was gone, gone, gone.

Over four trillion dollars was lost in the stock market. Another trillion dollars in pension funds and university endowments is now no longer there.

But here's what's still here: rich people. They are still with us and they are do-

Cuckoo Nutty World of Business

If CEOs whose behavior has raised questions of criminal wrongdoing were not in business, they would be considered sociopaths, a psychoanalyst contends.

"Analyzed as individuals, they might easily be seen as sociopathic," Kenneth Eisold, president of the International Society for the Psychoanalytic Study of Organizations, said of business executives such as Kenneth Lay of Enron and Dennis Kozlowski of Tyco, in an address to psychiatrists. "But within the context of a group that never challenges them, their unethical behavior becomes normative—they have no internal conflict."

Because of a willingness to ignore ethical issues during the economic boom of the 1990s, when many Americans profited from the stock market, "we got the CEOs we deserved," Eisold said.

ing better than ever. They laughed all the way to the Swiss bank over the scam of the millennium. They pulled it off, mostly legally, and if they bent the law here and there, no problem, there aren't more than a small handful of them behind bars as I write this. The rest, they're on the private beach with the well-groomed sand.

So, here's my question: After fleecing the American public and destroying the American dream for most working people, how is it that, instead of being drawn and quartered and hung at dawn at the city gates, the rich got a big wet kiss from Congress in the form of a record tax break, and no one says a word? How can that be?

I think it's because we're still addicted to the Horatio Alger fantasy drug. Despite all the damage and all the evidence to the contrary, the average American still wants to hang on to this belief that maybe, just maybe, he or she (mostly he) just might make it big after all. So don't attack the rich man, because one day *that rich man may be me!*

Listen, friends, you have to face the truth: **You are never going to be rich.** The chance of that happening is about one in a million. Not only are you never going to be rich, but you are going to have to live the rest of your life busting your butt just to pay the cable bill and the music and art classes for your kid at the public school where they used to be free.

And it is only going to get worse. Whatever benefits you may have now are going to get whittled down to nothing. Forget about a pension, forget about Social Security, forget about your kids taking care of you when you get old because they are barely going to have the money to take care of themselves. And don't even think about taking a vacation, because odds are your job won't be there when you get back. You are expendable, you have no rights, and, by the way, "what's a union?"

I know, many of you don't think it's that bleak. Sure, times may be tough, but you think you'll survive. You'll be that one person who somehow escapes the madness. You are not going to give up the dream of some day having your slice of the pie. In fact, some of you believe the whole pie might some day be yours.

I have some news for you: You're not even going to get to lick the plate. The system is rigged in favor of the few, and your name is not among them, not now and not ever. It's rigged so well that it dupes many otherwise decent, sensible, hard-working people into believing that it works for them, too. It holds the carrot so close to their faces that they can smell it. And by promising that one day they will be able to eat the carrot, the system drafts an army of consumers and taxpayers who gladly, *passionately,* fight for the rights of the rich, whether it means giving them billions in tax breaks while they send their own children into dilapidated schools, or whether it means sending those children off to die in wars to protect the rich man's oil. Yes, that's right: The workers/consumers will even sacrifice the lives of their own flesh and blood if it means keeping the rich fat and happy because the rich have promised them that some day they can *join them at the table!*

But that day never comes, and by the time the working stiff has this figured out, he's in an old-age home spewing a lot of bitter mumbo jumbo about authority and taking it out on the aide who is just trying to empty his sorry bedpan. There might have been a more humane way to spend his final days, but the money that would have financed that was spent by him on all that fantastic AOL Time Warner and WorldCom stock—and the rest was spent by the government on that outer space weapons system that never did quite seem to work.

If you are still clinging to the belief that not all of Corporate America is that bad, consider these three examples of what our good captains of industry have been up to of late.

First, are you aware that your company may have taken a life insurance policy out on you? Oh, how nice of them, you say? Yeah, here's how nice it is:

During the past twenty years, companies including Disney, Nestlé,

Procter & Gamble, Dow Chemical, JP Morgan Chase, and Wal-Mart have been secretly taking out life insurance policies on their low- and mid-level employees *and then naming themselves—the Corporation—as the beneficiary!* That's right: When you die, the company—not your survivors—gets to cash in. If you die on the job, all the better, as most life insurance policies are geared to pay out more when someone dies young. And if you live to a ripe old age, even long after you've left the company, the company still gets to collect on your death. The money does not go to help your grieving relatives through hard times or to pay for the funeral and burial; it goes to the corporate executives. And regardless of when you croak, the company is able to borrow against the policy and deduct the interest from its corporate taxes.

Many of these companies have set up a system for the money to go to pay for executive bonuses, cars, homes, trips to the Caribbean. Your death goes to helping make your boss a very happy man sitting in his Jacuzzi on St. Barts.

And what does Corporate America privately call this special form of life insurance?

Dead Peasants Insurance.

That's right. "Dead Peasants." Because that's what you are to them—peasants. And you are sometimes worth more to them dead than alive. (It's also sometimes referred to as "Dead Janitors" insurance.)

When I read about this in *The Wall Street Journal* last year, I thought I had mistakenly picked up one of those parody versions of that newspaper. But, no, this was the real deal, and the writers, Ellen Schultz and Theo Francis, told some heartbreaking stories of employees who died and whose families could have used the money.

They wrote of a man who died at twenty-nine of complications of AIDS, who had no life insurance of his own. His family received no death benefits, but CM Holdings, the parent company of the music store where he worked, collected $339,302 at his death.

Another CM Holdings policy was taken out on an administrative assistant who earned $21,000 a year, who died from Amyotrophic

Lateral Sclerosis (Lou Gehrig's disease). According to the *Journal* story, the company turned down a request from her grown children, who cared for her during her illness, to help buy a $5,000 wheelchair so they could take their mother to church. When the woman died in 1998 the company received a payout of $180,000.

Some of the companies—Wal-Mart among them—have stopped the practice. Some states have enacted laws banning "Dead Peasants" policies, and others are considering similar actions. And numerous lawsuits have been filed against companies by survivors of deceased employees seeking to be named the beneficiaries of the policies. But, for now, the policies continue at many companies. Is yours one of them? You might want to find out. It's good to know that, after you die, your corpse could in fact mean a new Porsche for the chairman.

Still not convinced that the rich could care less about you? Here's another example of just how little you mean to your corporate masters once they've got your vote and your obedience. Congress is considering a bill that will let companies put less money into your pension funds if you work in a blue-collar job because, they say, as a result of the filthy, unsafe working conditions they've created for you, you aren't going to live that long anyway. So companies don't need to really be planning to give you all your retirement money because, heck, you ain't going to be around to use it! You'll be dead because they didn't install enough ventilation or they made you work so hard you'll be lucky if you're not coughing up blood by the time you're fifty-eight. So why make them set aside all this pension money for you?

What's even more disgusting about this legislation is that it is backed by unions such as the UAW who want to see the pension money used now in the form of higher wages for their workers. But the numbers don't add up: Blue-collar workers who are *union members* actually live longer than nonunion industrial workers because they are paid better and have good health benefits. People with more money who have access to health care tend to stick around longer in this life and thus need more, not less, money put into pensions to support them during their lengthy retirements.

The third example of how expendable you are comes from our good friends in the Bush administration's Environmental Protection Agency. They have a plan called the "Senior Death Discount." Corporate polluters have complained for a long time about how the government figures the actual cost, in human lives, of their poisoning of the air and water. The EPA develops its regulations—and establishes fines—in part by calculating how many people will die as a result of the pollution. So, they came up with a number for the actual "worth" of a human life—$3.7 million. (See, you are worth millions, after all!)

But the business community complained. They said, "No way are all these schmucks worth nearly $4 million!" So, the Bush EPA came up with a neat little math trick: They said, okay, in order to reduce your costs and your efforts to clean up your pollution, we'll now say that anyone over seventy is only worth $2.3 million. After all, they're almost finished anyway, and they aren't producing anything for you anymore, so their lives just aren't worth as much.

That's when critics coined the policy the "Senior Death Discount." The elderly protested, and EPA Director Christie Whitman claimed the agency would stop using the calculation. And then she resigned.

So, you slaved your life away, you worked long hours, you gave everything you had to help your company earn record profits. When you went into the voting booth you voted for their Republican (and Democratic) candidates just like they asked you to—and after you retired, this is the thanks you got. A senior discount—not just at the movies or at McDonald's, but on your very life.

Look, I don't know how to put it any gentler than to say that these bastards who run our country are a bunch of conniving, thieving, smug pricks who need to be brought down and removed and replaced with a whole new system that **we** control. That is what democracy is supposed to be about—we, the people, *in fucking charge.* What happened to us? Perhaps we never were really in charge and those words just sounded good at Independence Hall on that sweltering day in 1776. Maybe if the Founding Fathers had air conditioning and a corporate jet they never would have written such a foolish thing. But they did, and that's what we're left to work with.

So how did we let the bad people win out, the ones who would've been blowing George III back then if they had half a chance? When are we going to get this country and its economy in *our hands,* electing representatives who will split the pie fairly and see that *no one* gets more than their fair share?

Instead, what we have are sad realities like this one: the two bosom buddies, George W. Bush (CEO of America), and Kenneth Lay (Chairman of Enron, the seventh largest company in the U.S.). Before its collapse, Houston-based Enron was raking in a monstrous $100 billion a year, mostly by trading contracts for commodities including oil, gas and electricity around the world. The increasingly deregulated energy market was a gold mine for the company, which was known for aggressive deal-making.

Lay, affectionately nicknamed "Kenny Boy" by Bush, was never shy about public displays of friendship. Enron donated $736,800 to Bush from 1993 on. Between 1999 and 2001, CEO Lay raised $100,000 for his pal, and personally contributed $283,000 to the Republican National Committee. Lay also graciously gave candidate Bush use of the Enron corporate jet during the presidential campaign so he could fly his family around the country and talk about his plan to "restore dignity to the White House."

This friendship was truly a two-way street. Bush interrupted an important campaign trip in April 2000 to fly back to Houston to watch Lay throw out the first pitch at the Astros opening day game at the new Enron Field. Who said men aren't sentimental?

After Bush became president, he invited Lay to come to Washington to personally conduct the interviews of people who would serve in the Bush administration, primarily for high-level positions in the Energy Department—the very regulatory agency overseeing Enron.

Harvey Pitt—the chairman of the Securities and Exchange Commission at the time—was a former lawyer for Enron's accountant, Arthur Andersen. Lay and the Andersen team also worked to make sure that accounting firms would be exempt from numerous regulations and would not be held liable for any "funny bookkeeping"—arrangements that would come in handy later.

The rest of Lay's time in Washington was spent next door with his old buddy, Vice President Dick Cheney. The two formed an "energy task force" responsible for drafting the country's new "energy policy," a policy that could affect virtually all of Enron's business dealings. Cheney and/or his aides met with Enron executives at least six times during this period, but no one knows the full extent of the meetings because Cheney has refused to make public the records of those meetings. Meanwhile, Enron's wheeler-dealers were cooking up schemes to manipulate an energy crisis in California that would end up adding millions to their own pockets.

Does any of this ring a bell? You may have forgotten, with all the military distractions that have taken the focus off of Enron, that this was one of the greatest corporate scandals in the history of the United States. And it was committed by one of the "president's" closest friends. I'm sure Bush thanks God every night, for the War on Terror!, 9/11, Afghanistan, Iraq, and the Axis of Evil all but assured that Enron would disappear from the news and from the minds of the voting public. This scandal should have resulted in Bush's early impeachment and removal from our White House, but fate often has a way of working in Bush's favor and letting him escape the consequences of his actions. As I've pointed out before, when you've had three run-ins with the law, as he has, and never spent a single night in jail, you have the lucky touch, and for people like him it rarely goes away.

But I, for one, will not forget Enron, and neither should you. It's an event that goes beyond corporate malfeasance to a concerted plan to wreck our economy and elect political hacks who would protect them in their scheme to attack America from within.

When things were good at Enron, they were very, very good. Lay and other high-ranking honchos took home huge paychecks, and enjoyed generous expense accounts and lavish perks. The sweet life at Enron helped them afford to make significant donations to politicians in both major parties—politicians who were able to ensure that the regulatory climate stayed very, very sympathetic to Enron's interests. According to the Center for Responsive Politics, Enron gave nearly $6 million to the Republican and Democratic parties since 1989, with 74 percent going to the Republicans. This meant that when Congress began investigating Enron at the beginning of 2002, 212 of the 248 members of the House and Senate on the investigating committees had taken campaign contributions from Enron or its crooked accountant, Arthur Andersen.

Even lower-level Enron employees thought they had a good deal going: They sat back and watched their retirement plans, heavily invested in Enron stock, grow and grow.

But the company's phenomenal success was fleeting . . . and fraudulent. Much of Enron's profitability was achieved through the creation of shell partnerships, and was propped up by dubious (and possibly criminal) accounting practices. It's unclear how much of the true story will ever be known, as important documents were shredded before investigators could see them.

By the fall of 2001, the pyramid scheme that was Enron imploded. And while the rest of the country was in a state of shock over 9/11, Enron executives were busy bailing out, selling stocks, and shredding documents.

And a national crisis didn't stop them from reaching out to their buddies in the Bush administration. Calls were placed by Enron executives to Commerce Secretary Don Evans and then-Treasury Secretary Paul O'Neill, seeking help as the company was on the brink of collapse.

Evans and O'Neill said they did nothing when Enron told them

It Slices, It Dices

Are you a CEO who may soon need to be shredding some documents in order to avoid prison showers for the next ten years? Then, as a service to you, may I suggest that you invest in one of these heavy-duty, industrial-strength beauties and kiss your incriminating documents good-bye:

The DestroyIt Crosscut 5009

Features include a shred cart with two 52-gallon sections for paper collection, conveyer belt, capacity of 500 sheets at a time, output of 7,000 pounds per hour. Price: $26,999 http://www.destroyit-shredders.com

The Ameri-Shred Corp AMS 10000

With a shredding speed of 176 feet per minute, output of 10,000 pounds per hour, can handle up to 1,100 sheets at a time. Also shreds mylar, microfilm, microfiche, paper clips, and staples.

Price: $88,066
http://machinerunner.com/Industrial-Paper-Shredders-Strip-Cut-2502000-Sheet/Ameri-Shred-Corp-AMS-10000.html

of the company's shell game and impending failure, and the administration proudly used that as evidence that no special favors were granted to one of the president's biggest supporters.

That's right—they were proud of doing *nothing* while millions of Americans were swindled. And the fleecing was made possible to a large degree by the Bush administration's willingness to let Enron run amok.

When he finally had to go before the press, George W. Bush tried to distance himself from his old friend and said, essentially, "Ken who?" Bush explained that his good buddy wasn't *really* a good buddy, but was instead just some businessman from Texas. "He [Kenny Boy] was a supporter of Ann Richards in my run [for governor] in 1994!" Bush told the media. (In fact, Lay contributed almost four times as much money to Bush's campaign for governor.)

When Enron officially went bankrupt in December 2001, Wall Street pundits and investors throughout the country were stunned.

But "bankrupt" has a different meaning for Enron's top executives than it does for the rest of us. The company's bankruptcy filing in 2001 shows 144 top executives received a total of $310 million in compensation and another $435 million in stock. That's an average of over $2 million each in compensation and another $3 million in stock.

And while the big guns counted their millions, thousands of Enron workers lost their jobs and much of their savings. Enron had established three savings plans for its employees and at the time of the bankruptcy, 20,000 of them were members of these plans. Sixty percent of the plans were made up of Enron stock. When the stock evaporated to pennies from an August 2000 high of $90, these employees were left with next to nothing. Losses in 401(k) plans totaled more than $1 billion.

But huge losses from the Enron collapse extended far beyond its employees, to thousands of others who owned Enron stock in public retirement funds, which, according to a *New York Times* article, lost at least $1.5 billion.

And the Enron collapse sent the entire stock market into a down-turn, with a negative ripple effect that is still being felt today.

But as I write this, in the summer of 2003, fewer than two dozen people have been charged with Enron-related crimes. Five of those have entered into plea agreements and are awaiting sentencing, and fifteen others are awaiting trial.

No charges have been filed against former Chairman Ken Lay or CEO Jeff Skilling.

So, what do we do?

The only true value your life has to the wealthy is that they need your vote every election day in order to get the politicians they've funded into office. They can't do that by themselves. This damnable system of ours that allows for the country to be run by the will of the people is a rotten deal for them as they represent only 1 percent of "the people." You can't get tax cuts for the rich passed when the rich don't have enough votes to pull it off. This is why they truly hate democracy: because it puts them at the distinct disadvantage of being in the smallest of the smallest minorities. So they need to somehow dupe or buy off 50 percent of the people to get the majority they need to run the show. That is no simple task. The easy part is buying the politicians, first with campaign donations, then with special favors and perks once in office, and then with a good-paying consulting job once out of office. And the best way to ensure that your politician *always* wins is to give money to both sides, which is what nearly every corporate PAC does.

Fooling the majority of the voters into voting for the rich man's candidate (or candidates) is much harder, but they've proven it can be done. Getting the media to repeat your words as if they were truth, with hardly a question being asked, is one method. As we've seen, scaring people works well, too. As does religion. The rich have thus had a hardcore army of conservatives, right-wingers, and Christian Coalition-types to act as their foot soldiers. It's an odd marriage of sorts because the rich, by and large, are neither conservative nor liberal, neither right nor left, nor are they devout Christians or Jews.

Their real political party is called Greed, and their religion is Capitalism. But they are more than happy to see millions of poor whites and even millions more middle-class people cheerfully pulling the lever in the voting booth for the candidates who will only screw these poor-white and middle-class people once they're in office.

So, our challenge, our mission, is to find ways to reach out to these millions of working people and show them how they are voting against their own best interests. It took the bankruptcy of Enron before thousands of its conservative employees, many of whom have said they proudly voted for George W. Bush and the Republicans, woke up. How many of them do you think will be voting for Ken Lay's best friend in the next election? But that's a painful way to build an opposition party. These otherwise good people should not be punished because they thought Rush Limbaugh and Tom DeLay were looking out for them. They were deceived and used. I truly believe that when they find out about tricks like dead peasants insurance and the senior death discount, when they learn what this latest tax cut has cost them in the form of reduced services and higher local taxes, they will wise up and be mad, very mad. And once they realize their name will never be Horatio Alger and that fairy tales are for children, they will grow up—and rise up—mighty fast.

CHAPTER

8

Woo Hoo!
I Got Me a Tax Cut!

George W. Bush
Bush Ranch
Crawford, Texas

Dear George:

I have to admit that when I first heard about your latest
$350 billion tax cut, like many Americans, I started thinking,
"Well, there he goes again, helping out his rich buddies."

But then one day I went to the mailbox and, along with the
usual junk mail, there was a check from my publisher for all
the books I sold last year. George, I just sat there and stared
at the number on this check, and then I got out my calculator
and I did the math figuring out your new tax break and . . .

Oh . . . my . . . God . . . George! MY SHIP HAS COME
IN! Hallelujah! Thank you! Thank you! THANK YOU!
Man, I had you judged *all* wrong. I thought you were doing
this tax cut just for Cheney, Kenny Lay, and yourself. After

all, you'll gain about $33,000 from the cut this year, and Dick Cheney's going to pocket a cool $85,924. (Cheney's really going to clean up in 2004, with a $171,850 tax cut.)

But, here's the thing I fear no one will give you credit for: You weren't just doing this for them; you were actually doing it for ME! There you were, sitting in the White House for the last year and half, when each week someone would give you the bad news summary: "Well, sir, unemployment is up over 6 percent, we've just lost another two million jobs, thirteen more countries now officially hate us, the Texas Rangers have the worst record in the American League West, none of your relatives have been arrested *this* week—oh, and the biggest-selling book of the year is still, um, *Stupid White Men*, which is, um, mostly about you, sir, and written by that guy who got up on the stage at the Oscars and yelled at you, Our Leader." Boy, do I feel sorry for the poor slob who had to bring you *that* news!

Man, you would have had every reason to call in the boys from Langley and have me disposed of the way Clinton had all those forty-seven people mysteriously killed! You would have had every right to make my life a living, miserable hell, complete with twice-a-year IRS audits and full body cavity checks every time I left the house. You could have done all that—and more—but you didn't.

Instead, you said to your economic advisers, "You know, we could have pushed through this big tax break last year, but Mike was broke then and he wouldn't have been eligible for it. Or, we could wait until next year, which will give us enough time to start so many rumors about him on Fox-MSNBC that no one will ever buy a book or movie ticket from him again. But, boys, I think the Christian thing to do is to put our tax break into effect *this* year, when Mike is making more than me AND Cheney. Let's just turn our cheek and give that bastard the biggest check he's ever seen!"

George, I don't know what to say. You are not the man I thought you were. Instead of punishing me, you have opened your heart—and the government's checkbook—to me. ME!

The Congressional Budget Office has added it all up and expects that the 2003 federal deficit will exceed $401 billion. Way to go, George—you're going to break the previous record of $290 billion, set in 1992 by your daddy. USA! USA! And in early 2003, the Treasury Department projected even *larger* deficits in coming years, totaling more than $44 *trillion*. But you guys at the White House chose not to release the findings until after the new tax cut was passed. Smooth move!

With the government's books leaking red ink by the bucketfuls, you could clearly use a few of my dollars now more than ever. But *you* didn't want them; *you* wouldn't take them. It was as if you said, "No, Mike, you keep your money and spend it whatever way you want. We'll be fine; don't worry about us. The next generation will figure out a way to pull themselves out of debt, so don't you look a gift horse in the mouth." What a pal!

This latest tax cut—the MIKE MOORE TAX CUT!—was incredible. Not only did you reduce the rate a guy like me pays in federal income tax, from 39 percent to 35 percent, you managed to do absolutely nothing for people in the lower brackets! You weren't lying when you said: "My jobs and growth plan will reduce tax rates for everyone who pays income tax." You just weren't telling the truth. People who used to pay 10 percent to 15 percent still pay 10 percent to 15 percent. Yes, you completely left out 8.1 million people from your "tax relief." And why not? That's just more money for guys like you and me! While the poor schmucks in the bottom half of the income bracket will keep about $100 a year, the richest 5 percent will be banking a whopping 50 percent of your tax cut.

Now, sure, I understand that a lot of people are suffering from all this, but, hey, let's face it, somebody's gotta suffer and why should it be you or me? So what if the tax cut will cost the individual states an estimated $3 billion over the next two years and $16 billion over the next decade! It's a big country!

Take the kids in Oregon, whose schools were shut down early this year because they ran out of tax money. I can guarantee you that we just made a lot of youngsters happy to have a longer summer vacation! Or, I'm sure you've heard about that new state library in Hawaii that can't even open because the federal tax funds ran out? Well, what the hell were they doing building a library in *Hawaii*? You go to Hawaii to be outside in the beautiful weather; you don't go there to sit inside and read a book! Everyone knows that! And I'm sure you saw the story about how they ordered most government buildings in Missouri to unscrew every third light bulb in order to save money after the tax cuts. Every third light bulb? Whiners! They've still got the other two! It's crybaby stuff like this that makes me sick.

Look, there are lots of sad-sack stories out there. God only knows I had my own share of them not that long ago. Nobody listened much then but—look at me now! See, ignoring people like me who were having hard times is not such a bad thing. Sooner or later the poor get tired of being ignored and decide to get rich! I'm sure this is what your senior political strategist, Karl Rove, had in mind when he said you were a "populist" whose elimination of dividend taxes was aimed at "the little guy."

Perhaps the genius move in this most recent tax cut is how you were able to tell the American public, "We're help-ing families with children who will receive immediate relief." The only problem was, you and the Republicans saw to it that the bill excluded 12 million children whose parents

With so many millionaires getting back so many millions, thanks to George W., the IRS has an actual form just for them . . .

Form **8302**	**Direct Deposit of Tax Refund of $1 Million or More**	OMB No. 1545-1763
(Rev. December 2001) Department of the Treasury Internal Revenue Service	▶ Attach to your income tax return (other than Forms 1040, 1120, 1120-A, or 1120S), Form 1045, or Form 1139.	

Name(s) shown on income tax return

Identifying number

Phone number (optional)
(   )

1. **Routing number (must be nine digits).** The first two digits must be between 01 and 12 or 21 through 32.

2. **Account number (include hyphens but omit spaces and special symbols):**

3. **Type of account (one box must be checked):**

☐ Checking   ☐ Savings

General Instructions

Purpose of Form

File Form 8302 to request that the IRS deposit a tax refund of $1 million or more directly into an account at any U.S. bank or other financial institution (such as a mutual fund, credit union, or brokerage firm) that accepts direct deposits.

The benefits of a direct deposit include a faster refund, the added security of a paperless payment, and the savings of tax dollars associated with the reduced processing costs.

Who May File

Form 8302 may be filed with any tax return other than Form 1040, 1120, 1120-A, or 1120S to request a direct deposit of a refund of $1 million or more. You are not eligible to request a direct deposit if:

- The receiving financial institution is a foreign bank or a foreign branch of a U.S. bank or
- You have applied for an employer identification number but are filing your tax return before receiving one.

If Form 8302 is filed with **Form 1045,** Application for Tentative Refund, or **Form 1139,** Corporation Application for Tentative Refund, both of which allow for more than one year's reporting, direct deposits may be made only for a year for which the refund is at least $1 million.

Note. *Filers of Form 1040 must request a direct deposit of refund by completing the account information on that form. Filers of Forms 1120, 1120-A, or 1120S must request a direct deposit of a refund using* **Form 8050,** *Direct Deposit of Corporate Tax Refund. This includes a request for a refund of $1 million or more.*

Conditions Resulting in a Refund by Check

If we are unable to process this request for a direct deposit, a refund by check will be generated. Reasons for not processing a request include:

- The name on the tax return does not match the name on the account.
- The financial institution rejects the direct deposit because of an incorrect routing or account number.

- You fail to indicate the type of account the deposit is to be made to (i.e., checking or savings).
- There is an outstanding liability the offset of which reduces the refund to less than $1 million.

How To File

Attach Form 8302 to the applicable return. To ensure that your tax return is correctly processed, see **Assembling the Return** in the instructions for the form with which the Form 8302 is filed.

Specific Instructions

Identifying number. Enter the employer identification number or social security number shown on the tax return to which Form 8302 is attached.

Line 1. Enter the financial institution's routing number and verify that the institution will accept a direct deposit.

For accounts payable through a financial institution other than the one at which the account is located, check with your financial institution for the correct routing number. Do **not** use a deposit slip to verify the routing number.

Line 2. Enter the taxpayer's account number. Enter the number from left to right and leave any unused boxes blank.

Privacy Act and Paperwork Reduction Act Notice

We ask for the information on this form to carry out the Internal Revenue laws of the United States. You are required to give us the information. We need it to ensure that you are complying with these laws and to allow us to figure and collect the right amount of tax.

In addition, the Privacy Act requires that when we ask you for information we must first tell you our legal right to ask for the information, why we are asking for it, and how it will be used. We must also tell you what could happen if we do not receive it and whether your response is voluntary, required to obtain a benefit, or mandatory under the law.

Our authority to ask for information is sections 6001, 6011, and 6012(a) and their regulations, which require you to file a return or statement with us for any tax for which you are liable. Your response is mandatory under these sections. Section 6109 requires that you provide your social security number or employer identification number on what you file. This is so we know who you are, and can process your return and other papers. You must fill in all parts of the tax form that apply to you.

You are not required to provide the information requested on a form that is subject to the Paperwork Reduction Act unless the form displays a valid OMB control number. Books or records relating to a form or its instructions must be retained as long as their contents may become material in the administration of any Internal Revenue law. Generally, tax returns and return information are confidential, as required by section 6103. However, section 6103 allows or requires the Internal Revenue Service to disclose or give the information shown on your tax return to others as described in the Code. For example, we may disclose your tax information to the Department of Justice to enforce the tax laws, both civil and criminal, and to cities, states, the District of Columbia, U.S. commonwealths or possessions, and certain foreign governments to carry out their tax laws. We may also disclose this information to Federal, state, or local agencies that investigate or respond to acts or threats of terrorism or participate in intelligence or counterintelligence activities concerning terrorism.

Please keep this notice with your records. It may help you if we ask you for other information. If you have any questions about the rules for filing and giving information, please call or visit any Internal Revenue Service office.

The time needed to complete and file this form will vary depending on individual circumstances. The estimated average times are: **Recordkeeping,** 1 hr., 25 minutes; **Learning about the law or the form,** 30 minutes; **Preparing, copying, assembling, and sending the form to the IRS,** 33 minutes.

If you have comments concerning the accuracy of these time estimates or suggestions for making this form simpler, we would be happy to hear from you. You can write to the IRS at the address listed in the instructions of the tax return with which this form is filed.

Cat. No. 62280S

Form **8302** (Rev. 12-2001)

make between $10,000 and $26,000 a year—including one million children in military families. Those who needed the money the most were the ones who got the shaft. But, after all, how much did those low-income people contribute to the Bush campaign? Lesson learned: If you want to get, you better give.

But, hey, I got ME, ME, ME a tax cut! Now, what will I do with it? According to you, George, I will voluntarily recycle it into our economy and it will trickle down to the less fortunate, resulting in more jobs and better wages for them.

And that is exactly what I am going to do. I am going to put my entire tax cut toward something that will benefit those who got left behind, those who work hard and have nothing to show for it, those who are sent to fight your wars and die. I have an idea that I think will go a long way to making America a better place, to building a better future for our children, to insuring that the planet we inhabit gets a fighting chance to make it to the twenty-second century.

How will I spend my tax cut?

George, I'm going to spend it all to get rid of you!

That's right. Every last dime from my tax cut is going to trickle down on your pointy little head in the hopes that, come election night, you will join the ranks of the unemployed and be sent packing back to the ranch. I will give the maximum legal amount to the candidate who has the best chance of defeating you. I will give the maximum legal amount to any congressional candidate who has a chance of helping to take back the House or Senate from the Republicans. I will write check after check after check after check until there is no more of my tax cut left to spend. I will ask the readers of this book to send me their ideas on how to best spend my tax cut, including which candidates in their area would be the best to support. I have established a Web site, www.SpendMikesTaxCut.com, and I will ask people to visit it and help me spend the thousands of dollars you have given me to toss you out of office. I will ask others who can do without their tax cuts to join me and use their bonus money to get our country back from those who seek to undermine all that we have stood for.

I hope you understand that none of this is personal and that I am still grateful to you for giving me this gift. It will be money well spent.

Yours,
Michael Moore

CHAPTER

A Liberal Paradise

THERE IS A COUNTRY I would like to tell you about. It is a country like no other on the planet. Many of you, I am certain, would love to live there.

It is a very, very liberal, liberated, and free-thinking country.

Its people hate the thought of going to war. The vast majority of its men have never served in any kind of military and they aren't rushing to sign up now. They abhor guns and support any and all efforts to restrict the usage of personal firearms.

Its citizens are strong supporters of labor unions and workers' rights. They believe that corporations are up to no good and should not be trusted.

The majority of its residents strongly believe in equal rights for women and oppose any attempt by the government or religious groups who would seek to control their reproductive organs.

In overwhelming numbers, the people of this country I speak of believe that gay and lesbian people should have the same opportunities as straight people and they should not be discriminated against in any way.

In this country nearly everyone wants to have the strongest protections necessary to ensure a clean environment. And they take personal responsibility by doing a number of things every single day to cut down on pollution and waste.

This country is so far to the left that 80 percent of its people believe in universal health care and racial diversity on college campuses.

This country I know of is so hippy-dippy-free-love and all that jazz that only a quarter of its people believe that drug users should go straight to jail—perhaps because, as their president has, 41 percent of the citizens have admitted to using illegal drugs themselves! And when it comes to holy matrimony, the number of people who live together and don't get married is up 72 percent in the past decade, and 43 percent of them have children.

I'm telling you, this country is so commie-pinko-weirdo, its conservative party can never get more than 25 percent of its recurring voters to join it, while the vast majority of its citizens define themselves as either members of the liberal party, or worse—independent or anarchist (the latter just simply refusing ever to vote!).

So, where is this utopia I write about, this land of liberal-lefty, peacenik tree-huggers (and how soon can you and I move there)?

Is it Sweden?

Tibet?

The Moon?

No! You don't have to go to the moon because . . . **you're already there!** This Land O' Left paradise I speak of is none other than . . . *the United States of America!*

Surprised? Don't believe it? Finally convinced my last screw has come loose? I don't blame you. It's hard to think of the U.S. of A. as anything but a country that is ruled by a conservative majority, a nation whose moral agenda seems set by the Christian Coalition, a people who appear to be cut from the cloth of their Puritan ancestors. After all, look who's in charge at the White House! And look at the approval ratings he gets!

But the cold bitter truth—and the best kept political secret of our time—is that Americans are *more* liberal than ever when it comes to both the lifestyles they lead and the positions they take on the great social and political issues of the day. And you don't have to take my word for it—it's all there in the polls, just the facts and nothing but.

Now, say this to any liberal and they won't just snicker (liberals stopped laughing a long time ago, which is part of the problem), they'll shake their heads and repeat the mantra they've learned from a media with a vested interest in making them believe they're on the losing side every miserable day of their lives: *"America has gone conservative!"* Ask any liberal-leaning person to describe this country and you'll hear a series of invectives about how we live in a nation of pickup trucks and gun racks and flags flying everywhere. They will speak with a tone of defeat about how much worse things are going to get, and resign themselves to four more years of whatever crap we've been eating for the last four (or fourteen or forty) years.

The right must rejoice every time they hear this surrender—and then they reinforce it with whatever sledgehammer they can grab. Yes! America supports the war! Yes! America loves its Leader! Yes! All of America was watching *The Bachelorette* last night! So, if *you* are not part of All-of-America, then just shut the fuck up and go crawl into that phone booth with the Noam Chomsky fan club, you miserable loser!

The reason the right is so aggressive in trying to squash any and all dissent is because they're in on the dirty little secret the left doesn't get: that **more Americans agree with the *left* than the right.** The right knows this because they look at the numbers, they read the reports, and they live in the real world that has become increasingly liberal in the last decade or so. And they hate it. So, in the tradition of all propagandists, they lie. They create an opposite truth: AMERICA IS CONSERVATIVE. Then they pound away with that false message so hard and so often that even their political opponents come to believe that it's true.

I want everyone reading this book to stop repeating this Big Lie. And to help you break this habit, I am going to give you the simple, indisputable facts. What I am about to share with you is not information that comes from liberal think tanks, the pages of the *People's Daily* or my handlers in Havana (to whom I report on an hourly basis). It is from sources that are as straight and mainstream as the Gallup Organization and as American as the members of the National Rifle Association. The polls were taken by organizations including the Harris Poll, *The Washington Post*, *The Wall Street Journal*, *USA Today*, Harvard University, National Opinion Research Center, PBS's *NewsHour with Jim Lehrer*, *The Los Angeles Times*, ABC News and, yes, Fox News (for the complete list of poll sources, see Notes and Sources).

Please, allow me to introduce you to **your fellow Americans:**

Fifty-seven percent of the American public believes that abortion should be legal in all or most cases. Fifty-nine percent think abortion should be decided between a woman and her doctor, while 62 percent don't want to see the Supreme Court overturn *Roe v. Wade*. In fact, a solid 53 percent think the legalization of abortion was a GOOD THING for the country (compared to just 30 percent who thought it was bad), and a full 56 percent of us want to leave a woman's access to an abortion as it is now or—get this—*make it easier*!

No wonder the right has lost its marbles—*THE MAJORITY OF AMERICANS ARE BABY-KILLERS!*

Since it became legal in 1973, there have been 40 million abortions in this country. One in three women will have an abortion by the time she's 45, and of those who do, almost half will have more than one.

What does this mean to conservatives? It means that *women* are deciding when life will be brought into this world. *Women* are in complete control of this decision. That is a tough pill for conservatives to swallow; after all, it's only been eighty-three years since women were even allowed to vote. To give them the power to decide which of us will get to be born—whoa! That means the next Sean Hannity might be getting flushed down into some medical waste jar right now as we speak! Imagine how helpless this makes right-wing men feel. We Impregnate, You Don't Decide. That's the way it always was until just a few years ago. A multi-millennial change takes some getting used to.

A whopping 86 percent of the American public say they "*agree* with the goals of the Civil Rights movement." Four out of five Americans say "it is important for colleges to have racially diverse student bodies." Hell, even the U.S. Supreme Court has come around on this one! And more than half of us believe affirmative action is necessary to help those who have been historically denied these opportunities. Seventy-four percent *disagree* with this statement: "I don't have much in common with people of other ethnic groups and races"—which puts us ahead of Great Britain, France, Germany, and Russia, when the same question is asked in those countries. Seventy-seven percent of us would adopt a child of another race, and 61 percent say they have friends or family members who are dating or are married to someone of another race. And, in fact, in the last twenty years, the number of interracial marriages has more than doubled, from 651,000 to 1.46 million.

THAT'S RIGHT! WE AMERICANS ARE A BUNCH OF RACE MIXERS AND RACE TRAITORS!

Oh, you can just see the conservative blood boiling, can't you?

What happened to everyone knowing their own place and sticking with their own kind? J.Lo! That's who's responsible for this! Taking all the good, white men with her. Next they'll start having kids and we won't know how to identify them by race, and if that happens, we might realize how ridiculous race is and start working together on the problems that really matter. And that, my friends, does not include much that is on the right wing's agenda.

Eighty-three percent of Americans say they are in agreement with the goals of the environmental movement. Three-quarters of us think environmental problems pose a serious threat to the quality of life in the United States. Eighty-five percent are worried about pollution of rivers and lakes, 82 percent worry about toxic waste and polluted drinking water, 78 percent worry about air pollution, and 67 percent worry about damage to the ozone. Eighty-nine percent of the people recycle and 72 percent check the label to avoid buying toxic products, while 60 percent would rather see the government push for more energy conservation than an increase in production of oil, gas and coal. When given the choice between "economic growth" or "environmental protection," assuming you couldn't have one without the other, Americans choose environmental protection. Even two-thirds of Republicans in one poll responded by saying they would vote for an environmentalist candidate over a non-environmentalist. Four times as many Americans trust environmental organizations to know what's better for the ecology than they do the government.

THAT'S RIGHT, AMERICANS ARE ECO-WACKOS! They would actually put the survival of some spotted snail fish over having a few more dollars in their pocket each week. How misguided is that? Don't they get it—this is OUR planet and we can do with it what we damn well please! Give these Americans a chance to buy more fuel-efficient vehicles (industry experts expect hybrid cars to soon make up 10–15 percent of America's annual car sales), and they flock to the showroom floor! What's the world coming to—*the world?*

Ninety-four percent of the American public want federal safety regulations enacted on the manufacture and use of all handguns—and 86 percent want this even if it makes guns more expensive! Seventy-three percent of Americans want a mandatory background check on anyone buying a gun. They want a five-day waiting period before you can actually get a handgun. They believe that you must have a police permit before you can own a handgun, that guns should be childproof, and that if you beat up your spouse, you shouldn't be able to own any gun. And in states like New York, 59 percent want an outright ban on all handguns.

In the 2000 election, The Brady Campaign to Prevent Gun Violence was able to defeat nine of the twelve candidates on their "Dangerous Dozen" list of elected officials who were deep in the pocket of the gun lobby. The NRA spent more than $20 million that year, focusing most of it on two of the largest hunting states in the country—Michigan and Pennsylvania—in the hopes of electing pro-gun governors and defeating Al Gore. What happened? Gore won both states, and the people of Michigan and Pennsylvania elected governors whom the NRA labeled as "anti-gun." This came two years after the NRA-backed Republican incumbent in Michigan, U.S. Senator Spencer Abraham, was defeated by anti-gun forces.

The NRA is so out of touch with even their own members, that, when NRA members in Michigan were polled, this is what the Lansing-based market-research company EPIC-MRA found out:

- 64 percent of NRA members favored mandatory reporting of private handgun sales;
- 59 percent favored regulations requiring that guns be stored unloaded;
- 68 percent supported creating uniform safety standards for domestic and imported guns;
- 56 percent supported a law requiring a five-day waiting period before purchasing a gun;
- 55 percent were in favor of banning high-capacity magazines that hold the ammo.

AMERICANS WANT THE GUNS PRIED FROM THEIR COLD, DEAD HANDS! Only 25 percent of us own a gun. The majority know they are less safe with a gun in the house. Why is this? Because more than a million of us have been killed by guns since Kennedy was assassinated. We couldn't have killed that many of our countrymen if we'd fought the Vietnam War another fifteen times! That means *everybody* knows somebody who at one time or another was shot with a gun. And you know what happens when that many people see firsthand the tragedy of gun violence—they end up hating guns! And that's the majority of the country.

Eight in ten Americans believe that health insurance should be provided equally to everyone in the country. And 52 percent say they would be willing to pay more in taxes or insurance premiums to see that happen. It's not surprising we want national health insurance since, per capita, we spend $4,200 a year on it already, while countries with universal health care pay far less: $2,400 in Germany; $2,300 in Canada; and $1,400 in the United Kingdom.

YES, AMERICANS ARE SOCIALISTS AND THEY WANT SOCIALIZED MEDICINE! Why? Because they get sick! Who doesn't get sick—and who doesn't want to get better? C'mon, this one's a no-brainer. So many millions by now have seen their life savings go up in smoke because of one accident or one horrible illness. They don't give a damn what it costs at this point. They just want it fixed. As the baby boomers' joints start to ache with arthritis and they lose a testicle or two, watch how quick we get universal health care. The only reason we don't have it already is that the politicians who oppose it are all covered 100 percent by very generous health plans. They've rarely paid a doctor bill in their lives and they don't intend to have you stop paying your bills now. Nothing seems crueler—or more ironic—than these upper crusters who never pay a dime for their high-priced shrinks or reflexology sessions to call those who just want that tumor removed from their uterus a bunch of commies. Well, the revolution is at hand and let's hope all those uninsured commies give the rich such a headache that a whole bottle of Advil won't be enough to take away the pain.

Sixty-two percent of the people you share this country with support changing current laws so that *fewer* nonviolent offenders are sent to prison. That's right, they want criminals roaming the streets! Eighty percent want more community service for those who break the law and 76 percent believe that offenders would do better being on the outside making restitution to their victims than by being locked away. Seventy-four percent prefer treatment and probation for nonviolent drug users.

AMERICANS ARE SOFT ON CRIME! They are a bunch of bleeding hearts! And they are dopers themselves! Ninety-four million Americans have used illegal drugs at least once in their lives. No wonder they want to let the potheads run amok!

Eighty-five percent of Americans support equal opportunity in the workplace for gays and lesbians. And 68 percent want laws enacted to punish anyone who would discriminate against homosexual employees. Seventy-three percent support hate crime laws and banning discrimination in housing. Half now say that gay and lesbian couples should receive the same benefits enjoyed by married couples, and 68 percent think gay couples should be entitled to Social Security benefits while 70 percent support employee-sponsored health insurance coverage for gay spouses. And half of us have no problem with gay and lesbian couples adopting children.

AMERICANS ARE A BUNCH OF LIMP-WRISTED PANSY-LOVERS! The country has gone to the fags! The U.S. Supreme Court has just legalized sex between consenting homosexuals. What's next—gay priests?! How are we going to get all macho for the next war if our men have all gone soft on the soft men? Not everybody can have David Crosby's baby!

According to a 2002 Gallup Poll, 58 percent thought labor unions were a good idea. An AFL-CIO poll put union approval ratings at 56 percent and even a fair and balanced poll from Fox News (Oops! Don't sue me! No, *sue me!*) showed that half the country had a favorable impression of unions (while only 32 percent were opposed). With only 13.2 percent of the country's workers belonging to a union, all this extra support must be coming from half of the non-union workers who would join one if given the choice. On top of all that, 72 percent believe that Washington gives too little consideration to working Americans.

The average working American has come to completely distrust Corporate America: Eighty-eight percent have little to no trust in corporate executives; 68 percent think these executives are less honest and trustworthy than they were a decade ago; 52 percent have very little or no trust in corporate accounting, while 31 percent have only some trust; 65 percent think there needs to be major reform of Corporate America; and 74 percent think the problems in Corporate America are due to greed and a lack of morals. They know that these bastards are constantly up to no good and should be watched every waking moment of every bloody day.

AMERICANS HATE THE MAN! Especially the boss-man! They believe they should get their fair share of the pie. They believe that the workplace should not be the place where they die. They believe that the employers must be forced to behave properly.

As you can see, we live in a nation of people who believe in racial equality, women's rights, labor unions, a clean environment, and fair treatment for gays and lesbians. Even on the one issue where Americans skew conservative—the death penalty—support for capital punishment has dropped dramatically in the past five years (thanks, in part, to the work of those students at Northwestern University who found at least eleven innocent people on death row in Illinois). While over 80 percent of the public used to believe in the death penalty, that number has dropped to 64 percent. When asked how they felt about capital punishment if it was guaranteed that a first-degree murderer received a sentence that would never let him out of prison, support for the death penalty drops to only 46 percent. This is a stunning drop in support of one of our nation's weirdest and cruelest activities, one that is practiced by no other Western industrialized country on this planet. In fact, a recent CNN poll found that 60 percent of Americans now support a nationwide moratorium on executions while a commission studies whether the death penalty is applied fairly.

How did this happen? It happened because the American people have a good heart and an active conscience. The majority will never support the killing of an innocent human being, even if they still believe in the death penalty as a concept. That is why we will see an end to capital punishment in the not too distant future. As people become educated about how we may be putting innocent people to death, they will not continue to support such a risky endeavor.

This goodness that I believe is at the core of most of my fellow Americans is what leads them down the liberal road more often than not. They do not want others to suffer. They want everyone to get a fair break in life. They want their planet to be around for their grandchildren to enjoy.

Conservatives know this is the real America—and it drives them crazy to live in such a liberal nation. You can hear them any day of the week on talk radio or the Fox News Channel; screaming, foaming-at-the-mouth right-wingers. Have you ever wondered why they're all so *angry*? I mean, listen to them. They spend all day, every day, just spewing so much bile about traitors, liberals, faggots, liberals, weasels, liberals, the French, liberals—I sometimes worry that they are going to choke on their own venom and then someone is going to have to invent a Heimlich maneuver for hate. Here are a few examples from our sacred airwaves:

"OH, YOU'RE ONE OF THE SODOMITES. YOU SHOULD ONLY GET AIDS AND DIE, YOU PIG. HOW'S

THAT? WHY DON'T YOU SEE IF YOU CAN SUE ME, YOU PIG. YOU GOT NOTHING BETTER TO DO THAN PUT ME DOWN, YOU PIECE OF GARBAGE? YOU HAVE GOT NOTHING TO DO TODAY, GO EAT A SAUSAGE AND CHOKE ON IT."

—Michael Savage

"ANYTHING [liberals] CAN DO TO BRING DOWN CHRISTIANITY AND JUDAISM IS GOOD FOR THEM. BECAUSE THEIR MINDS ARE WARPED, BECAUSE LIBERALISM IS NOT A PHILOSOPHY, LIBERALISM IS A MENTAL DISORDER."

—Michael Savage

"GOD SAYS, 'EARTH IS YOURS. TAKE IT. RAPE IT. IT'S YOURS.'"

—Ann Coulter

"WE NEED TO EXECUTE PEOPLE LIKE JOHN WALKER IN ORDER TO PHYSICALLY INTIMIDATE LIBERALS, BY MAKING THEM REALIZE THAT THEY CAN BE KILLED, TOO. OTHERWISE THEY WILL TURN OUT TO BE OUTRIGHT TRAITORS!"

—Ann Coulter

"WE SHOULD INVADE THEIR COUNTRIES, KILL THEIR LEADERS AND CONVERT THEM TO CHRISTIANITY!"

—Ann Coulter (on September 11 terrorists)

"I WILL TELL YOU, WHEN MICHAEL MOORE SAYS THAT THIS PRESIDENT IS AN ILLEGITIMATE PRESI-

DENT HE CROSSES THE LINE, HE CROSSES THE LINE
. . . HE CROSSES THE LINE INTO ANARCHY ALL
RIGHT."

—Bill O'Reilly

"IT IS TRUE THAT IF YOU ARE POOR AND CAN'T
AFFORD A GOOD LAWYER, YOUR ODDS OF GOING
TO PRISON SKYROCKET. BUT YOU KNOW WHAT?
TOUGH!"

—Bill O'Reilly

"FEMINISM WAS ESTABLISHED SO AS TO ALLOW
UNATTRACTIVE WOMEN EASIER ACCESS TO THE
MAINSTREAM OF SOCIETY!"

—Rush Limbaugh

"YOU GUYS ON THE LEFT, YOU WEREN'T THERE IN
THE COLD WAR, YOU'RE NOT HERE NOW. IF WE EVER
LISTEN TO YOU, WE'RE ALL GOING TO BE BOWING AT
THE FEET OF SOME DICTATOR SOMEPLACE ELSE!"

—Sean Hannity

"THEY'RE A BUNCH OF GUTLESS, SPINELESS COW-
ARDS!"

—Sean Hannity (on Hollywood leftists)

"CANADA IS A LEFT-WING, SOCIALIST BASKET
CASE. WHAT KIND OF FRIENDS ARE THEY?"

—Sean Hannity

One day, I was talking to the actor Tim Robbins—often an ob-
ject of the right's bellicose babbling—and he said, "Why is it that

they are so mad and angry all the time when they already control the White House, the Senate, the House of Representatives, the Supreme Court, Wall Street, all of talk radio, and three of the four cable news channels? They got their war, they got their tax cut, and their commander in chief has a 70 percent approval rating! You'd think they'd be happy, but they're not."

It does seem pathological to be unhappy when you are in charge of just about everything. Imagine how we would behave if Jesse Jackson were president, the liberal Democrats controlled both houses of Congress, Mario Cuomo and Ted Kennedy sat on the Supreme Court, and *The Nation* had the biggest news channel on TV. Man, we would be in seventh—no, eighth!—heaven, and you'd hear the joy in our voices and see the smiles on our faces.

And that's when it hit me: The right wing is so upset precisely because *they know* they are in the minority. They know Americans, in their hearts, do not really agree with their side, and they never will. Americans, like most humans, don't want to be around people who are filled with hate and meanness of spirit. And that is why they are so angry, because they know they are a dying species. They know the chicks and spics and the fags are taking over and so they are trying to get as much damage done as possible before their political breed becomes extinct. They howl the howl of a dying dog and they wail as the dinosaurs must have in their final days. Instead of fighting them, we should pity them.

Of course, most Americans would never describe themselves as "liberal." In the last two decades, it has become the dirtiest word in American politics. All a Republican has to do is brand an opponent "a liberal," and that's supposed to be the end of that loser. It hasn't helped that liberals have played right into their hands, first by stopping their own use of the word and then by acting as minimally liberal as possible. Liberals have acted and voted conservatively so often that they have redefined the term "wimp."

This is why Americans usually hate to vote for liberals. A "liberal leader" is often an oxymoron—liberals don't lead, they follow. Conservatives are real leaders. They have the courage of their convictions. They don't bend, they don't break, and they never give in. They are relentless in pursuit of their ideals. They are fearless and they take shit from no one. In other words, they actually *believe* in something. When's the last time you ran into a liberal or a Democrat who stuck to a principle just because it was right?

That is why most Americans don't trust liberals. You never know which way they will bend. At least with Republicans and conservatives, what you see is what you get, and in these scary times, that reassurance is comforting to millions.

The other problem is that many liberals aren't much fun and they certainly don't look like they're having a very good time. Who wants to hang out with that crowd?

But *Webster's Collegiate Dictionary* defines the word liberal this way: "Not narrow or contracted in mind; not selfish" and "not bound by orthodox tenets or established forms in political or religious philosophy; independent in opinion; not conservative; friendly to great freedom in the institution or administration of government. . . ." Liberal is also defined as generous, "and implies largeness of spirit in giving, judging, acting, etc."

And *that* is exactly how the majority of Americans think, act, and behave these days. Though they won't use the word itself, they are the living, breathing definition of liberal in their everyday words and deeds. Just as most independent, free-thinking women rarely use the word "feminist" anymore; their actions speak louder than their lack of a label, and feminist is exactly what they are.

So let's not get hung up on the terms. Most Americans don't approach the world with labels, but with common sense. To the majority of Americans it just makes sense that the air and water should not be trashed, that the government has no business poking around an adult's bedroom or genitals, that it isn't right to deny people a chance simply because of the pigmentation of their skin. Americans don't define these as political issues, but as basic logic. While this attitude may actually be a textbook definition of "liberal," why don't we start to look at it and define this cultural shift in an entirely different light?

Let's start saying the following: A new *Common Sense Majority* rules the land. Is it *common sense* to have 75 million people go without health insurance for most, if not all, of the past two years? Of course it isn't; that makes *no sense.* Is it *common sense* to let just five companies own all the major sources of information and news in America? Absolutely not. Is it *common sense* to see that every person has a job and makes a livable wage? You bet—that makes *good sense.*

What decent-thinking person wouldn't be for these things? We need to set the common-sense agenda and start calling the shots. The small group of right-wingers who now control most facets of our lives are the No Sense—or nonsense—Minority. **They do not represent the vast bulk of this country.**

You may be thinking, "Yeah, well, if that's true, then why does Bush have such high approval ratings?"

To me, the answer is simple. America was attacked. More than 3,000 people died. It's basic human nature that if you have been attacked, you will rally behind your leader—*no matter who that leader is.* The high ratings for Bush are not an endorsement of his policies. Rather, it is the response of a frightened country that has no choice but to back the man charged with protecting them. America has *not* fallen in love with Bush—it's more like "love the one you're (stuck) with."

Let me say it again: The overwhelming support for the war in Iraq only came *after* the war began. Before the war, the *majority* of Americans said that we should not be invading Iraq unless we have the backing and participation of all our allies *and* the United Nations. But once the war began, the average American wanted to support the troops, and wanted the troops to come home alive. After all, it is *their* children who were sent over there. What else were they going to say to the pollster on the phone when it was *their* son or daughter or *their* neighbors' kids who were in harm's way?

Support for Bush is actually very weak. The economy is in the crapper. People are struggling every day. And there is no way Bush can keep them *and* his rich buddies happy at the same time. Although the citizens of America love their country, and want to support it, if they don't have a job—or one that pays all the bills—that is what will be on their minds come Election Day.

So, take heart. And take a look around you. You live in a nation full of progressive-thinking, liberal-leaning, good-hearted people. Give yourself a pat on the back—you won! We won! Let's take a victory lap together and then get to work on fixing the Great Disconnect—how it is that, in a nation of lefties, the right hand controls everything. They do not represent the will of the people, and that has to change. Start acting like the victors you are and get out there to claim the country that is truly ours.

CHAPTER

10

How to Talk to Your Conservative Brother-in-Law

YOU KNOW the scene all too well. Thanksgiving dinner. The large extended family has gathered once again around the table to share good times and a hearty meal. The cranberries are ripe, the bird is plump, and that brother-in-law of yours at the other end of the table is at it again. "The Bush tax cut is going to put this country back on the road to prosperity!" The room goes uncomfortably silent and somebody tries to change the subject. The brother-in-law—a know-it-all who treats your sister nice but is an obnoxious ass nonetheless—continues. He goes through the familiar litany: "too many deadbeats are on welfare," "affirmative action is reverse discrimination," "they should build more prisons and throw away the key." Finally, your cousin Lydia, who is home on holiday break from Antioch College, has heard enough and calls him a "racist" and a "dick." Suddenly Grandma's special dilled mashed potatoes are flying across the table like an American missile on a sunny morning in residential Baghdad—and a nice, warm gathering of family and friends has turned into the culinary version of *Crossfire*.

Let's face it, almost every family has at least one right-wing reactionary of its very own, and there's not much you can do about it. It's a statistical certainty that for every two liberals, there will be one person who longs for the days of Strom Thurmond and legally accepted date rape.

I seem to have encountered most of these guys in the past year. Many of them have written me long letters filled with a passion rarely seen on our side of the political fence. Some stop me on the street and try to engage me in some form of heated debate. A few of these times I have asked if they would like to sit down and have a cup of coffee with me (though I don't even drink coffee, and they themselves clearly have had way too much of it). I don't engage them in argument but, rather, listen to them rant and rave about Bush, liberals, towelheads and welfare queens. It's quite a spiel they spew. Their litanies of grievances are long, and they all sound remarkably similar, as if they get their daily talking points straight from *Conan the Barbarian*. They seek nothing less than ridding the planet of bleeding-heart multi-culturalists wherever they may be having gay sex.

But, if you listen long and hard enough, you can hear their faint and distant cries for help. It's clear that they suffer from a unique pathology that is slowly driving them insane. They are, at their core, very, VERY afraid. They are afraid because, ultimately, they are ignorant. They are ignorant of much of the world that exists outside their own. They haven't a clue what it's like to be black or hopelessly poor or wishing to kiss someone of their own gender. This basic ignorance leads to their overwhelming and permanent state of fear. The fear quickly manifests itself into hate, which eventually leads to a very dark place. They become consumed with a desire to actually harm others, if not by their own hands (they are usually too afraid to do it themselves), then by having the state act in their stead: *"TAKE AWAY THEIR FUNDING! ELIMI-NATE THEIR JOBS! EXECUTE THE BASTARDS!"*

This hate becomes not just political but personal, as anyone who has ever been married to one of these guys or had one as a relative or neighbor or boss knows. It is a rough road to hoe when you begin your day with an inherent anger toward everyone who isn't *YOU*.

There is no school of therapy I know of to cure this illness; no medication developed yet by pharmaceutical companies for this conservative rage. (Actually, the drug companies need these Republican voters to insure that they will never truly be regulated; so it's in their best interest to make sure that these angry white guys are never healed.)

I firmly believe that many of these conservatives can be shown the error of their ways. They can be encouraged to think differently about the issues we are concerned about, to see them in a new light that will neither threaten them nor take away the core values they hold dear. I believe that many are lost in their own anger and have been manipulated by propaganda intended to get their blood boiling. The corporate, religious, and political chieftains know just which buttons to push to get otherwise decent and well-meaning people on their side.

I think there is a way to turn this around, to *convert* that brother-in-law of yours.

Now, you might say, "Whoa, wait a minute—I'm not into missionary work! Not if it means I have to walk among these cretins!"

But don't you want to see change—real, lasting progressive change—in your lifetime? Don't you want to pull the rug out from under this supposedly conservative movement that infects our Congress with so many Republicans? Don't you wanna have a little fun?

I'm not talking about trying to change the minds of the terminally bigoted. This is not about trying to win over the lunatic right. They're already too far gone. And frankly, they're too small to worry about.

I'm referring to the people you know and, yes, love. They take good care of their kids, they keep their houses fixed up nice, they volunteer at the church—and they always, incredibly, vote Republican. You can't figure it out. If he seems to be a good guy, why does he align himself with the party of Atila the Hun?

Here's my theory: I don't believe these people really are Republicans. They are just using a word they heard because the word was associated with tradition, common sense, and saving money. So they stuck the label on themselves. After all, who was the first Republican you heard about in history class? Honest Abe Lincoln—the guy good enough to be on the penny AND the five dollar bill! Plus, he got you a day off from school.

These people are, in truth, Republican In Name Only—RINOs. Ask them a series of questions: Do you want a clean environment? Would you live in a neighborhood with black people? Do you believe in going to war to resolve our differences with others? Most of the time they will not give the standard Republican answers. I have a friend who refers to herself as a Republican, but when I ask her if women should be paid as much as men, she responds, "We should be paid more!" When I ask her if people should be allowed to dump waste into the lake where she lives, she reminds me that she sits on the board of the local nature preserve. When I ask her how her mutual fund is doing since she was able to get rid of "That Liar Clinton," she says, "Don't ask."

So, I say to her, if Bush has driven the economy into the ground and cost you untold thousands of dollars, if the Republicans want to make it easier for people to dump shit into your lake, and if you think you should have the same rights as men—then why on earth do you call yourself a Republican?!

"Because the Democrats will raise my taxes," she responds, without missing a beat.

That is the RINO mantra. Even though these "Republicans" clearly do not believe in much of the Republican platform, and they know the Republicans will make many parts of their lives more miserable, they hold on to that Republican label because of just one thing: They think the Democrats are out to steal their hard-earned money.

As I've said, I believe we live in a liberal-majority nation, but if we really want to pull off a slam dunk of permanent change, we need to bring a few million of these RINOs over to our side. They are waiting there, wanting to jump the fence—just as long as they can take their money with them.

I've come up with a bunch of suggestions for how we can enlarge our majority by reaching out to our RINO friends and relatives. Some of these will require a bit of humility on your part. Many of them, I'm convinced, will work. It's time to raid the conservative right of this vast pool of soft support they have enjoyed for far too long.

At the very least, following my suggestions will lead to a much more peaceful Thanksgiving dinner:

1. First and foremost, assure your conservative friends or relatives that you do not want their money. You do not want them to make less money nor do you want them to lose what money they have. Right off the bat, let them know that you know that they love their money and that's just fine by you because you love yours, too (it's just a different sort of love).

2. Second, every political argument you make must be about *them* and for *them*. They base every decision on "How does this benefit ME?" Instead of fighting this self-centeredness, just go with it, embrace it, feed it. Yes, you say to them, this is *good* for YOU. The conservative lives life in the first person singular—I, ME, MINE—and that is the pronoun-centric language you must speak if you are to be heard.

3. Journey into the mind of the conservative. This is the dark continent you must venture to if the conversion is to be successful. What you will encounter in the conservative mind is fear. Fear of crime. Fear of enemies. Fear of change. Fear of people not exactly like them. And, of course, fear of losing any money on anything. If they can't see it (interracial couples don't live in their neighborhood), they are afraid of it. If they can't touch it (300 years of slavery that happened long ago), then they can't understand why things are the way they are. If they can't smell it (no industrial incinerators in their part of town), then they think the planet is in good shape.

4. Respect them the way you would like to be respected. We are asking them to be decent people and care about something other than just their money. If we ourselves are not decent, especially in the way we treat and talk to them, what are we asking them to become? Like us? I hope not.

5. Tell them what you *like* about conservatives. Be honest. You know there are many things about conservatives that we like and believe in ourselves—even though we usually wouldn't be caught dead saying them out loud. **Say them out loud** to your conservative brother-in-law. Tell him you, too, are afraid of being a victim of crime and want to prevent criminals from getting away with their actions. Tell him that if America is actually attacked you will be the first to defend the defenseless. Tell him you don't like freeloaders, either, especially that roommate you had in college who never lifted a finger to pick up a damn thing and turned your place into a pigsty.

He will see that you are, in some ways, just like him.

Tell him how dependable conservatives are. When you need something fixed, you call your redneck brother-in-law, don't you? You yourself can't fix a damn thing—and neither can any of your whiny liberal friends. Also, when you need a job, who hires you? The conservative who owns the business, that's who. You don't go hit up your slacker liberal brother-in-law for a job, do you? And if you need someone beat up, that bully who's been picking on you, you certainly aren't going to ask your uncle at the Unitarian Church to do it for you. You never know when you are going to need that conservative relative.

Conservatives are organized, on-time, efficient, well-groomed, and consistent. These are all good qualities and attributes, and we wish we were more that way. C'mon, admit it—where has being disorganized, inefficient, disheveled, erratic, and always late gotten us? Nowhere! Give a RINO his due, and you'll find him more willing to listen to what's coming next.

6. Admit that the left has made mistakes. Ouch. This is a tough one. I know, screw them, we're not the ones who need to confess! But, if you admit that, on occasion, you have been wrong, it's easier for the other person to consider what they have been wrong about, too. It also makes you appear more human and less of a jerk. I sat here for two full days staring at the computer before I could bring myself to continue on this point, but here's a start on what we've been wrong about:

- Mumia probably killed that guy. There, I said it. That does not mean he should be denied a fair trial or that he should be put to death. But because we don't want to see him or anyone executed, the efforts to defend him may have overlooked the fact that he did indeed kill that cop. This takes nothing away from the eloquence of his writings or commentary, or the important place he now holds on the international political stage. But he probably did kill that guy.

- Drugs are bad. They fuck you up, slow you down, and ruin your daily existence. Even though Nancy Reagan can kiss my ass, you really should just say no.

- Men and women *are* different. We are *not* the same gender. Do I have to show you the drawings? We are conditioned, whether through nature or society, to have our own peculiar quirks and desires and habits. The trick is how to make sure that those quirks are not too annoying to the other gender. For instance, very few women pull out a gun and shoot someone on the street. The chance that a woman will mug you tonight on the way home from work is somewhere around nil. That is a quirk specific to my gender. Likewise, very few men could give a shit about making the bed. Why make the bed? Who is going to see it? What are we doing, protecting the sheets from something we don't want them to see during the day while we're at work?

• It's really a bad idea to have sex before you're eighteen. Okay, maybe I'm just jealous because I had to wait until I was thirty-two. Nonetheless, the price to pay for teenage sex is pretty high—unwanted pregnancy, disease, and ending up with one ear bigger than the other because it's always cocked toward the front door in case the parents come home early. Who needs this? And, if possible, no one these days should have a baby until they are well into their twenties or thirties. There is practically no way, in our serf-based economy, for you to pull this off without a lot of pain and suffering.

• MTV sucks. Watching dumb-ass images of women, violence, and *The Real World* actors who have seen one too many episodes of *The Real World* themselves is the worst possible way to spend an afternoon. You'd be better off having teenage sex and then reading a book together.

• Granola is bad for you. It is filled with sugar and fat. One study found that many brands of breakfast granola are higher per serving in saturated fat and sugar than five chocolate chip cookies or one slice of orange-carrot cake. Vegetarianism is unhealthy. Humans need protein, and lots of it. Put down those sprouts and pick up a T-bone!

• The sun is *good* for you. Your skin needs at least ten minutes of direct sunlight a day for a much-needed shot of Vitamin D. Quit slapping all that sunblock over your kids. If you really are concerned about UV rays and skin cancer, then ask yourself, "When was the last time I attended a Greenpeace meeting in order to help make things better?"

• People who commit violent crimes should be locked up. Dangerous people should not be out on the street. Yes, they should get help. Yes, they should get rehabilitation. Yes, we should look for ways to reduce the root causes of crime. But no one has the right to assault you or rip you off and if you can't bring yourself to show at least an ounce of outrage against those who would harm you, then you just look like a wimp or a nut to most normal people. In fact, I want to assault you right now.

• Your children do not have a right to privacy and you better pay attention to what they are up to. Right now, as you are reading this, they are doing something. What are they doing? See, you don't even have a clue! Put down this book and head upstairs immediately!

• Not all unions are good, and, in fact, many of them are just plain lousy. They got their members to sign up for the company's 401(k) plan, and then—*poof!*—the money vanished. They adopted right-wing nationalism and turned "Buy USA" into a racist movement. There are two good unions: SEIU (Service Employees International Union) and UE (United Electrical, Radio and Machine Workers of America). Contact them if you want to organize your workplace, or for some general online guidance in how to unionize, check out www.aflcio.org/aboutunions/howto/. If you belong to one of the lazy, ineffective unions who are in bed with management or Bush, then you need to get your sorry ass down to the next union meeting and run for office.

• SUVs are not inherently evil; the fact that they use so much gas, that they are constructed to be killer machines, and that yuppie weasels drive them in urban areas *is* evil. Mostly SUVs are just horribly uncomfortable and the ride is too bumpy.

• Getting back to nature is a dumb idea. Nature doesn't want *you* anywhere near it. That's why nature created cities— to keep *you* as far away as possible!

- Bill O'Reilly makes a few good points. He's against the death penalty, he's an advocate for kids, and he opposes NAFTA. Okay, he's still a jerk, but even a jerk can be right some of the time.

- Too many of us hold a hoity-toity view of religion and think the religious are superstitious fifteenth-century ignoramuses. We're wrong, and they have as much a right to their religion as those among us who have no religion. This arrogance is a big reason the lower classes will always side with the Republicans.

- We have a namby-pamby way of saying things. It's like we invented our own language—and it annoys the hell out of anyone we're trying to get to listen to us. Knock off the PC mumbo jumbo, quit trying to be so sensitive and just say what is on your mind. Less wimp and more OOMPH!

- Why are you still bitching about right-wing author Ann Coulter? Sure, she's as crazy as a loon, but she's got more balls than the entire Democratic Leadership Council. You're just jealous because we don't have an Ann Coulter. And stop looking at her damn legs! That's why she's got you so jumbled up!

- The proposed "Liberal Radio Network?" What a stupid waste of time. Radio? Are you serious? What century are you in? Gee, why stop there—let's set up a Liberal Pony Express! How about a Liberal Morse Code? S-O-S! Get into the twenty-first century! Get a TV network. Get an Internet network. Get Snoop Dogg and 50 Cent to run for office!

- Animals don't have rights. Yes, they should be treated "humanely." Yes, Tyson Foods and all the others that "harvest" chickens are disgusting. But "freeing" chickens from their factory farms is idiotic. They don't know how to survive in the wild and they're just going to get hit by a truck. And lay off carrying on about the milk, no matter how bad it is for you. You just look like a dumbass if you go on national TV, like PETA does, to argue that beer is better for the body than milk. This shit just makes me wanna go kick my dog.

• Nixon was more liberal than the last five presidents we've had. His administration opened up a dialogue with China. He was instrumental in establishing affirmative action in hiring and protecting the rights of women. He was the first president to sign agreements on nuclear weapons control. Nixon was responsible for the 1970 Clean Air Act and created the Department of Natural Resources and the Environmental Protection Agency. He gave us Title IX to force tax monies to go to women's sports. He also attempted a type of welfare reform that would have guaranteed an income for the poor. Nixon still should have been run out of office, and the millions of dead in Southeast Asia will haunt him throughout eternity. But to think that he was the last "liberal" in office just makes me want to puke.

After admitting that you're not always right, you will find your conservative friend a lot less defensive and more willing to listen. Then it's time to make the case for why he or she should consider looking at things in a different light. The most important thing is to NEVER make the "moral" argument about why the Pentagon should get less money or why a sick child deserves to see a doctor. We have tried those arguments for ages and they don't work with conservatives. So save your breath and keep in mind that it's all about THEM. Begin every point with this one sentence: "I want **you** to make more MONEY!" Then take a stab at discussing the issues with them, using the following statements:

"Paying workers more money makes you money!"

Dear brother-in-law, when you don't pay people enough for them to take care of life's essentials, it ends up costing you and everybody else a lot of money. If workers have to take a second or third job, their productivity suffers on all three jobs. They aren't able to concentrate on one specific goal—making <u>you</u> a lot of money! They're preoccupied, thinking about how they have to get to that other job to make that <u>other</u> guy a lot of money. So your employee's tired, he makes more mistakes, he has more accidents, he leaves early, and his overall job performance is lower than if he was just concentrating on you. Why do you want him helping some other schmuck make money? If you paid him a decent wage, he'd only be thinking about <u>you</u>!

When employees are not making a living wage, they often end up having to seek food stamps or other public assistance. Who is paying for that? YOU. Why do you want to pay higher taxes for stuff like that when you can pay them directly and look like the good guy? Cut out the middleman and reap the benefits.

When you pay your employees more money, what do you think they do with it? Invest it in stocks? Horde it in offshore accounts? No! They spend it! And what do they spend it on? The stuff you make and sell! The working class is the consumer class that gives you your profits because they are not saving anything—they are roaming the aisles of Sam's Club buying things they don't really need. So every dollar you and other bosses put out there in wages is almost immediately recycled right back to you, improving your profit margin and making your stock rise. You get doubly rewarded.

If you pay people squat, or lay them off, they can't buy your stuff. They become a drain on the economy; some turn to crime, and when they turn to crime, it's your Mercedes they want, not some junker Oldsmobile in their poor neighbor's driveway. Why put yourself in a position where you might become a victim? Pay a living wage, give raises, provide good benefits—and then you can go home to your palace knowing that right now those happy workers are not taking the hood ornament off your car but rather they're out tossing all their cash right back at ya.

"Health Insurance for everyone will make you money!"

Brother-in-law, you are an employer, and your employees don't have health coverage, this costs you a lot of profit. They miss work—you lose money. They're absent longer—you lose money. Others work overtime to pick up the slack—you lose money. They get other people sick—you lose money. They work sick—you lose money. But employees who have health insurance go to the doctor right away and get medicine and get better quickly. If they are given paid sick days, they stay at home for a couple days and are back at work in no time making you money—and they feel better about their jobs because they're treated well, so they will work even harder. Employees whose health insurance allows them to see a shrink or avail themselves of preventive medicine are more productive and contribute more to the company. The short-term outlay of money for a group health plan has enormous long-term benefits that, in the end, will save you a bundle of money.

"Providing day care for your employees will make you money!"

Absenteeism is a huge drain on our gross national product. Estimates put its cost to our economy as high as $50 billion a year. The average employer loses almost $800 a year per employee due to unscheduled absences. Forty-five percent of the time an employee is a no-show for personal or family reasons. Which means that mom or dad has taken time off from work because the babysitter didn't show up, or the babysitter got sick and needed to go home early, or the kids were sick and needed to go to the doctor, or the babysitter's kid got in trouble at school and the babysitter had to leave, etc., etc. This, my conservative friend, costs your business money. For the price of an on-site day care room or facility, the company can make more money, you can make more money, and the babysitters can get real jobs with benefits. And millions of lawbreakers who pay their child care people under the table can stop leading a life of crime!

"Joining a union will make you money!"

If you are a worker, and not a boss, who considers himself a conservative and hates unions, I have one question: Why? If you want to make more money, "union" is the way to go. According to the U.S. Department of Labor, union workers make an average of $717 a week. *Non-union* workers like you make an average of $573 a week. Being a conservative is about you and you making as much money as you can. So why stay non-union? Because you don't want to be part of a group? What do you have against democracy? Some unions aren't democratic? Don't join those unions. Start one yourself. That free country you're always yakking about—that's what it means, the right to freely assemble. That right is so important, they made it Number One in the Bill of Rights.

"Clean air and water save you money!"

Each year in the United States air pollution kills 70,000 people—equal to the combined number of deaths from breast and prostate cancer. The related health care costs from air pollution have been estimated by the government at between $40 and $50 billion annually.

A 2003 study found that people living near one of thirty-eight Superfund toxic waste sites in New York City show significantly higher rates of asthma, respiratory diseases, and cancer. If you're not in New York, don't worry—you're still getting burned. The Superfund was established in 1980 and drew its money from specially imposed corporate taxes (mostly on chemical and oil giants) and is used to pay for the cleanup of contaminated industrial sites. In 1995, the taxes were not renewed, thanks to Washington's collusion with the corporate lobby groups who were tired of paying to clean up their own messes. With no new money coming in, the Superfund is nearly gone, and will be completely gone by 2004. And that means that we—you and I—will be paying to clean up *their* toxic dumps. We paid 20 percent of the cleanup costs in 1994, while the rest were covered by the Superfund. By 1999, the costs were split evenly between the fund and the taxpayers. The projected cost to taxpayers for this year: $700 million. That's money out of *your* pocket. But, hey, on the bright side, Bush is trying to limit the number of sites that get cleaned up. And while this may save you money, if you're lucky enough to live near one of the nearly 1,200 contaminated sites spread out across this country, it may also kill you.

We are falling behind other industrialized nations when it comes to investment in energy efficiency. Britain, Denmark, and Germany are moving increasingly to wind power, while we, with the world's fourth longest coastline, are doing next to nothing.

If we could get mileage standards in our cars to 40 miles per gallon by 2012, by 2024 we will have saved more oil than is in the Arctic National Wildlife Reserve, where Bush is so eager to start drilling. The easiest way to be less reliant on foreign oil is to *use less foreign oil*! This can be easily achieved by forcing the car manufacturers to produce cars that get more miles to the gallon.

Who cares that it's a good thing for the environment, it'll save you thousands of dollars each year, and possibly more!

"Stopping the Drug War will save you money!"

Rounding up drug users and putting them in prison is a huge waste of money. It costs $25,000 a year to lock up a doper; it costs only $3,000 to provide treatment. Even the most expensive treatment costs around $14,000 a year—still far less than prison. Every dollar spent on treatment will save you, the taxpayer, $3 not spent on cops, jails, and replacing that CD player stolen from your car. We are spending $20 billion annually for the war on drugs, a war that is lost year after year. All those police helicopters flying over Chico looking for pot plants could be catching the next nineteen hijackers. You are letting the government fight a war it can't win.

Plus, keeping drugs illegal doesn't stop their sale. All it means is that you, the conservative entrepreneur and investor, are making ZERO profit from the deal. All the profits go to scumbags. You hate scumbags. Why let them take YOUR money? Legalize the stuff and think of all the money you'll make from a depressed society desperate to get hooked. Americans spend an estimated $63 BILLION on illegal drugs each year and you've legislated yourself out of a piece of that action! Put down that martini and get with it!

"Giving lots of money to the public schools makes you money!"

When our pathetic schools send a generation of idiots and illiterates out into the work-a-day world, how in God's name do you expect to make any money? Right now, your office is full of people who cannot spell, who cannot do long division, who do not know how to ship a box to Bolivia because they haven't a friggin' clue what a Bolivia is.

Wondering why your wallet is gone and the punk in front of you is ready to shoot you? Try these statistics on for size: 40 percent of the U.S. prison population is functionally illiterate. Gee, how'd they get that way? From 1980 to 2000, states' expenditures on education went up 32 percent. In that same period of time, states' spending on prisons went up **189 percent**. Now that's smart thinking! And while they're in prison, are they making you any money? No! The state is actually taking license plate work away from your coffers. You want those workers free so they can come to work in your prison!

Seventy-five percent of welfare recipients are illiterate. Don't you think things might be a little different if they could read and write? I don't mean different for them, I mean different for YOU. That's a lot of welfare mothers who could be slaving away for you and making YOU money if they weren't stuck in the prison of their illiteracy. Educate them well and you will reap the rewards.

It totally boggles my mind that conservatives haven't demanded, purely out of self-interest, that our schools prepare young people to contribute and even excel in the workplace. Workers are supposed to bring you great ideas and make you filthy rich. Instead, they're sitting out there in their cubicles trying to figure out how to download the latest Weezer album. That's the result of all these years of chanting "leave no child behind" and demanding that your state keep testing kids with mandated exams. Teachers have stopped teaching anything useful and now teach for the test. Here's what it got you: a lot of kids who know how to beat a test but not much else. I've got a kid in my office right now who thought the U.K. was Russia, had never heard the name "George McGovern," and figured a legal pad was where you store legal court documents. And he's the smartest one in here! HELP!!!

"By never voting for a Republican again, <u>you</u> will make a ton of money!"

Look, I realize that at one time being a Republican and voting for Republicans seemed like the sure way to becoming wealthy. But that is not the way it works these days. Thirty years ago, if you made the equivalent of $50,000, you were rich. You lived in a big beautiful home. And there were hundreds, if not thousands, like you in every town in America. Roosevelt's New Deal had created a massive middle class and the gaps between rich and poor had actually decreased 7.4 percent from 1947 to 1968. It was not that hard to make the leap from working class to middle class or from middle class to well-to-do. The gap between those groups was not that wide. That's why all it took to be a rich kid back then was to have your dad be a family physician, a dentist, a lawyer, an accountant, a Realtor, the owner of a grocery store, or a mid-level management guy at the auto company. But all that began to crumble starting in the seventies when the income disparity really began to widen.

These days, the chance of you being rich, as I said earlier, is zip. Right now, the 13,000 families that make up the top .01 percent control the equivalent wealth of the poorest twenty million ones. And while those living it up in the top one percent have enjoyed income increases of 157 percent in the past twenty years, the middle class has only gotten a 10 percent increase. Only 10 percent for the mass of people who have powered the explosion in wealth we have seen in the past twenty years! The doctor is barely making ends meet, the lawyer is trying to scrounge up enough divorce cases to pay the bills, and the mid-management guy—well, now he tosses a mean tortilla down at Del Taco.

These very Republicans you say you are one of want nothing to do with you. They have either downsized you, fired you, or they've got you doing the jobs of two or three people. They have taken your money in the stock market and made it vanish. They have pushed through tax bills that truly benefit only that top one percent. You aren't going to see any real savings and, in fact, you are going to end up paying higher local and state taxes and see a noticeable drop in government services just as you start to hit middle age. They are spending your retirement money right now on boondoggle after boondoggle to make their buddies rich.

In short, they are using you like a sucker. They've got you mouthing all their platitudes while they slip their hand in your back pocket and steal you blind. Don't be a dope! The Republicans hate you, despise you, and sure enough never want to make their tent any bigger so that there's room for you. Get a clue!!

Now, this is not to say the Democrats are the answer, and if I had my way we'd have more alternatives on the ballot than them. But, ask yourself, honestly, weren't you doing better as a conservative under Clinton? Sure you hated his good looks and charm and how he almost got away with that blow job, but get over it! You are being taken for a ride. And you know it. You just can't bring yourself to admit it 'cause you don't want to look stupid.

You won't look stupid. No one will blame you. Everyone got snookered. Drop all this "Republican" nonsense, declare yourself an independent, and then go shopping for a party or for people running for office who are going to try to help you make more money. Any representative who delivers on making our schools and libraries a top priority, who sees to it that everyone has health care, who demands that we not live in a society of illiterates, who backs any bill that increases people's wages, and who taxes the wealthy for duping an entire country into bankruptcy—well, that is who you should be working for and voting for, because, in the end, it will all benefit <u>you</u>.

Being "Republican" is suicide.

C'mon, brother-in-law! Take a walk on the wild side. It ain't all that bad. Plus, who knows, you might just have a happier Thanksgiving dinner this year!

CHAPTER
11

Bush Removal and Other Spring Cleaning Chores

THERE IS PROBABLY no greater imperative facing the nation than the defeat of George W. Bush in the 2004 election. All roads to ruin lead through him and his administration. Four more years of this insanity and suddenly Canada isn't going to look so cold. Four more years? I can't take four more minutes.

I've received thousands of e-mails and letters in the past year, and they all contain this desperate question: *"What are we going to do to get rid of him?!"*

Which leads to the even scarier question: ***"How in the hell are the Democrats going to be able to pull this off?"*** No one—*and I mean no one*—trusts the Democrats' ability to get this job done. They are professional losers. They can't get themselves elected out of a men's room. Even when they actually *win* an election—as they did in 2000—the Democrats *STILL* lose! How pathetic is that?

In the midterm elections of 2002, there were 196 Republican incumbents defending their seats in the House of Representatives.

The Democrats could only put up a real challenge to these Republicans in twelve of those districts, and the Democrats only managed to win three of those races. With nearly 210 million voting-age Americans to choose from, the best the Democrats could do is find twelve people worthy enough to run. What gives them the right to even still call themselves a party? Why are they guaranteed a slot on every ballot in America? My paperboy could find twelve people to run for office from just one paper route.

This is why we are scared, because we know the Democrats are not up to the job.

So, what do we do? The Greens are in much better shape when it comes to true commitment and passion, but let's be honest—this is not the year of the Greens (and even the Greens know it).

The Democrats wasted two years whining and moaning about the Greens, declaring Nader and Co. the enemy. That's the sure sign of a real loser—blame somebody else for your mistakes.

In an attempt to rebuild some bridges and mend the wounds of 2000, I have reached out to Democratic leaders in an attempt to forge a Democratic-Green alliance for 2004. The combined vote for Gore and Nader was over 51 percent, enough to win any election. I have suggested to Democrats that Greens may back a Democratic candidate for president who supports the essential elements of the Green agenda, and in turn Democrats should vote for Greens in districts where Democrats are not fielding a real candidate for Congress.

I have found few takers on this offer. In fact, what I discovered was even worse: Democratic Party leaders have told me something that they will not admit in public—that they have basically written off 2004; that they see little chance of defeating George W. Bush. They would rather save their energies for 2008 when Hillary or one of their bigger marquee names—whoever the hell that may be—will run and win.

You and I have to reject the defeatist nature of these sad, impotent Democrats. In truth, this is not their decision to make. We, the people, cannot endure another four years of Karl Rove's finger puppet. And we cannot wait around for the so-called opposition party—the Democrats—to get off their ass and do their job.

So what do we do? One thing we know is that people will vote for an independent candidate, as Jesse Ventura has shown us. Perot did incredibly well—imagine what a sane person could do! But we don't have the time in the next few months to mount a serious third party challenge. That work should have been done in the last two years. It wasn't. Time's up.

Our only hope is to get someone semi-decent on that disgustingly smug and totally unjustified Democratic line that sits on the ballot in all fifty states. And it must be someone who can beat Bush.

Now, there are two "seemingly" decent people officially running as I write this book—Dennis Kucinich and Howard Dean. Kucinich is by far the better candidate on the issues. Dean, who has in past elections been endorsed by the NRA and is for limited use of the death penalty, is strong on many other issues. I would like to believe that one of them could pull it off.

But I'm tired of always being in this spot—and I'm not alone. Just for once, wouldn't it be nice to win, especially considering how liberal most Americans are? It's time to start thinking outside the tiny box that exists in our minds. For starters, let's stop believing the president has to be a white guy. White guys are a shrinking minority in this country—making up just 38 percent of voters. Plus, as I've pointed out before, all the Democrats who've won the presidency since Franklin Roosevelt (with the exception of Lyndon Johnson's landslide in 1964) have won by *losing* the white male vote. They won by getting an overwhelming number of white women and black and Hispanic men and women to vote for them.

If the Democrats would stop watering down their beliefs to appeal to all the dumb white guys out there, they'd win. Women of all colors are 53 percent of the electorate. Black and Hispanic men make up nearly 8 percent of the vote. That means that women and these minority men represent about 60 percent of the entire nation, an overwhelming majority and a powerful winning combination.

Americans are ready for a female president. How about one of our woman governors or senators running for president? The voters *want* to vote for women—we have gone from having only two women to fourteen women in the U.S. Senate in a little more than a decade. The electorate is fed up with the same old tired men who look like a bunch of hustlers and liars. Isn't there one woman of the 66 million voting-age women in this country who could beat the pants off this frat boy? *Is there not one?*

I also believe the country is ready for a black president. We've already got one on TV on *24,* one of the most-watched shows on Fox. Then there was Morgan Freeman as president in *Deep Impact* (and the last time I saw him, he was playing God in *Bruce Almighty*!). Hollywood wouldn't make a black man God if they thought that it couldn't play in Pittsburgh. And *12 million* Americans in 2003 cast their votes for our next "American Idol" for a black man, Ruben Studdard.

Whether it's the 2004 election, or ones to come, we need to find fresh candidates who can kick some Republican butt. The assumption is that a presidential candidate has to be a senator or a governor. If a candidate isn't a professional politician, but is a citizen like Al Sharpton, no one will give him the time of day (though Sharpton has said some of the most lucid—and hilarious—things in this campaign).

What we need now is a Bushwhacker! Someone who is already so beloved by the American people that, come Inauguration Day 2005, we'll be liberated from The Smirk. Someone who is *our* Reagan, an already well-known figure who will lead with his or her heart and pick the right people to do the day-to-day work.

Who is this person who could lead us to the promised land?

Her name is Oprah.

OPRAH!

That's right, Oprah Winfrey.

Oprah could beat Bush. Hands down. C'mon—you know she could! America loves her. She's got good politics, she's got a good heart, and she'd have us all up at six in the morning jazzercising! This cannot be a bad thing. And she'd get us all reading a book a month! ("Good evening. This is your president. This month we are all going to read *Brave New World*.") How cool would that be?

Here's another plus—Oprah can't be bought. She's already a billionaire! Imagine a president who owes no favors to lobbyists or oil companies or Ken Lay. She only answers to Steadman! And us! With a salary of only $400,000 a year in the White House, being president would certainly be a step down for Oprah, but it be would okay with me if she were president *and* she kept her show on the air. Every afternoon at 4 p.m., broadcast live from the East Room of the White House, we could watch President Oprah with an audience of average Americans talking about what they are going through, how they are in need of this or that—with Oprah there to help them. Except, unlike her current show from Chicago, *Oprah at 1600 Pennsylvania Avenue* could actually fix people's problems right then and there. Can't pay the bills? President Oprah orders the arrest of credit card executives who charge outrageous interest rates. Your kids acting up again? Not after they get hauled into the Oval Office for a good talking to. Your husband no longer paying attention to you? Maybe he will after his mug ends up on the post office wall on a **"Men Who Don't Shut Up and Listen"** poster.

I have been on *Oprah* three times. I've seen firsthand how the average citizen responds to her. Men and women of all races connect to her. She's like Bruce Springsteen, Mother Teresa, and Princess Di all rolled into one. I saw grown adults break down and sob after being able to shake her hand. Why this response? I think it's because Oprah is a real person who is not afraid to say what she wants to say and be who she wants to be. She's one of us who somehow made it. We like it when someone from our team wins! Her whole thing is about "I'm trying to do my best. I have my ups and downs, but I get up every day and give life another go."

Oprah's campaign to encourage people to perform simple acts of kindness—and the ripple effect those good deeds can create—is just one example of her belief in the power of the individual to change the world.

Now, this may all sound like a bunch of sappy nonsense to the cynics among you, but, hey—nothing *else* has worked! Why not try a new path? Why not go with someone who really cares about people? Someone who tries to help the common woman or man have it a bit easier today, just today, in a world that is increasingly cruel, complicated, and empty.

I know, you probably thought I was just writing this stuff about Oprah for a laugh. I'm dead serious. This is the time for bold moves, the time to think in new ways if we are ever going to win and turn things around. Oprah would beat Bush. Imagine the debates—Bush vs. Oprah! She'll have him twisted in so many knots he won't know what hit him. She'll look directly into the camera and she'll tell America, "I will take care of you. I will protect you. You will join me in this work. I will bring all the right people in who will see that no one who lives in this country suffers any more abuse, and the world will know us as the generous and peaceful people that we are." She will then turn to W. and tell him that he is on his way to the time-out room and a visit with Dr. Phil.

And she'll win in a landslide.

Now, how do we convince Oprah to run? I will start by posting a "Draft Oprah" petition on my Web site. When I first floated this idea in early 2003, the media asked her for a response and she said, smiling, "People say, 'Never say never.'" But when it comes to politics, Oprah continued, "I can say, 'Never.'" We can change her mind. You can write her by logging onto www.oprah.com. She is probably not going to like this idea at first and I have probably ensured that I will not be appearing on her show any time soon. But it is my hope that she will answer the call to lead us out of our national misery. Oprah! Oprah! Oprah!

Okay, so what if Oprah won't run? Who else do we have who is already so popular and beloved that they could announce tomorrow and beat Bush by next November? Well, they're not all black women, but there *are* other Oprahs waiting in the wings. How about Tom Hanks? Everybody loves Tom Hanks! He's one of the good guys. He cares about people. He loves his country. He would trounce Bush.

And, of course, there's Martin Sheen. People love him playing the *role* of president on TV. Let's stop the pretend act and have him do the real thing!

Or what about Paul Newman? He'd beat Bush, too. If Reagan could do it at his age, just think of how cool it would be to have the elder statesman Paul Newman calling the shots. Free salad dressing for everyone! And Joanne Woodward as first lady! No, wait—Joanne Woodward for president!

How about Caroline Kennedy? A Kennedy with no scandals! Just a generous, decent person who is also a mom!

Or any one of the Dixie Chicks! No one has made the right more afraid than the Dixie Chicks. They spoke out first, when it wasn't popular. They've got guts and they sing songs about getting rid of dead-wood boyfriends and husbands who drag you down. That has to be a lock on the female vote right there! Let's make them proud to be from Texas again! They could take turns and serve one year each, and then in the fourth year they can hand over the office to their vice president—Oprah!

But let's say none of these celebrities is willing to give up their nice lives to go live in a hornet's nest. Who could blame them? Then where does that leave us?

Many months ago, in the days leading up to the Iraq invasion, I was flipping through the channels and I came across a general talking on CNN. Assuming this was just another one of those talking ex-military heads who had sprung up all over our networks, I was ready to keep flipping. But he said something that caught my ear, and I continued to listen. He was actually questioning the wisdom of Bush attacking Iraq. Long before it came out that Bush & Co. were purposefully deceiving the American people about "weapons of mass destruction" in Iraq, he was questioning whether, in fact, Iraq was a true threat to the United States. Whoa. Who was this guy?

His name was Wesley Clark. Gen. Wesley Clark. First in his class at West Point, a Rhodes Scholar at Oxford, former Supreme Allied Commander of NATO, and a registered Democrat from Arkansas. I started checking him out. And here is what I discovered:

• He is pro-choice and a strong advocate for women's rights. Asked on *Crossfire* if he thought abortion should remain legal, he answered simply and to the point: "I am pro-choice."

• He is against the Bush tax cut. Here is what he says: "I thought this country was founded on a principle of progressive taxation. In other words, it's not only that the more you make, the more you give, but *proportionately* more because when you don't have very much money, you need to spend it on the necessities of life. When you have more money, you have room for the luxuries. . . . One of the luxuries and one of the privileges we enjoy is living in this great country. So I think that the tax cuts were unfair."

• He is against Patriot Act II and wants the first one re-examined. Here's what he said: "One of the risks you have in this operation is that you're giving up some of the essentials of what it is in America to have justice, liberty, and the rule of law. I think you've got to be very, very careful when you abridge those rights to prosecute the war on terrorists."

• He is for gun control. Says Clark: "In general, I have got twenty some odd guns in the house. I like to hunt. I have grown up with guns all my life, but people who like assault weapons—they should join the United States Army, we have them."

• He is for affirmative action. Speaking of the brief he filed with the Supreme Court to support the University of Michigan in its efforts to have affirmative action, he said, "I'm in favor of the principle of affirmative action. . . . What you can't have is, you can't have a society in which we're not acknowledging that there is a problem in this society with racial discrimination. . . . We saw the benefits of affirmative action in the United States armed forces. It was essential in restoring the integrity and the effectiveness of the armed forces."

• He is not for sending the troops into Iran or continuing with this axis of evil nonsense. "Number one is that we need to use multilateralism for what it can do," says Clark. "Multilateralism, if you use it effectively, can put a lot of economic pressure and diplomatic pressure to bear. Number two, I think we need to be very careful about jumping to a military option too quickly, especially in the case of Iran, because we can overturn the government there, perhaps, we could certainly blow up some facilities. But that doesn't necessarily solve the problem."

• He is pro-environment: "Human beings do affect the environment and all you have to do is fly along the Andes and look at the disappearing glaciers down there and you recognize that there is something called global warming and it's just getting started as China and India modernize."

• He favors working with our allies instead of pissing them off: "[This is] an administration which really hasn't respected our allies. . . . If you really want allies, [you've] got to listen to their opinions, you've got to take them seriously, you've got to work with their issues."

So, here's my question to the lame-o Democrats: *Why the hell aren't you running this guy?* Is it because he might WIN? Yeah, how bizarre would that be—a winner! Don't want to try that, do you?

Well, if I were looking for a strategy to beat Bush the deserter, I'd run a friggin' four-star general against him! Bush wouldn't stand a chance. This may be the only way to beat Bush, beat him at his own game. Bush's political strategist, Karl Rove, will try to convince the American people that this is a wartime election—and you don't change presidents during wartime. That's what they're counting on—scaring the American people into four more years of Bush II. If they've succeeded in frightening voters into believing that there really is some enemy threat out there, it may not be possible for us to undo that kind of damage. Instead, why don't we just roll with it and tell the American people, well, yes there *is* a threat out there— and who would you rather have protecting you: a guy who ran and hid in Omaha, or one of the top generals in the land? Clark has been awarded the Silver Star, the Bronze Star, the Purple Heart, and the Presidential Medal of Freedom. Thanks to the British and the Dutch, he's also got a couple honorary Knighthoods!

I know this will come as a shock to many of you. "Mike, how could you be for a general?!"

Well, first of all, as I write this, I'm not endorsing anyone (except Oprah. Run, Oprah, Run!). This is how I see it. I had four years to help build a Green Party or some other independent alternative. I didn't do it. No one did it. Sure, I made my contributions, but it wasn't enough. As I sit here typing these words, the Green Party still is not on a majority of ballots in the country. And now we have an even greater task in front of us—stopping George W. Bush from totally dismantling our Constitution and the freedoms we so dearly cherish. We're stuck in a dilemma, and sometimes desperate times call for desperate measures.

If it takes a pro-choice, pro-environment general who believes in universal health care and who thinks war is never the first answer to a conflict, if that is what it takes to remove these bastards and do the job the Democrats should have done in 2000—then that is what I am prepared to do. This involves a huge compromise on my part—will the losers who run the Democratic Party be willing to admit their mistakes and meet the millions like me halfway? Whether it's Kucinich or Dean, Oprah or Hanks, or the Good General, I'm ready for a win.

Who wants to join me?

We cannot leave this election to the Democrats to screw it up again. It will require the active participation of all of us to get out there and snatch our country back. I am writing this as best I can, as personally as I can, to each of you who read *Stupid White Men* (more than 2 million Americans), each of you who saw *Bowling for Columbine* (over 30 million of you) and all of you who have come to my Web site (over a million a day). That's enough for a small army, and so I once again want to call out Mike's Militia to rise up and beat back the Invasion of the Bushies. True, we don't have the money and the media outlets they have—but we've got something better: We've got the people on our side. And unless they declare martial law or suspend the elections, unless they've got Katherine Harris sucking chads in all fifty states, then there is no good reason why we shouldn't be able to beat them.

As your commander in chief, I hereby instruct you to engage in "Operation 10-Minute Oil Change." By doing something for just ten minutes each day, we will be able to remove the oil slick of Bush and his oil buddies who now sit in the White House. I ask each of you to perform the following guerrilla activities between now and November 2004. They will take only ten minutes each day:

1. Talk to anyone and everyone who will listen about every which way Bush has been bad for the country and bad for them. This election, like all elections with incumbents, is more a referendum on the incumbent than on the opponent. If the electorate comes to believe that the incumbent has hurt the country or the pocket-book of the average citizen, then the voters will usually vote for whoever is running against him. So the first focus must be to convince people you know that a change is in order.

2. Join the campaign of the person you believe has the best chance of beating Bush. Join more than one if you can't make up your mind right now.

3. Download a **poster** from your candidate's Web site and stick it in your window or your yard. Order a bumper sticker and put it on your car.

4. Sign up to **run for precinct delegate** (if there's still time for the 2004 caucuses and primaries. If not, see if you can attend the caucus meetings or the county convention). You must find a way to get in on the ground floor with those who will ultimately pick the candidate at the national convention.

5. There is still time for YOU to run for **local office** in the upcoming election. Why not YOU? It's not like there's a great brain trust lining up to be on the village council. Just do it!

6. Buy a few copies of the **following books** and pass them around to your friends and family and your conservative brothers-in-law: *The Best Democracy Money Can Buy; Perpetual War for Perpetual Peace; Bushwhacked!; Thieves in High Places; The Great Unraveling;* and *Lies and the Lying Liars Who Tell Them.* They all contain great bits of useful information that, once shared with any sane person, will only increase the size of Mike's Militia.

7. I need each person who reads this book to pledge to **give up their four Saturdays** in October 2004 to go out and work for the candidates who are going to put an end to the Bush regime in D.C. Just four Saturday afternoons for your country. I know this is more than the ten minutes I asked of you—but you're in too deep now to quit! There are a number of things you can do: Go door to door for a congressional candidate, hand out literature on the street, make phone calls from a candidate's headquarters to get out the vote, put up yard signs, lick stamps, send e-mails, call in to talk shows, hound the opponents, hold rallies, host neighborhood potlucks. This election will be about one thing—Getting Out the Vote.

8. For the more committed among you, why not **travel to a congressional district** that is one of the swing districts where there's a chance to boot a Republican out? Many of us think nothing of getting on a bus and traveling a thousand miles to Washington, D.C., for a demonstration. Why not travel to Paducah, Kentucky, to work for a week or a weekend for a candidate who has a shot at winning? Your presence could make the difference. It's a little more work than carrying a sign and chanting slogans, but the results may be worth it. (You can go to my Web site to find out those districts I've targeted where they need our help.)

9. Election Day: **Take a Nonvoter to Lunch—and to Vote!** What if each one of you who plans to vote in 2004 convinced just **one person** who isn't planning to vote to go with you to the polls? Do not try to convince someone who has completely checked out of voting to check back in; it doesn't work that way. People don't usually re-marry their first spouse and they usually don't go to the same movie twice. So skip the moral argument or the good citizen speech and just say to Bob—who has been bitching about everything from Bush to his 401(k)—"Hey, I'm heading over to vote. Let's get the hell outta here!" When you get to the polls, ask him to come on in with you, *it'll only take ten minutes*. Trust me, he'll go along. It's just like when someone says, "Here-have-a-beer." You often aren't in the mood for one but you don't want to turn your friend down, and, besides, what can it hurt? Your job, between now and next election day, is to identify one friend, family member, co-worker or fellow

student who has views similar to yours but will probably not bother to vote unless you actually go with him or her to the polling place. In many congressional races, the outcome is decided by only a few thousand votes. If I'm lucky, there are over a million of you reading this book right now. All it would take to switch the balance of power is for just 10 percent of you to take one or two of your non-voting friends to the polls with you. It really is that simple.

10. Finally, **here's an idea to get even more nonvoters out to the polls.** We used to do this back home in Flint. Everyone who votes (in most states) is given a receipt with a number on it when their ballot is deposited in the ballot box (some states also hand out little "I Voted" stickers). Hold a big concert or party in your town on election night where the admission ticket is simply the voter receipt stub or sticker. Announce that you are going to hold a raffle with these voter stubs and the winner will receive whatever prize you and your cohorts are able to give (we used to give out $1,000, though one year someone donated a car to give away). This was especially effective in getting young people out to vote, and I've seen black and Hispanic communities have a lot of success in getting people who otherwise feel disenfranchised to give it one last chance. Make sure you follow your local election and raffle laws, but if you try it, you may be surprised how well it works. Sure, it would be nice if people voted just because it is their sacred right, but, let's face it, we live in twenty-first-century America and, unless it's a phone-in vote on *Total Request Live,* the majority has no enthusiasm to get involved. Whatever it takes to jumpstart their batteries again, I'm for it.

There you go. You have your marching orders. Don't fail me, and don't fail yourself. They outsmarted us once—and *they're* supposed to be the *stupid white men*! Let's not let it happen again. There're just too damn many of us to have it end up any other way. We love our country and we care about the world in which our country exists. There is no reason to sink into some self-centered despair or cynicism. There is every reason to put this book down right now, pick up the phone, walk out the door, and make a difference.

Dude, where's your country? It's right outside your window, just waiting for you to bring it home.

Notes and Sources

2. Home of the Whopper

President Clinton made his angry denial of infidelity on January 26, 1998, following a presentation on child-care policy in the White House with his wife and the vice president at his side. The text of his statement is on record with the National Archives and Records Administration, and can be read online at: http://clinton4.nara.gov/WH/New/html/19980126–3087.html.

Most of President Bush's remarks cited in this chapter are posted online at the official White House Web site: www.whitehouse.gov. Tricky to get away with those whoppers, even the little ones, with some damn minion writing down every word you say and putting it on the Internet for everyone to see!

• The various versions of the president's often-repeated whopper about the threat posed by Iraq's weapons of mass destruction can be read in their entirety there: January 21, 2003, "President Bush Meets with Leading Economists;" September 12, 2001, "President's remarks at the United Nations General Assembly;" February 8, 2003, "President's Radio Address."

• Making a pitch for Senate hopeful John Cornyn at a fundraising dinner in Houston on September 26, 2002, Bush hinted at a personal vendetta against Saddam: "[T]here's no doubt his hatred is mainly directed at us. There's no doubt he can't stand us. In fact, this is a guy that tried to kill my dad."

• Bush personally peddled the stories that Iraq attempted to obtain enriched uranium in Africa, and had also attempted to purchase aluminum tubes to help build a nuclear weapons program, in a televised October 7, 2002, speech in Cincinnati, "President Outlines Iraqi Threat."

- In his Fall 2002 multi-state campaign to drum up support for the Iraq war during October and November, 2002, the president worked to link Saddam Hussein and al Qaeda. See: October 28, 2002, "Remarks by the President at New Mexico Welcome;" October 28, 2002, "Remarks by the President in Colorado Welcome;" October 31, 2002, "Remarks by the President at South Dakota Welcome;" November 1, 2002, "Remarks by the President at New Hampshire Welcome;" November 2, 2002, "Remarks by the President in Florida Welcome;" November 3, 2002, "Remarks by the President in Minnesota Welcome;" November 4, 2002, "Remarks by the President at Missouri Welcome;" "November 4, 2002, "Remarks by the President at Arkansas Welcome;" November 4, 2002, "Remarks by the President in Texas Welcome."

For more information about the companies landing the post-war reconstruction contracts in Iraq worth hundreds of billions of dollars, and their financial contributions to George W. Bush and the Republican Party, check with the Center for Responsive Politics. In particular, check out the report, "Rebuilding Iraq—The Contractors," at www.opensecrets.org/news/rebuilding-iraq.

Ambassador Joseph Wilson's credentials are established in his biography provided by the Middle East Institute, a Washington, D.C. think-tank. Over nearly three decades, Wilson served in posts with the National Security Council, the U.S. Armed Forces, Foreign Service, and State Department, and was the last official American to meet with Saddam Hussein before the launching of "Desert Storm." Wilson's own account of his trip to Niger in 2002 was published by the *New York Times*, "What I didn't find in Africa," July 6, 2003.

Further accounts of the Wilson investigation, and the Bush Administration's persistent repetition of the Iraq-nuke stories, in the face of contradictory evidence, are reported by Nicholas D. Kristof, "White House in Denial," *New York Times*, June 13, 2003; Richard Leiby, "Retired Envoy: Nuclear Report Ignored; Bush cited alleged Iraqi purchases, even though CIA raised doubts in 2002," *Washington Post*, July 6, 2003; *ABC World News Tonight*, "White House knew Iraq-Africa claim was false; Bush administration forced into contrition by discovery of paper trail," July 22, 2003; Dana Priest & Karen DeYoung, "CIA questioned documents linking Iraq, uranium ore," *Washington Post*, March 22, 2003; Michael Isikoff, et al., "Follow the yellowcake road," *Newsweek*, July 28, 2003; Walter Pincus, "Bush faced dwindling data on Iraq nuclear bid," *Washington Post*, July 16, 2003; and Evan Thomas, et al., "(Over)selling the World on War," *Newsweek*, June 9, 2003.

Sixty-two million people watched Bush make his ultimate pitch for war in his 2003 State of the Union address, according to *Washington Times* reporter Jennifer Harper, "Bush's speech resonates with public, polls show," January 30, 2003. The speech is online at the White House Web site: "State of the Union Address," January 28, 2003.

CIA Director George Tenet's statement taking "responsibility" for Bush's use of the disproved intelligence that Iraq was seeking uranium in Africa in his 2003 State of the Union address can be read at www.cia.gov

The disclosure about the October memos showing the CIA had warned the White House the Iraq-Niger uranium story was based on faulty intelligence was reported on July 23, 2003 by David E. Sanger and Judith Miller of the *New York Times,* "After the War: Intelligence; National Security Aide Says He's to Blame for Speech Error," and Tom Raum, "White House official apologizes for role in State of Union speech flap," Associated Press; and on August 8, 2003 by Walter Pincus, "Bush team kept airing Iraq allegataion; officials made uranium assertions before and after President's speech," *Washington Post.*

Secretary of State Powell's address to the UN referenced here was made on February 5, 2003. The official transcript is posted by the U.S. mission to the UN: www.un.int/usa.

The report that two trailers found in northern Iraq were for the production of hydrogen to be used to inflate balloons—not chemical weapons as asserted by the president—was made in the British newspaper *The Observer*, by Peter Beaumont, et al. "Iraqi mobile labs nothing to do with germ warfare, report finds," June 15, 2003. This was further confirmed when the Defense Intelligence Agency, part of the Department of Defense, came to same conclusion, as reported by Doughlas Jehl, "Iraqi trailers said to make hydrogen, not biological arms," *New York Times*, August 9, 2003.

The remarks by Lt. Gen. James Conway about the failure of U.S. troops to find chemical weapons in Iraq were reported by the Associated Press, Robert Burns, "Commander of U.S. marines in Iraq cites surprise at not finding weapons of mass destruction," May 30, 2003.

Information about the U.S. cooperation with Iraq in its war against Iran, and Iraq's use of chemical or biological weapons in that conflict, comes from a multitude of sources, including: Patrick E. Tyler, "Officers say U.S. aided Iraq in war despite use of gas," *New York Times*, August 18, 2002; "Chemical weapons in Iran: confirmation by specialists, condemnation by Security Council," *UN Chronicle*, March 1984; Henry Kamm, "New Gulf War issue: Chemical Arms," *New York Times*, March 5, 1984; Reginald Dale, "U.S. and Iraq to resume diplomatic relations," *Financial Times*, November 27, 1984.

The list of chemical agents sold by U.S. corporations to Saddam Hussein from 1985–1990 is included in the Senate report: "U.S. Chemical and Biological Warfare-Related Dual Use Exports to Iraq and their possible impact on health consequences of the Gulf War," Report by Chairman Donald W. Riegle Jr. and ranking member Alfonse M. D'Amato of the Committee on Banking, Housing and Urban Affiars with respect to export administration, United States Senate, 103d Congress, 2d session, May 25, 1994.

For more on the export of chemical and biological agents by U.S. corporations to Iraq, including a list of the companies, see William Blum's cover story in the April 1998 issue of *The Progressive*, "Anthrax for Export," and Jim Crogan's April 25—May 1, 2003 report in the *LA Weekly*, "Made in the USA, Part III: The Dishonor Roll," *LA Weekly*.

The information about the export from the U.S. to Iraq of dual-use technologies comes from the government's own watchdog in a report: "Iraq: U.S. military items exported or transferred to Iraq in the 1980s," United States General Accounting Office, released February 7, 1994, though published in 1992.

The Reagan administration's commitment to ensuring an Iraqi victory over Iran is well-documented in the following sources: Seymour M. Hersh, "U.S. secretly gave aid to Iraq early in its war against Iran," *New York Times*, January 26, 1992; sworn court declaration of former National Security Council official Howard Teicher, January 31, 1995; and Michael Dobbs, "U.S. had key role in Iraq buildup; trade in chemical arms allowed despite their use on Iranians and Kurds," *Washington Post*, December 30, 2002.

The information about the Saudi arms transfers to Iraq in the 1980s comes from the February 1994 GAO report cited above.

An excellent resource for the classified history of U.S. policy in Iraq is the National Security Archive, a non-profit research institute and library of declassified U.S. documents obtained through the Freedom of Information Act. The Archive obtained documents showing the White House opposed Congressional efforts to sanction Iraq for its chemical weapons use, in part to protect potential postwar reconstruction contracts: "Iraqgate: Saddam Hussein, U.S. policy and the prelude to the Persian Gulf War, 1980–1994," *The National Security Archive*, 2003. Many of the Archive's document collections are online at www.gwu.edu/~nsarchiv.

Rumsfeld's efforts to connect the September 11 attacks to Saddam Hussein was reported by CBS News on September 4 , 2002: "Plans for Iraq attack began on 9/11." General Wesley Clark spoke about the pressure he received to connect September 11 to Saddam in an appearance on *NBC News: Meet the Press,* on June 15, 2003.

The BBC first reported on February 5, 2003 that British intelligence had concluded there was no current relationship between Saddam Hussein and al Qaeda: "Leaked report rejects Iraqi al-Qaeda link," *BBC News*.

The background about the alleged al Qaeda base in northern Iraq comes from Jeffrey Fleishman, "Iraqi terror camp cracks its doors," *Los Angeles Times*, February 9, 2003; and Jonathan S. Landay, "Alleged weapons site found deserted," *Philadelphia Inquirer*, February 9, 2003.

Among the many polls showing Americans believing Saddam Hussein was involved in the September 11th attacks: *Newsweek* poll, July 24–25, 2003; Program on International Policy Attitudes/Knowledge Networks Poll, July 2003; Harris Interactive Poll, June 18, 2003; CNN/*USA Today*/Gallup Poll, June 9, 2003 and another on February 9, 2003; *Christian Science Monitor* Poll, April 9, 2003; CBS News/*New York Times* Poll, February 10, 2003; Knight-Ridder Poll, January 12, 2003.

Saddam's alienation of fundamentalists (like Osama bin Laden) with the creation of a secular state has been widely reported by, among others: John J. Mearsheimer & Stephen M. Walt, "An unnecessary war; U.S.-Iraq conflict," *Foreign Policy*, January 1, 2003; Warren P. Strobel, "Analysts: No evidence of Iraq, al-Qaida cooperation," *Knight Ridder Washington Bureau*, January 29, 2003; Paul Haven, "Saddam, al-Qaida would be unusual allies," Associated Press, January 29, 2003; Patrick Comerford, "Will Christians of Iraq be denied the promise of peace?" *Irish Times*, January 6, 2003; Daniel Trotta, "Safe under Saddam, Iraqi Jews fear for their future," *Fort Lauderdale Sun-Sentinel*, July 4, 2003; Matthew McAllester, "New fear for Iraq Jews," *Newsday*, May 9, 2003.

The information about U.S. complicity with Pol Pot and the Khmer Rouge in Cambodia comes from: John Pilger, "The Friends of Pol Pot," *The Nation*, May 11, 1998; Philip Bowring, "Today's friends, tomorrow's mess," *Time International*, October 8, 2001; Andrew Wells-Dang, "Problems with Current U.S. Policy," *Foreign Policy in Focus*, July 30, 2001.

The U.S. role in the coup that led to the death of Patrice Lumumba and brought Mobuto to power in Congo/Zaire is detailed in: Howard W. French, "An anatomy of autocracy: Mobutu's Era," *New York Times*, May 17; Peter Ford, "Regime Change," *Christian Science Monitor*, January 27, 2003; Ian Stewart, "Colonial and Cold War past fuels anti-West anger in Congo," Associated Press, August 24, 1998; and Stephen R. Weissman, "Addicted to Mobutu: why America can't learn from its foreign policy mistakes," *Washington Monthly*, September 1997.

Background on the ouster of Brazil's Joao Goulart can be found in the June 15, 2001 report by the *National Catholic Reporter*, "It's time for a good national confession; Truth commissions to heal war atrocities." See also A. J. Langguth, "U.S. Policies in hemisphere precede Kissinger and Pinochet," *Los Angeles Times*, July 15, 2001.

America's complicity in Indonesia, first with the overthrow of an elected president, and then the invasion of East Timor, is documented by Jane Perlez, "Indonesians say they suspect CIA in Bali Blast," *New York Times*, November 7, 2002; James Risen, "Official history describes U.S. policy in Indonesia in the 60s," *New York Times*, July 28, 2001; "East Timor Revisited," *National Security Archive*, December 6, 2001; "CIA Stalling State Department Histories," *National Security Archive*, July 27, 2001; Seth Mydans, "Indonesia Inquiry: Digging up agonies of the past," *New York Times*, May 31, 2000.

For an overall view of human rights in China, see "World Report 2003: China and Tibet," from *Human Rights Watch* and "Report 2003: China," from *Amnesty International*. Richard McGregor reported the number of fast food chains in China in "KFC adds fast food to fast life in China," *Financial Times*, January 20, 2003. Information on Kodak, and growing Chinese market can be found in Joseph Kahn's "Made in China, Bought in China," *New York Times*, January 5, 2003. Wal-Mart's extensive dealings with China are detailed by Michael Forsythe, "Wal-Mart fuels U.S.-China trade gap," *Bloomberg News*, July 8, 2003.

China's use of mobile execution vans was reported by Amnesty International, "Chinese use mobile death van to execute prisoners," and by Hamish McDonald, "Chinese try mobile death vans," *The Age* (Melbourne), March 13, 2003.

For information on all the countries around the world who suffer under dictators, authoritarian governments, or for human rights progress for any given country, check with International Centre for Human Rights and Democracy, www.ichrdd.ca; Human Rights Watch, www.hrw.org; and Amnesty International, www.amnesty.org.

Paul Wolfowitz was interviewed by journalist Sam Tannenhaus for *Vanity Fair* in May 2003. The Department of Defense objected to Tannenhaus's version of the interview, and posted their own transcript of the conversation. As the DOD's version doesn't make Wolfowitz look any better, I decided to use it rather than *Vanity Fair*'s.

Professor Fatin Al-Rifai appeared on ABC's *Nightline*, on July 14, 2003, where she expressed her reservations about American rule. Reports on clerics gaining political stature were found in David Rohde, "GI and Cleric vie for hearts and minds," *New York Times*, June 8, 2003; Anthony Browne, "Radical Islam starts to fill Iraq's power vacuum," *London Times*, June 4, 2003. Nicholas D. Kristof's article in the *New York Times* on June 24, 2003, "Cover your hair," and Tina Susman's "In Baghdad, a flood of fear," *Newsday*, June 9, 2003 are just two reports of the emerging backlash against "westernization" in Iraq.

Dominique de Villepin's speech to the United Nations was delivered on March 19, 2003, and can be read in full here: www.un.int/france/documents_anglais/030319_cs_villepin_irak.htm

The "Coalition of the Willing" was listed, as of April 3, 2003, on the White House Web site, www.whitehouse.gov.

Stories of the Bush administration lashing out at the French are found in the following: William Douglas, "Paris will face consequences," *Newsday*, April 24, 2003; "Rumsfeld dismisses 'old Europe' defiance on Iraq," *CBC News*, January 23, 2003; and "Commander-in-Chief," *Dateline NBC*, April 25, 2003.

The more ridiculous and petty attacks on the French come from many different sources, and are only a small sampling of the anti-French backlash. John Kerry and his alleged-"French" look was reported by Adam Nagourney & Richard W. Stevenson, "Bush's aides plan late sprint in '04," *New York Times*, April 22, 2003. For more about Jim Saxton's proposed bill to punish the French economically, see "Congress slow to act on anti-France bill," Associated Press, March 10, 2003. Ginny Brown-Waite's absolutely ludicrous call to dig up the bones of the WWII dead buried in France deserves only the most colorful coverage, so I will point you to the *New York Post*'s March 14, 2003 article "Dig up our D-Day Dead," written by Malcolm Balfour. Richard Ruelas's *Arizona Republic* article "McCain isn't saying 'oui' to Bush's tax cut plan," of April 25, 2003 discusses the attack ads on the two Republican weasels who were having second thoughts about Bush's disastrous tax cut. The always level-headed Sean Hannity let his emotions get the best of him in talking about Jacques Chirac's betrayal on his one-sided debate show, *Hannity & Colmes*, on June 11, 2003.

From pouring French wine down the toilet, to the wonders of the Freedom Fry, to the satisfaction of rolling over photocopied French flags in an armored car, and much more, see the following: Deborah Orin & Brian Blomquist, "White House just says Non," *New York Post*, March 14, 2003; John Lichfield, "French tourism counts cost as Americans stay away," *The Independent*, July 29, 2003; Sheryl Gay Stolberg, "An Order of Fries, Please, But Do Hold the French," *New York Times*, March 12, 2003; "Fuddruckers jumps on 'Freedom fry' bandwagon," *PR Newswire*, March 14, 2003; Brian Skoloff, "Central Valley dry cleaners called French Cleaners vandalized," Associated Press, March 20, 2003; Rob Kaiser, "Sofitel surrenders, lowers French flag," *Chicago Tribune*, March 1, 2003; "Merchant stands his ground as Americans boycott fromage.com,"

Toronto Star, February 16, 2003; J.M. Kalil, "Everything French Fried," *Las Vegas Review-Journal*, February 19, 2003; Floyd Norris, "French's has an unmentioned British flavor," *New York Times*, March 28, 2003; Alison Leigh Cowan, "French exchange students get the cold shoulder," *New York Times*, July 4, 2003; and finally, for the French weasel embedded in the White House—Elisabeth Bumiller, "From the President's patisserie, building a coalition of the filling," *New York Times*, May 5, 2003

If you would like to find out more about the life, and genealogy, of Paul Rivoire, visit the Paul Revere House online, www.paulreverehouse.org/father.html

For more on the integral helping hand the French gave the colonists during the Revolutionary War, track down Stacy Schiff's article, "Making France our best friend," from the July 7, 2003 issue of *Time*.

Figures on Iraq's oil exports to various countries comes from the Energy Information Administration's "International Petroleum Monthly," for July 2003. Our overall trade numbers with Iraq for 2001 can be found through the Foreign Trade Division of the Census Bureau.

Jennifer Brooks wrote of Saddam's receiving a key to Detroit in the *Detroit News*, March 26, 2003. Rumsfeld's visit to Iraq is well documented, and the National Security Archive at George Washington University (cited above) has a cute picture of the two men shaking hands. For a quick look, however, see Michael Dobbs, "U.S. had key role in Iraq buildup," *Washington Post*, December 30, 2002.

Statistics on telephones per capita in Albania, along with many other fun facts, can be found in the CIA's *World Fact Book, 2003*, available online at www.cia.gov. This is also a great place to start on the bare facts for any country you feel like learning a little bit more about.

Poll numbers cited for international opposition to the war in Iraq can be found in the following: Peter Morton, "U.S. citizens at odds with world on war," *National Post*, March 12, 2003; Derrick Z. Jackson, "World is saying 'no' to war," *Chicago Tribune*, March 17, 2003; "People power on world stage," Reuters, March 6, 2003; "Japanese premier says not always right to follow public opinion," *BBC Worldwide Monitoring*, March 5, 2003; Susan Taylor Martin, "Business of war rolls on in Turkey, opposition or no," *St. Petersburg Times*, March 2, 2003; and George Jones, "Poll shows most Britons still against the war," *Daily Telegraph*, February 13, 2003. The not-so-twisted British view of the biggest threat to world peace comes from a survey done for *The Times* (London), "Bush 'as big a threat as Saddam,'" February 23, 2003.

For a look at the role trade deals played in the "Coalition of the Willing," see Tom Skotnicki's "Coalition of the Winning," *Business Review Weekly*, June 26, 2003, Claire Harvey's "NZ leader seeks peace in her time," *The Weekend Australian*, April 26, 2003, Linda McQuaig's "Rebuffed president recklessly saddles up for war," *Toronto Star*, March 9, 2003, and David Armstrong's "U.S. pays back nations that supported war," *San Francisco Chronicle*, May 11, 2003.

For a general view of some of the members of the "Coalition," check out Dana Milbank's "Many willing, but only a few are able," *Washington Post*, March 25, 2003. Milbank's article also reports on Morocco's offer of 2,000 monkeys to help with the invasion. An interesting sidenote, while the monkeys may not have made it into war, various other non-simians did. Siobhan McDonough reported in the Associated Press on April 2, 2003, that among the ranks there were chickens, pigeons, dogs and dolphins. And while Poland did come up short on farm animals, they managed to round up a few soldiers to commit to the cause, as reported in "Poland to commit up to 200 troops in war with Iraq," Associated Press, March 17, 2003.

The estimate for the percentage of world population that the "Coalition" represented comes from Ivo Daalder's "Bush's coalition doesn't add up where it counts," *Newsday*, March 24, 2003 and the U.S. Census Bureau's Population Clock, World Population estimate.

Information on the Lockheed Martin war machine comes from the following sources: "Liquidmetal Technologies and Lockheed Martin establish product development partnership," *Business Wire*, January 27, 2003; Barbara Correa, "War machine grows quickly," *Daily News* (Los Angeles), March 23, 2003; United States Air Force, "USAF Fact Sheet: Milstar satellite Communications System," March 2003; Craig Covault, "Milstar pivotal to war," *Aviation Week*, April 28, 2003; "Air Force launches a military communications satellite," Associated Press, April 8, 2003; Tom McGhee, "Bibles to bomb fins," *Denver Post*, April 6, 2003; Heather Draper, "Lockheed Martin set to launch 6th Milstar," *Rocky Mountain News*, January 22, 2003; Dick Foster, "Springs base controls 'eyes and ears' of war," *Rocky Mountain News*, March 22, 2003; Robert S. Dudney, "U.S. dominance in space helped win operation Iraqi Freedom," *Chattanooga Times Free Press*, May 25, 2003; Richard Williamson, "Wired for war," *Rocky Mountain News*, January 3, 2000; Tim Friend, "Search for bin Laden extends to Earth orbit," *USA Today*, October 5, 2001; and Heather Draper, "Liftoff: Defense stocks soar," *Rocky Mountain News*, October 9, 2001

Estimates for the deaths in Iraq and Afghanistan come from related projects. For Afghanistan, see Marc Herold's "Daily Casualty Count of Afghan Civilians Killed by U.S. Bombing." Herold is a professor at the University of New Hampshire, and his report, based on an extensive and thorough study of media reported civilian deaths from the begin-

ning of the Afghan campaign through the present can be viewed at
http://pubpages.unh.edu/~mwherold/. For the war in Iraq, an identical
system was set up through the Iraq Body Count, which can be found
online at www.iraqbodycount.net.

Reports on affected Iraqi civilians come from Paul Reynolds,
"Analysis: Risk to civilians mounts," *BBC News*, April 2, 2003; Lara
Marlowe, "33 civilians die in Babylon bombing," *Irish Times*, April 2,
2003; Zeina Karam, "Injured Iraqi boy making progress: 'I feel good,'"
Toronto Star, June 10, 2003; Corky Siemaszko, "Is he under the rubble?" *New York Daily News*, April 9, 2003; William Branigin, "A gruesome scene on Highway 9," *Washington Post*, April 1, 2003;
Christopher Marquis, "U.S. military chiefs express regret over civilian
deaths," *New York Times*, April 2, 2003.

Information on cluster bombs can be found in Jack Epstein's *San Francisco Chronicle* article "U.S. under fire for use of cluster bombs in Iraq,"
May 15, 2003; and also via Human Rights Watch, in particular, "U.S. use
of clusters in Baghdad condemned," April 16, 2003, and "Cluster
bomblets litter Afghanistan," November 16, 2001.

Steve Johnson wrote an excellent article on the "embedded journalists" in the *Chicago Tribune*, "Media: with embedded reporters, 24-hour
access and live satellite feeds," April 20, 2003. Also check out Jim
Rutenberg's "Cable's war coverage suggests a new 'Fox Effect' on television journalism," *New York Times*, April 16, 2003. To see the full report
from Fairness and Accuracy in Reporting on the pro-war bias in evening
newscasts, refer to the watch group's Web site, www.fair.org. It was
published in June 2003. Neil Cavuto's comments on why he threw jour-
nalistic objectivity out the window can be found at www.foxnews.com in
an article he wrote March 28, 2003, titled "American first, journalist
second," Fox News.com, March 28, 2003. Brian Williams sat through
shock and awe and commented on how far we'd come since fire-bombing
Dresden on NBC's *Nightly News* on April 2, 2003. The Army's $470 mil-
lion deal with Microsoft was reported in the *Seattle Post-Intelligencer*,
"Microsoft wins biggest order ever," *Seattle Post-Intelligencer*, June 25,
2003. ABC's *World News Tonight* erroneously reported the discovery of
a weapons site on April 26, 2003. The September *New York Times* article that reheated the propaganda from the White House was reported by
Michael Gordon and Judith Miller. The title of that article was, "U.S. says
Hussein intensifies quest for A-bomb parts," and it appeared in print September 8, 2002.

Source articles on the story of Jessica Lynch are: Susan Schmidt &
Vernon Loeb, "She was fighting to the death," *Washington Post*, April 3,
2003; Thom Shanker, "The Rescue of Private Lynch," *New York Times*,

April 3, 2003; Mark Bowden, "Sometimes heroism is a moving target," *New York Times*, June 8, 2003; Mitch Potter, "The Real 'Saving of Private Lynch,'" *Toronto Star*, May 4, 2003; John Kampfner, "Saving Private Lynch story 'flawed,'" *BBC News Correspondent*, May 15, 2003; and Lisa de Moraes, "CBS News chief defends approach to Lynch," *Washington Post*, July 22, 2003.

Powell's disgust with the quality of intelligence he was to present to the United Nations was first reported by Bruce B. Auster, and others, in "Truth & Consequences," published in *U.S. News & World Report*, June 9, 2003. Reports of Britain's plagiarized "intelligence" were widespread, but in particular there is Sarah Lyall's "Britain admits that much of its report on Iraq came from magazines," *New York Times*, February 8, 2003.

Statements from Ari Fleischer and George W. Bush concerning the "yellow cake" whopper can be found at www.whitehouse.gov. George Tenet took responsibility first, as was reported by Barry Schweid, "After discredited report, finger-pointing abounds inside Bush administration," Associated Press, July 11, 2003. The October memos from the CIA surfaced and were reported by, among others, Dana Milbank & Walter Pincus, "Bush aides disclose warnings from CIA," *Washington Post*, July 23, 2003.

Rumsfeld's charming incoherence was in full effect on NBC's *Meet the Press*, July 13, 2003. Condoleezza Rice appeared on *Late Edition with Wolf Blitzer*, on CNN the same day, and she also showed up that busy Sunday on CBS's *Face the Nation*.

Former Nixon aide John Dean wrote his impressions of the whoppers Bush and his buddies had served us over the preceding months on www.findlaw.com. His article, "Missing weapons of mass destruction: Is lying about the reason for war an impeachable offense?" appeared there June 6, 2003.

3. Oil's Well That Ends Well

The oil industry tells you exactly what everyday products are derived from oil on their company Web sites. The American Petroleum Institute, www.api.org, which is the industry's largest trade and lobby group, and Arctic Power, www.anwr.com, a front group that sounds "green," but actually promotes drilling in the Arctic National Wildlife Refuge, are two places to go for that information. Before you log off, learn more about what you can do to promote energy awareness and alternatives to oil by visiting Greenpeace, www.greenpeaceusa.org, and the Sierra Club, www.sierraclub.org.

"How Fuel Cells Work," a technical report by Karim Nice, explains the ABCs of fuel cells at www.howstuffworks.com. Additional information about the feasibility of hydrogen fuel cells is provided by Philip Ball, "Hydrogen fuel could widen ozone hole," *Nature*, June 13, 2003; David Adam, "Hydrogen: Fire and Ice," *Nature*, March 24, 2000. For more on the use of fossil fuels to create hydrogen energy, see "These Fuelish Things," *The Economist,* August 16, 2003.

In "Oil as a finite resource: When is global production likely to peak?" a study prepared for the World Resources Institute in 2000, Dr. James McKenzie projected that oil production could begin to decline as early as 2007, and as late as 2019. Other industry experts have drawn similar conclusions, as reported by David Robinson in "A new era for oil," *Buffalo News*, October 8, 2002, and Jim Motavalli in "Running on EMPTY," *E*, July 1, 2000.

For more on the Bush Administration's plan to expand nuclear energy production, see Dan Roberts's article, "Hydrogen: clean, safer than in the past and popular with politicians," *Financial Times*, May 13, 2003; and "Energy Policy," *NPR: Talk of the Nation*, June 13, 2003. Vice President Dick Cheney put it in his own words in an address to the Nuclear Energy Institute May 22, 2001: www.whitehouse.gov/vicepresident/news-speeches.

Visit these sites to **TAKE ACTION NOW** and join the fight for sustainable energy:

Climate Action Network: www.climatenetwork.org
Friends of the Earth: www.foe.org/act/takeaction/index.html
Greenpeace: www.greenpeaceusa.org/takeaction/
Natural Resources Defense Council: www.nrdc.org/action/default.asp
Physicians for Social Responsibility: www.capwiz.com/physicians/home/
Project Underground: www.moles.org
Sierra Club: www.sierraclub.org/energy
Sustainable Energy and Economy Network: www.seen.org
Union of Concerned Scientists: www.ucsaction.org
U.S. Public Interest Research Group: www.newenergyfuture.com
World Wildlife Fund: www.takeaction.worldwildlife.org

4. The United States of *BOO!*

George W. Bush, with a straight face, explained to us that the terrorists hated our democratically elected leaders on September 20, 2001. The speech was Bush's formal announcement that the two nouns "freedom" and "fear" were at war. A full transcript can be found through www .whitehouse.gov.

Cheney's views on our "new normalcy" a condition that "will become permanent in American life," are well documented, but for a little more information on this normalcy, check out "Barricades cover their muscle with warmth," Renee Tawa, *Los Angeles Times*, November 8, 2001—a report on the attempts to make concrete barricades more "elegant."

Statistics used to determine one's chance of dying in a terrorist incident are taken from the Population Estimates Program and Populations Projections Program of the Census Bureau report "Annual Projections of the Total Resident Population as of July 1. Middle, Lowest, Highest, and Zero International Migration Series, 1999–2100" on www.census.gov. Statistics on dying from flu, pneumonia, suicide, being a homicide victim, or in a car accident come from The Centers For Disease Control National Vital Statistics Reports: "Deaths: Preliminary Data for 2001, March 14, 2003.

For FBI terror alerts and information about shoe bombs and security on transportation go to www.fbi.gov. For more on shoe bombs, see Jack Hagel, "FBI identifies explosive used for shoe bomb," *Philadelphia Inquirer*, December 29, 2001.

Articles on terrorism and counterfeit goods can be found in *The International Herald Tribune* "Terrorist groups sell Sham Consumer Goods to Raise Money, Interpol Head Says," David Johnston, July 18, 2003; Congressional Testimony, Senate Governmental Affairs, Terrorism Financing, July 31, 2003; "Hearing of the House International Relations Committee," *Federal News Service*, July 16, 2003; Judd Slivka, "Terrorists planned to set wildfires, FBI memo warned," *Arizona Republic*, July 13, 2003; Amber Mobley, "U.S. citizen admits planning al Qaeda attack," *Boston Globe*, June 20, 2003; Randy Kennedy, "A conspicuous terror target is called hard to topple," *New York Times*, June 20, 2003; Rhonda Bell, "Suspicious package on porch a false alarm," *Times-Picayune* (New Orleans), October 13, 2001.

For information about the Project for the New American Century, visit www.newamericancentury.org. For more on Bush's doctrine of permanent war, and the immediate use of September 11 to set the stage for attacking even more countries, see: John Diamond, "Bush puts focus on protracted war with global goals," *Chicago Tribune*, September 14, 2001; "Deputy Defense Secretary Paul Wolfowitz discusses the course of action the U.S. may take after Tuesday's attacks," NPR's *All Things Considered*, September 14, 2001; Christopher Dickey, et al., "Next up: Saddam," *Newsweek*, December 31, 2001; "Votes in Congress," *New York Times*, May 25, 2003; Maureen Dowd, "Neocon coup at the Department d'Etat," *New York Times*, August 6, 2003.

Rumsfeld's promise of permanent war was made October 4, 2001. It can be found at www.defenselink.mil.

Information on Russell Feingold (D-Wisconsin) and his lone vote against the Patriot Act, see: Nick Anderson, "His 'No' vote on the Terror Bill earns respect," *Los Angeles Times*, October 31, 2001; Emily Pierce, "Feingold defiant over vote against anti-terrorism bill," *Congressional Quarterly*, November 2, 2001; Judy Mann, "Speeches and symbolism do little to solve our problems," *Washington Post*, October 31, 2001. Matthew Rothschild, "Russ Feingold," *The Progressive*, May 2002.

Russ Feingold's entire statement in opposition to the Patriot Act can be found at his Web site, www.russfeingold.org. For more on the Patriot Act, and the text of the act itself, visit the Electronic Privacy Information Center at www.epic.org/privacy/terrorism/usapatriot. Also visit the ACLU at www .aclu.org and the American Library Association at www.ala.org. For more on the White House pushing the act through Congress, and Congress not reading the final version before voting on it, check out Steven Brill's *After: Rebuilding and Defending America in the September 12 Era*, Simon & Schuster, 2003, and "Surveillance under the 'USA/Patriot Act,'" ACLU, 2002.

For specifics of the bill, refer to the Senate Judiciary hearings of October 9, 2002; "How the anti-terrorism bill puts financial privacy at risk," ACLU, October 23, 2001; *Imbalance of Power*, Lawyers Committee for Human Rights, September 2002-March 2003; Nat Hentoff, "No 'sneak and peak,'" *Washington Times*, August 4, 2003.

Dan Eggen and Robert O'Harrow Jr. reported on Ashcroft's "emergency" warrants and non-emergency warrants in the March 24, 2003, edition of the *Washington Post*, "U.S. steps up secret surveillance." Also see, Anne Gearan, "Supreme Court rejects attempt to appeal cases testing scope of secret spy court," Associated Press, March 24, 2003; Curt Anderson, "Ashcroft accelerates use of emergency spy warrants in antiterror fight," Associated Press, March 24, 2003; Evelyn Nieves, "Local officials rise up to defy the Patriot Act," *Washington Post*, April 21, 2003; Jerry Seper, "Congressmen seek clarifications of Patriot Act powers," *Washington Times*, April 3, 2003.

If you would like to read the Justice Department's report on detainees, "U.S. Department of Justice Office of the Inspector General: Report to Congress on Implementation of Section 1001 of the USA Patriot Act," July 17, 2003, check www.findlaw.com.

You can view the Defense Advanced Research Projects Agency Web site at www.darpa.mil. For more about Poindexter, DARPA, and the Policy Analysis Market, see Floyd Norris, "Betting on Terror: What Markets Can Reveal," *New York Times*, August 3, 2003; Stephen J. Hedges, "Poindexter to quit over terror futures plan," *Chicago Tribune*, August 1, 2003; Peter

Behr, "U.S. files new Enron complaints," *Washington Post*, March 13, 2003; and Allison Stevens, "Senators want 'Terrorism' futures market closed," *Congressional Quarterly Daily Monitor*, July 28, 2003.

If you would like to learn more about the situation at Guantanamo Bay, see "Imbalance of Power: How changes to U.S. law and policy since 9/11 erode human rights and civil liberties," from the Lawyers Committee for Human Rights, as well as Matthew Hay Brown, "At Camp Iquana, the enemies are children," *Hartford Courant*, July 20, 2003; Paisley Dodds, "Detainees giving information for incentives, general says," *Chicago Tribune*, July 25, 2003.

Reports on government abuses under the Patriot Act can be found in Philip Shenon, "Report on U.S. antiterrorism law alleges violations of civil rights," *New York Times*, July 21, 2003; "Code-red cartoonists," *USA Today*, July 24, 2003; and Tom Brune, "Rights abuses probed," *Newsday*, July 22, 2003.

John Clarke recounted his story of interrogation as he tried to reenter America from Canada in "Interrogation at the U.S. border," *Counterpunch*, February 25, 2002; Many of the other stories of a government out of control come from Neil Mackay, "Rage. Mistrust. Hatred. Fear. Uncle Sam's enemies within," *Sunday Herald*, June 29, 2003. Also see, "Judge steps down after admitting ethnic slur," Associated Press, June 18, 2003; "Six French journalists stopped in L.A., refused admission to U.S.," Associated Press, May 21, 2003; "Cop photographs class projects during 1:30 AM visit," Associated Press, May 5, 2003; Matthew Rothschild, "Enforced conformity," *The Progressive*, July 1, 2003; Dave Lindorff, "The Government's air passenger blacklist," *New Haven Advocate*; Matthew Norman, "Comment & Analysis," *The Guardian*, March 19, 2002; "Show doesn't make evil man sympathetic," *USA Today*, May 18, 2003; "Principal bans Oscar-winning documentary," *Hartford Courant*, April 6, 2003.

Ari Fleischer's Big Brother admonition to Americans can be found at www.whitehouse.gov, and was widely reported.

For more on the INS visas for terrorists debacle, see Bill Saporito, et al., "Deporting the INS: Granting visas for terrorists after 9/11 could be the last gaffe for the Immigration Service," *Time Magazine*, March 25, 2002.

5. How to Stop Terrorism? Stop Being Terrorists!

William Blum's *Killing Hope: U.S. Military and CIA Interventions Since World War II* offers accounts of the U.S.-engineered coups in Chile, Guatemala, and Indonesia. *Perpetual War for Perpetual Peace: How We*

Got to Be So Hated is an important collection of essays by Gore Vidal (as a bonus, get a handy twenty-page chart chronicling U.S. military interventions around the world since 1948). For a critical look at current U.S. foreign policy log onto Foreign Policy In Focus' Web site: www.foreign policy-infocus.org.

Israel is one of the United States's largest arms importers. In the last decade, the United States has sold Israel $7.2 billion in weaponry and military equipment, $762 million through Direct Commercial Sales (DCS), more than $6.5 billion through the Foreign Military Financing (FMF) program (William D. Hartung and Frida Berrigan "An Arms Trade Resource Center Fact Sheet," May 2002). The Middle East Research and Information Project has a primer on the current uprising in Palestine and a primer on Palestine, Israel and the Arab-Israeli Conflict: www.merip.org. Peace Now, the Israeli peace organization, believes that "only peace will bring security to Israel and ensure the future of our people." It presses the Israeli government to seek peace—through negotiations and mutual compromise—with its Arab neighbors and the Palestinian people (www.peacenow.org). The Arab Association for Human Rights (www.arabhra.org) works to promote and protect the political, civil, economic, and cultural rights of the Palestinian-Arab minority in Israel.

The U.S. energy consumption figures come from the U.S. Department of Energy's Energy Information Administration and the United Nations Development Program's Human Development Report. For a critical look at U.S. consumption habits, read *Affluenza: The All-Consuming Epidemic,* by John de Graaf, David Wann, Thomas H. Naylor & David Horsey. There are many guides to turning good intentions into everyday actions: *Culture Jam: How to Reverse America's Suicidal Consumer Binge—and Why We Must,* by Kalle Lasn; *The Complete Idiot's Guide to Simple Living,* by Georgene Lockwood; *50 Simple Things You Can Do to Save the Earth,* by The Earth Works Group; and *The Better World Handbook* by Ellis Jones, Ross Haenfler and Brett Johnson.

The figures on clean water come from the United Nations Environmental Program and the World Health Organization. Join Public Citizen's campaign to protect universal access to clean and affordable drinking water by keeping it in public hands (www.citizen.org/cmep/Water/).

The stories about sweatshop workers come from the watchdog group National Labor Committee and UNITE!, the union that represents garment workers in the U.S. and Canada. Hook up with them (www .nlcnet.org and www.behindthelabel.org) or with one of the many anti-sweatshop campaigns on the web: Sweatshopwatch: www.Sweatshop watch.org; Maquila Solidarity Network: www.maquilasolidarity.org and United Students Against Sweatshops: www.usasnet.org.

The International Labor Organization (ILO) has estimated that 250 million children between the ages of five and fourteen work in developing countries—at least 120 million on a full-time basis. The Children's Rights Division at Human Rights Watch documents the plight of forced and bonded child labor: www.hrw.org/children/labor.htm. Global March Against Child Labor is trying to eradicate child labor www.global march.org. Order your free anti-child-labor poster for hanging in your classroom, community center, or office at www.aft.org/international/child/. You can also sign an anti-child-labor petition.

The site www.iraqbodycount.org maintains a database of civilian deaths in the war on Iraq. "Casualty figures are derived from a comprehensive survey of online media reports," it says. "Where these sources report differing figures, the range (a minimum and a maximum) are given. All results are independently reviewed and error-checked by at least three members of the Iraq Body Count project team before publication."

The statistic on smart bombs in the Iraq war are taken from Jim Krane's report in the Associated Press, "U.S. Precision Weapons Not Foolproof," April 4, 2003.

According to Peace Action, the U.S. has more than 10,500 nuclear warheads in its stockpile. Log onto its Web site to learn more and campaign for a safer world: www.peace-action.org. The Plowshares movement has long used nonviolent civil disobedience to disarm our country, www.plowsharesactions.org. The Chemical Weapons Working Group is organizing to ensure the safe disposal of munitions and other chemical warfare and toxic material around the U.S.: www.cwwg.org.

If you would like to learn more about America's illustrious history of upending democracy and protecting cruel dictators, there is perhaps no better place to start—in terms of declassified government documents—than the National Security Archive at George Washington University. Their Web site address is: www.gwu.edu/~nsarchiv/.

6. Jesus W. Christ

God needs no sources and is offended at even the suggestion.

7. Horatio Alger Must Die

The statistics for corporate compensation come from: "Executive Pay," John A. Byrne et al., *Business Week*, May 6, 2002; "Executive Pay: A

Special Report," Alan Cowell, *The New York Times*, April 1, 2001. The *Business Week* report also noted: "In the past decade, as rank-and-file wages increased 36 percent, CEO pay climbed 340 percent, to $11 million."

Fortune's report on corporate crooks, "You Bought, They Sold," was published September 2, 2002. You can view it online at www.fortune.com.

The bulk of the information in the section on Dead Peasants Insurance, as was noted in the text, comes from the great work of Ellen E. Schultz and Theo Francis. "Valued Employees: Worker Dies, Firm Profits—Why?" appeared in *The Wall Street Journal* on April 19, 2002. Other subsequent reports include "Companies Gain a Death Benefit," Albert B. Crenshaw, *The Washington Post*, May 30, 2002; and "Bill to Limit Dead Peasants Policies Ignored to Death," L.M. Sixel, *Houston Chronicle*, October 4, 2002.

To find out more about the bill in Congress that would let companies put less money into the pension funds of blue-collar workers, see "Bill Reduces Blue-Collar Obligations for Pension," Mary Williams Walsh, *The New York Times*, May 6, 2003. You can read more about the "Senior Death Discount" controversy in "Life: The Cost-Benefit Analysis," John Tierney, *The New York Times*, May 18, 2003.

If you would like more specific information on Ken Lay's contributions to the Bush campaign, or if you're looking for information on campaign donations in general, check the excellent people at the Center for Responsive Politics, www.opensecrets.org. Information on Bush's use of the Enron jet see "Enron: Other Money in Politics Stats," Center for Responsive Politics, November 9, 2001; and "Flying High on Corporations," *Capital Eye*, Winter 2000. Reports of Bush's quick detour from campaigning to see Lay throw the opening pitch at Houston's Enron Field appeared in "Bush Visits Top Contributor for Houston Baseball Bash," Megan Stack, Associated Press, April 7, 2000.

For more on "Kenny Boy's" role in "helping" Bush select people for the new administration and his part in Cheney's "Energy Task Force," see "Mr. Dolan Goes to Washington," James Bernstein, *Newsday*, January 4, 2001; "Bush Advisers on Energy Report Ties to Industry," Joseph Kahn, *The New York Times*, June 3, 2001; "Power Trader Tied to Bush Finds Washington All Ears," Lowell Bergman and Jeff Gerth, *The New York Times*, May 25, 2001; "Bush Energy Paper Followed Industry Path," Don van Natta and Neela Banerjee, *The New York Times*, March 27, 2002; "Judge Questions U.S. Move in Cheney Suit," Henri E. Cauvin, *The Washington Post*, April 18, 2003.

Additional information about Enron can be found in the following: Richard A. Oppel Jr., "Enron Corp. Files Largest U.S. Claim for Bankruptcy," *The New York Times*, December 3, 2001; Steven Pearlstein &

Peter Behr, "At Enron, the fall came quickly; complexity, partnerships kept problems from public view," *The Washington Post*, December 2, 2001; Leslie Wayne, "Enron, preaching deregulation, worked the statehouse circuit," *The New York Times*, February 9, 2002; John Schwartz, "The cast of characters in the Enron drama is lengthy, and their relationships complex," *The New York Times*, January 13, 2003; Jim Drinkard & Greg Farrell, "Enron made a sound investment in Washington," *USA Today*, January 24, 2002; Stephen Labaton, "Balancing deregulation and Enron," *The New York Times*, January 17, 2002; Jerry Hirsch, et al., "Safeguards failed to detect warnings in Enron debacle," *The Los Angeles Times*, December 14, 2001; Mary Flood, "The Fall of Enron," *Houston Chronicle*, February 5, 2003; Jerry Hirsch, "Energy execs gain millions in stock sales," *The Los Angeles Times*, June 13, 2001; Stephanie Schorow, "Wealth of options," *Boston Herald*, September 30, 2002; Jake Tapper, "Secret hires warned Enron," *Salon*, January 20, 2002; Ben White and Peter Behr, "Enron paid creditors $3.6 billion before fall; filing also details payments to executives," *The Washington Post*, June 18, 2002; Jim Yardley, "Big burden for ex-workers of Enron," *New York Times*, March 3, 2002; Eric Berger, "Enron facing pension lawsuit," *Houston Chronicle*, June 26, 2003; Steven Greenhouse, "Public funds say losses top $1.5 billion," *The New York Times*, January 29, 2002; Mary Flood, et al., "Far from finished," *Houston Chronicle*, June 22, 2003.

Enron and Andersen's political donations and the conflicts of interest they ultimately caused in the government's "investigations" are discussed in Don Van Natta Jr., "Enron or Andersen made donations to almost all their congressional investigators," Don Van Natta Jr., *The New York Times*, January 25, 2002. Information on Enron's attempts to hide its law breaking, and the Bush administration's decision to do nothing about the impending collapse can be found in: "Shredded papers key in Enron case," Kurt Eichenwald, *The New York Times*, January 28, 2002; "Ken who?" Bennet Roth, et al., *Houston Chronicle*, January 11, 2002; "Bush aide was told of Enron's plea," Dana Milbank, *The Washington Post*, January 14, 2002; "Number of contacts grows," H. Josef Herbert, Associated Press, January 12, 2002.

"President" Bush's attempt to deny his close friendship with Ken Lay are documented, first and foremost, in the transcript of a question-and-answer session with reporters on January 10, 2002. This can be found at www.whitehouse.gov. Also see "Ken who?" Bennet Roth, et al., *Houston Chronicle*, January 11, 2002, "Enron spread contributions on both sides of the aisle," Don van Natta Jr., *The New York Times*, January 21, 2002 and "Despite President's Denials, Enron & Lay Were Early Backers of Bush," Texans for Public Justice (www.tpj.org), January 11, 2002.

8. Woo Hoo! I Got Me a Tax Cut!

For more information on the real effects of the Bush 2003 "Mike Moore Tax Cut," check out the Center on Budget and Policy Priorities' report, "New tax cut law uses gimmicks to mask cost; ultimate price tag likely to be $800 billion to $1 trillion." The Center can be found online at www.cbpp.org.

Bush and Cheney's projected tax-cut windfall was reported by James Toedtman in *Newsday*, "Tiebreaker's Tax Break," May 20, 2003.

As this is written, the Texas Rangers are in the cellar of the American League West, 19.5 games out of first place. (Okay, I know, they don't suck as bad as the Detroit Tigers.)

If you'd like to know more about the forty-seven people President Clinton had "killed," simply check your favorite Internet search engine and type in the words, "Clinton Body Count." Or, tune in to AM talk radio any day of the week. This urban legend is a favorite among the right.

In the summer of 2003, the Congressional Budget Office (www.cbo.gov) projected that the 2003 federal deficit would reach $401 billion. For more on that announcement, see Alan Fram's June 10 article, "CBO Expects Deficit to Shatter Record," from the Associated Press. You can read more about Bush's attempts to hide the Treasury Department's deficit projections until after Congress had approved his tax cut in "Bush Shelved Report on $44,200 Billion Deficit Fears," Peronet Despeignes, *Financial Times*, May 29, 2003.

Bush made his claim that every taxpayer would benefit from his tax cut in an April 26, 2003, radio address. You can find the transcript at www.whitehouse.gov. The Center on Budget and Policy Priorities revealed the truth in its June 1, 2003, report, "Tax cut law leaves out 8 million filers who pay income taxes." The Center also reported on the effect the federal tax cut would have on the states on June 5, 2003, "Federal tax changes likely to cost states billions of dollars in coming years." More information can be found through the Citizens for Tax Justice (www.ctj.org), specifically the May 30, 2003, report, "Most taxpayers get little help from the latest Bush tax plan."

For an excellent look at the inventive ways states are finding to save money, including the unscrewing of light bulbs and the shutting down of schools, see "Drip, Drip Drip," Matt Bai, *The New York Times*, June 8, 2003, and "States Facing Budget Shortfalls, Cut the Major and the Mundane," Timothy Egan, *The New York Times*, April 21, 2003.

If you are expecting a refund of $1 million or more from the IRS (and who isn't?), you can download the direct-deposit form from this IRS Web site: www.irs.gov/pub/irs-pdf/f8302.pdf.

Bush's comments on how the tax cut would help families with children were made during the May 28, 2003, signing ceremony for the tax cut. A transcript can be found at www.whitehouse.gov. If you would like to read more about how the tax cut Bush signed that day *did not* help families, including 1 million military families, check out "Tax Law Omits $40 Child Credit for Millions," David Firestone, *The New York Times*, May 29, 2003, and "One million military children left behind by massive new tax package," Children's Defense Fund (www.childrensdefense.org), June 6, 2003.

9. A Liberal Paradise

There are roughly 1.4 million men and women active in the military today according to the Department of Defense, "DoD Active Duty Military Personnel Strength Levels, fiscal years 1950–2002." Even during Vietnam, from 1965 to 1972, only 2,594,000 Americans served, as reported by David M. Halbfinger and Steven A. Holmes, "Military Mirrors a Working-Class America," *The New York Times*, March 30, 2003.

Even at the dawn of the unending "War on Terror," a poll of college students from the Americans for Victory Over Terrorism, released in the May 2002, found that 21 percent would evade the draft completely, while 37 percent were only willing to serve in the military if that service took place within the United States. Spokespeople for the Army and the Marines have said that September 11 did not bring an increase in recruitment, and cited internal research from the Marine Corps that showed the war has had a "neutral to slightly negative" effect on recruitment, according to Joyce Howard Price's report, "Marines, Army view war as recruitment aid," published in *The Washington Times*, March 31, 2003. David M. Halbfinger, in the article cited above, states that personnel numbers for the military have dropped 23 percent in the last decade.

For the poll numbers on Americans' view of health care, see the following: Henry J. Kaiser Family Foundation and *The News Hour with Jim Lehrer* Uninsured Survey, May 16, 2000; and Henry J. Kaiser Family Foundation/Harvard School of Public Health, February 12, 2003. International comparisons on health-care costs come from Robert H. LeBow, *Health Care Meltdown*, published 2003. For an extensive report on the numbers of Americans who do not have health insurance, check out "Going Without Health Insurance," from the Robert Wood Johnson Foundation and Families USA, March 2003.

Support for racial diversity, and our views on race in general, can be found in Will Lester's "Poll finds black-white agreement on diversity, disagreement on how to get there," Associated Press, March 7, 2003; Riley E. Dunlap's "Americans Have Positive Image of the Environmental Movement," Gallup News Service, April 18, 2000; the Pew Global Attitudes Project Poll, June 3, 2003; the Dave Thomas Foundation for Adoption's poll conducted by Harris Interactive, June 19, 2002; *Washington Post*/Kaiser Family Foundation/Harvard University, "Race and Ethnicity in 2001: Attitudes, Perceptions, and Experiences," August 2001.The rise in interracial marriages over the past two decades was reported by Cloe Cabrera, "Biracial marriages on rise as couples overcome differences," *Tampa Tribune*, January 1, 2000.

For more on our views of the women's movement and abortion rights, see: Riley E. Dunlap, "Americans Have Positive Image of the Environmental Movement," Gallup News Service, April 18, 2000; ABC News/ *Washington Post* Poll, January 21, 2003; NBC News/*Wall Street Journal*, January 28, 2003; Pew Research Center, January 16, 2003; Gallup/CNN/*USA Today* Poll, January 15, 2003; and ABC News/ *Washington Post* Poll, January 21, 2003. For statistics on abortion, visit the Alan Guttmacher Institute online at www.agi-usa.org. The increase of couples living together without getting married, and in many cases not having children, was reported by Laurent Belsie, "More couples live together, roiling debate on family," *Christian Science Monitor*, March 13, 2003.

Reports on the public's views of the criminalization of drugs, the sentencing of nonviolent offenders, views on how to deal with crime in general and our attitudes toward the death penalty can be found in: "Optimism, Pessimism and Jailhouse Redemption: American attitudes on Crime, Punishment, and Over-incarceration," findings from a national survey conducted for the American Civil Liberties Union by Belden Russonello & Stewart, January 22, 2001; Quinnipiac University Polling Institute, March 5, 2003; ABC News/*Washington Post* Poll, January 24, 2003; CNN/*Time* magazine Poll, through Harris Interactive, January 17, 2003.

You can find estimates on illegal drug use in the American population through the U.S. Department of Health and Human Services.

America's green, environmentally friendly underbelly is revealed in: Riley E. Dunlap, "Americans Have Positive Image of the Environmental Movement," Gallup News Service, April 18, 2000; Henry J. Kaiser Family Foundation/*Washington Post*/Harvard University, June 23, 2002; Gallup Poll, March 18, 2002; Gallup Poll, April 21, 2003; Gallup Poll, March 13, 2003; Pew Global Attitudes Project Poll, June 3, 2003; and Zogby International for National Environmental Trust, "A poll of likely

Republican primary or caucus voters in California, Iowa, New Hampshire, New York, and South Carolina," August 1999.

For the numbers on the true American attitude toward guns, see National Opinion Research Center, "2001 National Gun Policy Survey of the National Opinion Research Center: Research Findings," December 2001; Violence Policy Center, "New Survey Reveals More Americans Favor Handgun Ban Than Own Handguns," March 15, 2000; Michigan Partnership to Prevent Gun Violence, "Public Opinion: Opening the Door to Public Policy Change," conducted by market research and analysis firm EPIC-MRA, October 2000.

Aside from *Will & Grace, Queer Eye for the Straight Guy,* the sudden renewed popularity of musical theater, you can find even more proof of America's love affair with homosexuality to be found in these sources: Human Rights Campaign, "HRC Hails New Gallup Poll Showing Continuing Positive Trend in U.S. Public Opinion On Some Gay Issues," press release, June 4, 2001; *Los Angeles Times* poll, June 18, 2000; Henry J. Kaiser Family Foundation, November 2001; Gallup Poll, May 15, 2003; and *Newsweek*, April 27, 2002.

America's widespread support for unions, and distrust of corporations can be seen in the following: ABC News/*Washington Post* Poll, July 15, 2002; Gallup Poll, August 30, 2002; AFL-CIO Labor Day Survey, August 29, 2002; Fox News poll, October 25, 2002; Kent Hoover, "Labor unions aim to capitalize on public anti-corporate attitude," *Houston Business Journal*, September 9, 2002; Program on International Policy Attitudes, "Americans on globalization survey," November 16, 1999; Harris Poll, July 27, 2002; and the Democratic Leadership Council, "America's changing political geography survey," October 2002 (conducted by Penn, Schoen & Berland Associates). For more on union membership statistics nationwide, and to see how union members are paid better than non-union members, check out the Bureau of Labor Statistics at www.bls.gov.

Michael Savage expressed his charming view of sodomites, and his love of eating sausages, on his now-cancelled (because of this very comment) *MSNBC* show *Savage Nation* on July 5, 2003. Savage (whose real last name is Weiner) diagnosed the left with a mental disorder (and an unhealthy love of—OH NO!—Islam) on his MSNBC show on April 19, 2003. Our good friend Ann Coulter conveyed the message from God that we should "rape" the Earth on Fox News' *Hannity and Colmes,* on June 22, 2001. Coulter, who has in the past been identified by Fox News as a "constitutional scholar," suggested liberals should be killed at the 2002 Conservative Political Action Conference. Her profound understanding of the political, social, economic, and religious environment of Afghanistan, and her advice on what America should do there was posted on the Web site of the conservative magazine, the *National Review*, shortly after September 11. Pointing out the fact that George W. Bush is an illegitimate president at the Oscars spurred Bill O'Reilly to denounce me as an anarchist on his Fox News show, on April 14, 2003. His quote on the poor being shipped off to prison without a fair trial comes from his September 4, 2001, show. Rush Limbaugh's well-founded theory on the origins of feminism was pronounced on his syndicated July 28, 1995, show, *Rush Limbaugh*. Sean Hannity's temper-tantrum, name-calling fit was reported in *Crain's New York Business*, February 17, 2003, and his well-founded, issue-based dissection of Canadian culture was reported in the *Ottawa Citizen*, March 23, 2003.

10. How to Talk to Your Conservative Brother-in-Law

Regarding the case of Mumia Abu-Jamal, read Amnesty International's "Life in the Balance" at www.amnestyusa.org/abolish/reports/mumia/ as well as other anti-death-penalty activism through Amnesty. Also look at The National Coalition to Abolish the Death Penalty at www.ncadp.org and the Death Penalty Information Center at www.deathpenaltyinfo.org.

The information about unions and pensions comes from David Cay Johnston and Kenneth N. Gilpin, "A Case Sounds a Warning About Pension Safety," *The New York Times*, October 1, 2000; Peter G. Gosselin, "Labor's Love of 401(k)s Thwarts Bid for Reform," *Los Angeles Times*, April 22, 2002.

To read about the "buy American" campaign, look at Dana Frank's book *Buy American: The Untold Story of Economic Nationalism*, Beacon Press, 1999; Peter Gilmore, "The Untold Story (and Failure) of 'Buy American' Campaigns," *UE News*, United Electrical, Radio and Machine Workers of America; Lisa Hong, "Is It 'Buy American,' or 'Japan Bashing'?" *Asian Week*, February 7, 1992.

To help unionize your workplace, go to the SEIU (Service Employees International Union) at www.seiu.org or UE (United Electrical, Radio and Machine Workers of America) at http://www.ranknfile-ue.org.

Before you give Bill O'Reilly too much credit, remember the following: He is against the death penalty. Reason given: "It's not punitive enough." Similarly, he opposes NAFTA because he objects to Mexicans crossing into the U.S. Let's not forget that he has spoken about "Mexican wetbacks" on at least two occasions: *The O'Reilly Factor,* February 6, 2003, and in the Allentown, Pennsylvania, *Morning Call,* January 5, 2003.

Information about Nixon came from articles written by Deb Riechmann from the Associated Press: "Nixon Sought Release of Americans in China Before Historic Trip," April 5, 2001, and "U.S.—Tale of a Treaty," June 16, 2001; *USA Today*, "Title IX at 30: Still Under Fire," June 19, 2002; Huw Watkin, "Burying the Hatchet," *Time* magazine, November 20, 2000; *The American Experience*, PBS, 2002, as accessed on *www .pbs.org/wgbh/amex/presidents*.

Union and non-union worker salaries are found at the Bureau of Labor Statistics, United States Department of Labor, "Table 2. Median Weekly Earnings of Full-Time Wage and Salary Workers by Union Affiliation," February 25, 2003.

Numbers given for people killed each year in the U.S. from air pollution come from Harvard School of Public Health press release, "Air pollution deadlier than previously thought," March 2, 2000. The figures for health-care costs from air pollution are from the Centers for Disease Control, National Center for Environmental Health, Air Pollution and Respiratory Health Branch, www.cdc.gov/nceh/airpollution.

Discussions about Superfund come from a series of articles by Katherine Q. Seelye in *The New York Times*, "Bush Proposing Policy Changes on Toxic Sites," February 24, 2002 and "Bush Slashing Aid for EPA Cleanup at 33 Toxic Sites," July 1, 2002; Margaret Ramirez, "Report Links Superfund Sites, Illness," *Newsday*, June 15, 2003. To demand industry and government accountability, contact The Center for Health, Environment and Justice at www.chej.org.

Information about spending on energy in the U.S. comes from the United States Department of Energy, "Table 1.5 Energy Consumption and Expenditures Indicators, 1949–2001," and The American Council for an Energy-Efficient Economy Federal Fact Sheets, "Energy Efficiency Research, Development, and Deployment: Why Is Federal Support Necessary?" accessed on the fact sheets at www.aceee.org. For a look at the prospects of a more fuel-efficient fleet of cars and SUVs, check out "Increasing America's Fuel Economy," from the Alliance to Save Energy. They can be found online at www.ase.org.

For more on the costs of the drug war, read The Center for Substance Abuse Treatment, April 2000; Drug Policy Alliance, " 'Fuzzy Math' in New ONDCP Report," February 12, 2003. To get involved, contact the Prison Moratorium Project at www.nomoreprisons.org, a group working to stop prison expansion and put resources into communities most affected by criminal justice policies. Also look at New York Mothers of the Disappeared, an organization of family members fighting to put an end to the Rockefeller Drug Laws that target poor people and people of color (www.kunstler.org).

The statistic on money spent on illegal drugs each year is from "Prepared Remarks of Attorney General John Ashcroft, DEA/Drug Enforcement Rollout," John Ashcroft, United States Department of Justice, March 19, 2002.

The information on illiteracy in prisons and of welfare recipients comes from the most up-to-date National Center for Education statistics as reported in The Center on Crime Communities and Culture (Open Society Institute), "Education as Crime Prevention," September 1997; Verizon Reads Program at www.verizonreads.net; Lezlie McCoy, "Literacy in America," *The Philadelphia Tribune*, December 3, 2002. To become involved in programs fighting illiteracy, go to Literacy Volunteers of America at www.literacyvolunteers.org and Women in Literacy at www.womeninliteracy.org.

Statistics about spending on education and prisons comes from the Bureau of Justice Statistics, National Center for Education Statistics, National Association of State Budget Officers, U.S. Census Bureau as cited in *Mother Jones'* special report "Debt to Society," 2001.

For information on income disparity in the U.S., read the Census Bureau report, "A Brief Look at Postwar U.S. Income Inequality," June 1996 (covering years 1947 to 1992) and "The Changing Shape of the Nation's Income Distribution, 1947–1998," June 2000. Also look at Paul Krugman's *New York Times* article "For Richer," October 20, 2002.

11. Bush Removal and Other Spring Cleaning Chores

In 2000, Gore received 48.38 percent of the vote and Ralph Nader got 2.74 percent, according to the official results from the Federal Election Commission (www.fec.gov). Combined, this is 51.12 percent.

As *The New York Times* reported (David Rosenbaum, "Defying Labels Left or Right, Dean's '04 Run Is Making Gains," July 30, 2003), Dean "remains a fiscal conservative, he believes gun control should be left to the states and he favors the death penalty for some crimes."

According to the United States Census Bureau's February 2002 report "Voting and Registration in the Election of November 2000," 42,359,000 white non-Hispanic men voted in the 2000 election. A total of 110,826,000 votes were cast, making white men 38.22 percent. Women of all races accounted for 59,284,000 votes, or 53.49 percent. Black men cast 5,327,000 votes in 2000, comprising 4.81 percent, while Hispanic men cast 2,671,000 votes, equal to 2.41 percent—combined this is 7.22 percent. Thus, black men, Hispanic men, and women totaled 60.71 percent of all voters.

The two women senators as of 1991 were Nancy Kassebaum (R-Kansas), who served from 1978 to 1997, and Barbara Mikulski (D-Maryland), who has served 1987 to present. The other current women senators are: Lisa Murkowski (R-Alaska); Blanche Lincoln (D-Arkansas); Dianne Feinstein (D-California); Barbara Boxer (D-California); Mary Landrieu (D-Louisiana); Olympia Snowe (R-Maine); Susan Collins (R-Maine); Debbie Stabenow (D-Michigan); Hillary Rodham Clinton (D-New York); Elizabeth Dole (R-North Carolina); Kay Bailey Hutchison (R-Texas); Patty Murray (D-Washington); and Maria Cantwell (D-Washington). The first woman elected to the United States Senate was Hattie Wyatt Caraway (D-Arkansas). She was not, however, the first woman to serve in the Senate—that distinction belongs to Rebecca Latimer Felton (D-Georgia), who was appointed to fill a vacancy in 1922. In all, since 1922, the good people of the United States—who are about 51 percent female—have only managed to put thirty-three women in the Senate. For a full list of female senators, visit the Senate's Web site, www.senate.gov. For a full list of female presidents . . . well . . . why are you still reading this? The book is done! Go bug Oprah like I told you to!

While the Census Bureau estimates that there are 146 million women in this country, not all of them are eligible to run for president. To be the president of the United States, you must be born an American citizen, and you must be 35 or older. Again using estimates from the Census Bureau, there are 66,190,000 women eligible to be our next president.

Oprah's statement that she would "never" run for president was reported by, among others, Peggy Andersen, "Oprah for President? 'Never!'" Associated Press, May 31, 2003.

To find out more about Gen. Wesley K. Clark, and to see what he's up to, check out www.leadershipforamerica.org, the organization he set up to "foster a national dialogue about America's future." His statements about being pro-choice and for gun control were made on CNN's *Crossfire,* June 25, 2003. He spoke about Bush's tax cut, the Patriot Act, and affirmative action on NBC's *Meet the Press,* June 15, 2003. His comments on attacking Iran were made on FOX News' *Big Story,* June 23, 2003, while his ideas on working with our allies were made on NBC's *Meet the Press,* February 16, 2003. Finally, Clark's thoughts on the environment were delivered in a speech before the Council on Foreign Relations, February 20, 2003.

If you are interested in running for precinct delegate, or any other office, or if you'd just like to get busy taking back the Democratic Party, visit www.dnc.org, where the party has a handy map that can guide you to contact information for your state's party. Your state party will be able to provide you with all the details you will need to get the ball rolling. Just don't tell them what you're up to.

Whether you're running for office or you are looking for more information, or you just want to find out more about the candidates and what they stand for, a good place to begin is Project Vote Smart (www.votesmart.org). Through their Web site you can find your elected officials, links to candidates' Web sites, as well as a wealth of other voting information and links.

If you need to register to vote, or if you need to register the friends you are planning to drag with you to the voting booth on election day, visit www.rockthevote.com. You can register online through the site, and you can make your friends do it, too.

Most important, stay informed. Listen to National Public Radio, Pacifica Radio, read the newspaper, or try to regularly check out these Web sites: www.buzzflash.com, www.commondreams.org, or www.cursor.org for good daily updates on news stories you might be missing.

Acknowledgments

I would like to thank my wife, Kathleen, who, when I didn't feel like writing, would turn up the radio and start dancing. Suddenly I would find the inspiration to keep writing and keep living.

I'd also like to thank my daughter, Natalie. She graduated from college this year, something neither my wife nor I had done. We are so proud of her.

I'd like to thank my sister Anne. She has contributed so much to my work in the last two years, she has forgotten that she is still a lawyer. When the last publisher wouldn't organize a book tour, she did—and drove us in the minivan from city to city. When my film debuted in Cannes, she became my de facto manager. When I needed to nail certain parts of this book, she and her wonderful husband, John Hardesty, were there till the bitter end. All this, *and* she's the middle child!

I'd like to thank the guy who invented the dill pickle. It is my last remaining vice.

I'd like to thank my long-time buddy, Jeff Gibbs, who has bailed me out on more than one occasion in recent years. He sat with me looking up fact after fact while I wrote. He pushed me to keep the book a-blazing when, at times, I just wanted to write haikus. This guy is a genius. Though he had never worked on a movie before, he produced some of the most memorable scenes in *Bowling for Columbine*. Though he had never written a movie score, he scored my film in five days after the original music fell through. What's next? He's scaring me.

I would like to thank Ann Cohen and David Schankula, the brain trust behind this book. For months they labored with me over every word. They helped write, rewrite, reword, and redo the whole damn thing. They did the research, the proofreading, the fact checking. Then they rotated my wheels, blacktopped my driveway, and raised a herd of goats for me. How will I ever repay them?

Thanks also to Tia Lessin, Carl Deal, and Nicky Lazar for doing further fact checking and research when they should have been sneaking me into Afghanistan.

Also thanks to the interns—Brendon Fitzgibbons, Jason Kitchen, Sue Nelson, Stephanie Palumbo, Michael Pollock, Brad Thomson, and Doug Williams—to office staffers Rebecca Cohen and Emma Trask, and to those who read the manuscript and offered good suggestions: Al Hirvela, Joanne Doroshow, Rod Birleson, Terry George, Veronica Moore, Kelsey Binder, Leah Binder, Rocky Martineau, and Jason Pollock. Many thanks to the copyeditors: Lori Hall Steele, Mary Jo Zazueta, and Terry Allen.

I'd like to thank the Canadians. If you weren't there, we'd have no idea what was wrong with us.

I would definitely love to thank my new publisher, Warner Books—I couldn't ask for better people. First, thanks to Larry Kirshbaum, for saying that the most important thing was to "get the book right and for you to feel good about it—don't worry about the deadline!" I have never heard a person in authority say don't worry about the deadline! Don't tell me that! You are too cool.

I would also like to thank my editor at Warner Books, Jamie Raab. Her enthusiasm, her authentic *human* response to my writing was just the boost I needed this year. I thank her for her patience and rolling with the crazy way I work. She's the best.

I also want to thank all the other good people at Warner Books who had a hand in this project. Also, thanks to Paul Brown for his cover design. After the great job he did on *Stupid White Men*, there was no one else who could have made this cover (from an idea Schankula gave me) come to life.

Thanks also to the Jedi Master agent Mort Janklow. They'll never touch me as long as you're The Force!

I'd like to thank the musicians whose music I listened to while writing this book: Bruce, the Dixie Chicks, Patty Griffin, U2, Madonna, Alanis, Kasey Chambers, Steve Earle, Iris Dement, Nancy Griffith, Warren Zevon, R.E.M., Pearl Jam, Audioslave, and the Pretenders. It helps to write to a good beat.

I'd like to thank the Irish people in counties Donegal, Antrim, Derry, and Galway who invited us into their homes and let me hook up my laptop so I could finish the book while the publisher thought I was just down the street in New York.

Finally, thanks to my dad, who took care of me when I should have been taking care of him during this saddest of years.

About the Author

Michael Moore, who promised that, "barring success," his last book would definitely be his last, unfortunately had the success he was avoiding and was forced to write this book. He has written the bestsellers *Downsize This: Random Threats from an Unarmed American* and, with Kathleen Glynn, *Adventures in a TV Nation*. Spending fifty-eight weeks on *The New York Times* bestseller lists, his *Stupid White Men* became the largest-selling nonfiction book of 2002–03 in the U.S., with more than 4 million copies in print worldwide. It won the "Book of the Year" award in Great Britain and absolutely nothing in the United States, except there is a crazy online petition for him to run for president. Michael Moore is the Oscar-winning filmmaker of *Bowling for Columbine* and the groundbreaking classic *Roger & Me*. He also is the Emmy-winning writer/director/host of *TV Nation* and *The Awful Truth*. He has failed to win a Grammy or a Tony but hopes to resolve this as soon as he learns to sing and act. He recently lost fifty-two pounds by refusing to eat anything that says "nonfat" on it, and is working on his next film, titled *Fahrenheit 9/11*. He lives with his wife and daughter in Michigan and New York.

To contact the author, and to read more, go to
MichaelMoore.com